JULIE HOLLEDGE was born in 1950 and took a first-class degree in Drama at Bristol University in 1972. She has worked in the theatre for the past nine years, first as an actress in Theatre-in-Education projects at the Northcott Theatre, Exeter and the Belgrade Theatre, Coventry, now as a director. She has directed plays for the Sidewalk Theatre Company and the Broadside Mobile Worker's Theatre, is a founder member of Mrs Worthington's Daughters and from 1978–80 was associate director of the Women's Theatre Group. Her productions have run in London (the Royal Court Theatre Upstairs, The Young Vic Studio, the King's Head, the ICA) and throughout the country. At present she is a freelance director; she is writing a Ph.D and lives in London.

Based on original material gathered over five years from museums, private collections, newspapers and most particularly from autobiographical accounts and original playscripts, *Innocent Flowers* tells for the first time the story of actresses whose passionate love of the theatre was matched by their deep commitment to women's rights. Thousands of these women, some famous, others little known, set out at the turn of the century to change the conventional roles they played on stage, to fight for the vote and to change the world.

The new women's theatre became a countrywide movement involving amateurs and professionals, women and men. They wrote and produced hundreds of plays – many on taboo subjects such as sex, divorce, venereal disease – performing them in streets, church halls, West End theatres, ice rinks – anywhere. The First World War brought an abrupt end to their activities, but, by tracing the lives and loves of these strong and spirited women, Julie Holledge has recovered an inspiring time in the history of the theatre.

To beguile the time,
Look like the time; bear welcome in your eye,
Your hand, your tongue: look like the innocent flower,
But be the serpent under it.

Lady Macbeth
Macbeth Act 1 Sc. V

JULIE HOLLEDGE

INNOCENT FLOWERS

WOMEN IN THE EDWARDIAN THEATRE

Virago

FOR MY MOTHER AND FATHER

Published by VIRAGO PRESS Limited, 1981
Ely House, 37 Dover Street, London W1X 4HS

Copyright © Julie Holledge 1981

British Library Cataloguing in Publication Data

Holledge, Julie
   Innocent flowers.
    1. Theatre – Great Britain – History
   I. Title
   792'.0941   PN2595
   ISBN 0–86068–070–3
   ISBN 0–86068–071–1 Pbk

Typeset by Computacomp (UK) Ltd,
Fort William, Scotland.
Printed by Lowe and Brydone Printers Ltd
of Thetford, Norfolk.

CONTENTS

ACKNOWLEDGEMENTS

I would like to thank James Aubrey, Sarah and Ted Braun, Jill Craigie, Stacey Charlesworth, Anne Engel, Marilyn Milgrom, Mary Moore, Stef Pixner, Helen Rappaport and Michelene Wandor who all read and commented on the manuscript. I am also grateful to Athene Seyler, Jane Comfort, Jill Esmond and all the actresses at Denville Hall for allowing me to interview them and to Jane Marcus for her work on Elizabeth Robins and Jane Watson for her work on the Pioneer Players and Mrs Worthington's Daughters Theatre Company.

For permission to quote from Copyright sources I have to thank: Michael Joseph for quotations from Lena Ashwell's *Myself a Player*; Curtis Brown Ltd. for quotations from Edward Craig's *Gordon Craig*, Isadora Duncan's *My Life* and Cicely Hamilton's *Life Errant*; Chapman and Hall Ltd. for quotations from Eva Moore's *Exits and Entrances*; Hutchinson Publishing Group Ltd. for quotations from Charles Pearce's *Madame Vestris and Her Times* and Irene Vanbrugh's *To Tell My Story*; The Author's Literary Estate and The Hogarth Press Ltd. for quotations from Elizabeth Robins' *Ibsen and the Actress* and Virginia Woolf's *Between the Acts*; Methuen & Co. Ltd. for quotations from Chris St. John's *Hungerheart: The Story of a Soul*; The Society of Authors on behalf of the Bernard Shaw Estate; Victor Gollancz Ltd. for quotations from Elizabeth Sprigge's *Sybil Thorndike Casson*; Winant Towers Ltd. for quotations from Margaret Webster's *The Same Only Different*. My apologies to other copyright holders who may have been inadvertently omitted and to those I have been unable to trace.

INTRODUCTION

The actress's position in any society that is dominated by men is an ambiguous one. She is successful in so far as she can recreate male images of women. Yet she may be rewarded for this knack of pleasing with the freedom to reject and challenge these very fantasies. Her private life will be exposed in newspapers and magazines to shock and thrill her audience and her political views will be published, even if they attempt to subvert the society she serves. In the late nineteenth and early twentieth centuries a group of actresses used this political and sexual influence to further the cause of women's emancipation.

The early women's rights movement is remembered principally for the struggle for the vote, but it was concerned with many issues we now associate with a more recent scene: equal pay, equal job opportunities, equality before the law – particularly in the divorce and custody courts. The struggle to improve the political and legal status of women, while freeing them from the domestic tyranny of men, was reflected with astonishing variety on the stage of the late Victorian and Edwardian theatres. The music hall audiences of the 1890s were entertained by as many women impersonating men as male comedians. Vesta Tilley, Bessie Bonehill, Dr Crippen's wife Belle Elmore, Ella Shields and a host of other women dressed in top hats and tails, satirised men through song. Meanwhile, the middle classes were sitting in the red-plush stalls of the West End theatres watching 'society drama', so called because it depicted the lives of lords, ladies, duchesses and earls, and was invariably set in the drawing room of a London mansion or country house. Within each house-party a woman with a past lurked, ready to expose or be exposed for her sexual misdemeanours. Initially a secondary character, she moved to the centre of the stage in the 'new woman' plays of the 1890s. Arthur Wing Pinero, Henry Arthur Jones and Oscar Wilde were the successful exponents of this art, which played to immaculately dressed audiences. Athene Seyler recalls the scene at the beginning of her career as an actress:

> It was a glamorous job and everyone behaved so beautifully. What I remember now is going on and looking into the house as the curtain went up and the whole stalls looking as if it had snowed because all the men were in dinner jackets with white shirt-fronts. Well, no one was allowed into the stalls if they weren't in evening dress and it was so beautiful with the live orchestra.

While 'society drama' attracted the evening audience, the late Victorian equivalent to fringe theatre provided matinées and Sunday night performances of 'social drama'. Introduced to England by Ibsen and then practised by Shaw, this theatre of ideas exposed social ills, many of which concerned the sexual and financial exploitation of women and children. Of course, plays like *Ghosts* and *Mrs Warren's Profession* were considered obscene by the Lord Chamberlain, so in order to avoid censorship, theatre societies were formed to organise private performances for select memberships.

When I began researching this book, I anticipated writing about the indirect influence of actresses active in the women's rights movement on the playwrights of the time. For instance, Shaw wrote for his favourite actresses and confessed to using their personalities in the creation of his female characters. But when I began looking at the first performances of Ibsen in this country, I discovered to my surprise that they were staged by a small group of actresses who were disenchanted with the position of women both on and off the stage. By tracing the lives of these women into the Edwardian era, I discovered a suffrage society, known as the Actresses' Franchise League, founded in December 1908, which had over one thousand members.

I saw the League purely as a political organisation until I discovered advertisements for suffrage plays in the newspaper of the Women's Social and Political Union, *Votes for Women*. The plays were all about ten to thirty minutes long and were staged anywhere from a church hall to a skating rink. The men and women who wrote them were using a dramatic form to argue out topical issues. As the discussion about taxation or the position of married women was taken up by the women's movement, so a play was immediately written encapsulating the main arguments. These playwrights, a number of whom were actresses, were inexperienced writers and their plays are not literary masterpieces, but the encouragement they received persuaded some of them to continue writing. Having begun my research believing that there were no women playwrights writing between 1900 and 1920, I subsequently discovered over 400. Eventually, I managed to trace some of the actresses who had been active in the Actresses' Franchise League; when I spoke to them they painted a vivid picture of the first women's theatre of the twentieth century.

To tell the story of the women who developed this flourishing women's theatre, I have divided this book into three sections. In the first, I have tried to let the actresses of the late nineteenth century explain, in their own words, how they became involved in the theatre and aware of the women's rights movement. I have concentrated on the legitimate theatre rather than the music hall – the latter would need a separate book to do it justice. The second section deals with the Actresses' Franchise League and the emergence of the Women's Theatre Company just before the First World War. Finally, I have drawn a brief portrait of the first woman director of the twentieth-century English theatre. She was involved in the first productions of Ibsen, the suffrage theatre of the pre-war period and continued this tradition of women's theatre through the war into the 1920s.

At the end of the book I have included some suffrage plays. I would like to thank Sidewalk Theatre Company for performing them to a modern-day audience. They are not brilliantly constructed plays, but as a reviewer discovered, 'they are delightfully simple and powerful without being declamatory'.

ILLUSTRATIONS

Florence Farr (*by kind permission of Raymond Mander & Joe Mitchenson*).

Janet Achurch as Nora in *A Doll's House* (*by kind permission of Raymond Mander & Joe Mitchenson*).

Lillah McCarthy (*by kind permission of Raymond Mander & Joe Mitchenson*).

Lena Ashwell (*by kind permission of Raymond Mander & Joe Mitchenson*).

Eva Moore (*by kind permission of the Fawcett Library*).

Decima Moore (*by kind permission of the Fawcett Library*).

Diana of Dobson's by Cicely Hamilton (*from the collection of Julie Holledge*).

How the Vote was Won by Cicely Hamilton (*by kind permission of the Fawcett Library*).

The Actresses' Franchise League musicians contingent preparing for the demonstration on 17 June 1911 (*by kind permission of the London Museum*).

Lena Ashwell and C. M. Hallard in the final act of *Diana of Dobson's* by Cicely Hamilton (*by kind permission of Raymond Mander & Joe Mitchenson*).

Decima Moore entertaining suffragettes boycotting the National Census on the eve of April 2 1911 (*by kind permission of the London Museum*).

Vesta Tilley (*by kind permission of Raymond Mander & Joe Mitchenson*).

Ailsa Craig (*by kind permission of Raymond Mander & Joe Mitchenson*).

Kitty Marion on her release from prison (*by kind permission of the London Museum*).

Ellen Terry and Edy Craig (*by kind permission of Raymond Mander & Joe Mitchenson*).

Edy Craig and Cicely Hamilton (*by kind permission of the Fawcett Library*).

Edy Craig, Chris St John and Tony (Clare Atwood), 1943 (*from a photograph by the late Antony Marshall in his garden at Bethersden, Kent, 1943*).

Part One

THE ACTRESS

'What was wanted of women of the stage was,
first and mainly, what was wanted of women outside
– a knack of pleasing' – *Elizabeth Robins*

1. HEDDA IS ALL OF US

The early Victorian theatre was shunned by the bourgeoisie. They saw it as a place of decadent popular entertainment which promoted riots and social disturbance. This revulsion was based partly on fact — it was not unknown for an audience to stop a performance and demand a different play, or to riot over the price of seats. It was also based on a deep-rooted belief, stemming from the Puritan revolution, that any entertainment, short of Shakespeare and opera, was fundamentally immoral. Performers were equated with rogues and vagabonds, especially actresses, who were seen as scarlet women soliciting from the stage rather than the streets — an attitude which was reinforced by the knowledge that, ever since the first English actress had appeared in 1660, the aristocracy had selected mistresses from the stage. In an age when the paragon of womanhood was the humble, obedient wife, mother or sister of some man, a woman who flagrantly displayed herself in the theatre was anathema.

The task of wooing the middle classes back into the theatre was taken up by the actor-managers. It was these performers, rather than writers or producers, who dominated Victorian theatre. In order to go into management, actors had to convince a financial backer that their popularity with the theatre-going public was sufficient to warrant leasing a theatre. It was not unusual for the lease of a minor theatre to change hands within three years. In contrast, the major theatres were often leased by the same actor-manager for over twenty.

In 1865 Marie Wilton, who began her acting career in early childhood, and her husband Squire Bancroft borrowed £1,000 and leased the Scala Theatre — popularly known as the dust-hole of Tottenham Court. The venture seemed doomed to failure. But the Bancrofts transformed the dust-hole with rosebud chintz, carpets and elegant fittings into the Prince of Wales Theatre. Instead of presenting six hours of performance in one evening, which was the Victorian norm, they provided after-dinner entertainment for the middle classes from 8.00 to 10.30 p.m. Their success in attracting a new audience encouraged the other actor-managers to try similar innovations: Wyndham at the Criterion Theatre introduced programmes instead of cut-down bill posters, Hare at the Court Theatre began selling tea and coffee as well as alcohol in the intervals and Gilbert at the Savoy staged the first matinées for women and children. Not only were the old theatres refurbished, but new theatres were built in the 1860s with smaller, extravagantly furnished auditoriums providing between 500 and 800 seats.

The plays written for the new audience reflected their materialistic values and puritan morality. Melodrama, the staple diet of the early Victorian stage, was ousted by naturalistic domestic comedies, commonly known as 'cup-and-saucer' dramas. By the 1870s the working classes had been hived off to the music halls and theatre was becoming respectable. Even the attitude of the Church to dramatic entertainments was changing, or as the Rev. H. R. Hauvers of St James, Marylebone, put it: 'We have reached a critical time in the history of the stage, a time when prelates and playactors shake hands.'[1] Henry James, who was visiting London in 1877, gave a vivid picture of this new English theatre in an article he wrote for *The Galaxy*:

> The first step is to go to an agency in an expensive street out of Piccadilly, and there purchase a stall for the sum of eleven shillings. You receive your ticket from the hands of a smooth, sleek bottle-nosed clerk, who seems for all the world as if he had stepped straight out of a volume of Dickens or Thackeray. There is almost always an old lady taking seats for the play, with a heavy carriage in waiting at the door; the number of old ladies whom one has to squeeze past in the stalls is in fact very striking. 'Is it good?' asks the old lady of the gentleman I have described, with a very sweet voice and a perfectly expressionless face (she means the play, not the seat). 'It is thought very good, my lady,' says the clerk, as if he were uttering a 'response' in church. ... In the house itself everything seems to contribute to the impression which I have tried to indicate – the impression that the theatre in England is a social luxury and not an artistic necessity. The white-cravatted young man who inducts you into your stall, and having put you in possession of a programme, extracts from you, masterly but effectually, a sixpence

which, as a stranger, you have wondered whether you might venture to give him, and which has seemed a mockery of his grandeur – this excellent young man is somehow the keynote of the whole affair. An English audience is as different as possible from a French. ... It is well dressed, tranquil, motionless; it suggests domestic virtue and comfortable homes; it looks as if it had come to the play in its own carriage, after a dinner of beef and pudding.[2]

As the audience changed, so did the social status of the actors. In *Caste*, one of the first plays performed by the Bancrofts, the central character is an actress. Instead of being a scarlet woman, she is a virtuous wife and mother who believes her husband has died in India defending the British Empire. The transformation from rogues and vagabonds to respected professionals was completed in 1895, when Henry Irving, the actor-manager of the Lyceum, was knighted. By 1914, the same honour had been conferred on the other leading actor-managers: Squire Bancroft, Wyndham, Tree, Hare, Alexander and Forbes-Robertson.

Once the theatrical profession had achieved respectability the middle-class children who had been taken to the matinées at the Prince of Wales and had performed in endless drawing-room amateur dramatics, began to contemplate acting as a career. This was particularly true of girls who rebelled against their incarceration in the home and saw the theatre as a romantic alternative. They had been taught that women should be humble and obedient and that ambition and independence were unfeminine attributes, but on the stage they saw women expressing passion and achieving fame.

Such dissatisfaction with family life was a reflection of the growing influence of the early women's rights movement. In the same year as the Bancrofts opened the Prince of Wales, John Stuart Mill had been elected to parliament by the City of Westminster on a manifesto which included the demand for women's suffrage. Two years later he attempted to amend a reform bill to give women the vote. As well as fighting for suffrage, women were agitating for better education facilities and employment opportunities. The Association for the Promotion of the Employment of Women had been set up as early as 1858, to increase the number of careers open to impecunious middle-class women. The Association propagandised its views in a periodical, *The Englishwoman's Journal*. It asserted that women should be employed as hairdressers, hotel managers, wood engravers, dispensers, house decorators, watchmakers and telegraphists, but showed little interest in the theatrical profession.

Although the average middle-class father accepted, by the end of the century, that the theatre was suitable entertainment for his daughter, he reacted with horror at the thought of her becoming an actress. When Marie Tempest told her family that she was going on the stage, they were so incensed that they persuaded Gladstone, who was acquainted with her grandmother, to speak to her:

> I can remember his impressive, but very charming manner and his smooth, lovely voice, talking and talking. As he talked, he warmed up and I became interested. I relaxed my defiance, before the wonder of what he told me. He spoke of the Greek drama, and then of the monkish Mysteries and Moralities, of Restoration drama and then, clearly introduced by the grand preamble, he spoke of the advent of women on the stage. He frowned as he suggested the depravity of the life I wished to live. He talked of Macready, of Helen Forsyth and of Kean and Irving. He forgot his moralising for a moment and spoke of the power of good of the dramatist and the actor. Then he looked at me again, remembered his mission and drew all he had said into a final argument of warning.[3]

Less subtle methods of persuasion were used by other parents of would-be actresses. Eva Moore, a successful West End actress who began her career in the 1880s, was brought up in a typical Victorian family of nine girls and one boy, in which her father's word was law. The girls took it in turns to cook his breakfast:

> I remember, too, at breakfast how I would watch my father's face to see by his expression if it was 'all right'; the awful moment when, eyeing it with disfavour, he would give his verdict 'lumpy'. The cook for the day, after such a verdict, generally left the table in tears.[4]

When Eva got her first acting job, playing a small part in a matinée, she was too frightened to tell her father. Although he allowed his daughters to earn their living teaching ballet and elocution, they were not permitted to perform themselves. When he eventually discovered Eva was acting, he threw her out of the house. Other would-be actresses gave way to parental pressure: Mary Goulden, Emmeline Pankhurst's sister, was prevented from going on the stage by her father who, though an amateur actor himself, thought that an actress-daughter would be bad for his business.

If they succeeded in defying their parents, the young actresses found themselves outside the protection of their families, with no idea of how to embark on their careers. Violet Vanbrugh, who became a leading London actress after appearing with Henry Irving at the Lyceum Theatre, left her parents' home in Exeter in 1886, with fifty pounds:

> Very soon after my arrival in London I knew that I was up against a harder proposition than I had ever had to face. I knew no one who could help me, and I had not the slightest idea how to set about the achievement of my ambition. I looked in the papers and wrote to the theatrical managers asking for interviews, but no answer came to my letters. Among the many letters I wrote was one to Miss Ellen Terry. I had seen her at the Lyceum when I was a child, and I thought of course that she would remember me. How could she? I was only one of hundreds of little girls who had been introduced to her, so to this letter, as to the others I received no reply.[5]

Eventually Ellen Terry helped her get her first job, but in the interim Violet Vanbrugh decided to take acting classes. There was no drama training as such, only the possibility of a few lessons from actresses like Mrs Stirling, who had acted lead parts with Macready and Phelps, or Mrs Crow who had worked with Henry Irving. Jane Comfort, who began her career in 1909 and retired after her last engagement in *The Mousetrap* a few years ago, was one of the latter's pupils. She remembers how the class, which assembled in Mrs Crow's living room, 'used to lie on the rug in front of the fire, it was winter time, and watch while she showed us how she and Henry Irving took three minutes over an exit, which was very entertaining, but was a bit old-fashioned in method.'[6]

In 1896 the first acting academy was established by Ben Greet, who guaranteed successful students their first job in one of his touring companies, and in 1904, the famous actor-manager, Beerbohm Tree, established a school at His Majesty's Theatre which later became the Royal Academy of Dramatic Art. Athene Seyler was one of the first pupils:

> I went to the Academy in 1908 and won my gold medal in 1909. I was the third gold medallist. The Academy had only been in Gower

Street for three years when I went and it was quite a novelty. All the older generation looked down on it and thought it was dreadful because they'd learnt their job in little stock companies and they thought it was rather playing at it, I think.

I had to struggle for a year with my family before I was allowed to go on the stage at all, in fact I went into what the Victorians called a decline – which was utter boredom. My mother wanted me to be a pianist but I had no gift at all, it was just wishful thinking. We knew the great critic William Archer and he interviewed me and told my mother he thought I had a chance of getting into the Academy. So I went up a fortnight later than the exams to have an interview with Mr Bancroft who was running the Academy. When I went into the room he looked at me – I was a very plain little girl, I've been a plain lady all my life – and said, 'Miss Seyler, I'm sorry but you have no qualifications for the stage,' and I, with the courage of youth, said 'I know what you mean, Mr Bancroft, I'm very plain but I'm quite sure if you heard me recite, you'd change your mind.' And he did.

In those days accomplished actors and actresses came to give classes. They weren't professional teachers, they were working actors and actresses so you immediately got in touch with the feeling of the theatre. Of course the premises were idiotic. It was a little house in Gower Street and the double drawing room was the auditorium and the stage. When you made a good exit you went through the door and onto the landing where the stairs came in.[7]

Prior to the creation of the acting schools in the twentieth century, the only way into the theatre was through a personal introduction to one of the actor-managers. But once a letter of introduction had been secured there were few formalities, as May Whitty discovered in 1881 when she went to see Captain Bainbridge at the Court Theatre: 'All right,' he said, 'you can start tonight in *The Mountain Sylph.*' 'Tonight – what as?' 'A sylph of course. Just follow the others and do what they do. Be at the theatre half an hour before the show. They'll give you some clothes in the wardrobe.'[8]

Frequently, a young actress's second job was as difficult to find as her first. Irene Vanbrugh, Violet Vanbrugh's sister, explains:

We used in those days to leave cards at the stage doors so, with my very common little card, I called at the stage door of the Haymarket

Theatre and boldly asked to see Mr Beerbohm Tree. I was politely refused admission but left my card. I then went to the St James' Theatre and the same thing happened. A few days afterwards I had a note asking me to go down to see Mr Tree. Here was the opening of the Golden Doors! His first words to me were, 'Why do you want to see me? I thought you were acting with my friend Mr Toole.' I tried to explain to him, very shyly, that I thought it better to try my luck elsewhere. He also managed to suggest to me that I was being ungrateful, but by this time I had gained a little more courage and did not feel so crestfallen. He then said, 'Well, there is the part of a waiting maid in a play by Henry Arthur Jones called *The Tempter* I am going to produce here which I think you might be able to do. Rehearsals start in August.' He asked me what my salary had been with Mr Toole and I told him two guineas a week but that I should like him to give me three. This was eventually arranged, and feeling terribly pleased and proud I hurried back to tell the good news to Violet.[9]

Whether they began their careers in light opera, musicals or matinées, the actresses found themselves in a new and alien world. The theatre was a hierarchical institution and the new recruits had virtually no contact with the stars. There was no union to negotiate minimum wages or to provide contracts and they soon realised that their homes, which they had considered claustrophobic, were comfortable and secure. They found it hard to support themselves, pay for their costumes and their digs on a guinea a week, even though this wage was more than double that of an industrial worker. 'In those days,' wrote Eva Moore, 'after a matinée, there were only two things to do: either stay in the theatre or go out and walk the streets. Your rooms were generally a long way from the theatre, which meant 'bus riding (and every penny had to be considered) and there were no girls' clubs then.'[10] In her efforts to save money, Eva, who was just seventeen, used to walk home to her digs after the evening performance. One night she was attacked and her bag was stolen; she was so distraught that her father allowed her home to recover.

Having gained a little experience 'walking-on' in West End productions, most young actresses tried to get work in a touring company, where they had a chance to tackle larger parts. It was hard work, as Violet Vanbrugh discovered:

We used to play three or four dramas a week, touring through many of the little towns of the South of England, but in spite of rehearsing all day, playing in the evening and studying most of the night, I was very happy. My contract was to find my own dresses, and my salary was £1 a week, not exactly a princely salary, but I was being taught my business – and by sharing rooms with two other girls I managed to live on it, and by the end of six months tour had even saved a pound or two.[11]

The tours were divided into three separate categories: the No 1 tours played the major cities such as Manchester and Glasgow, while the No 2 and No 3 tours visited smaller provincial towns. Many of the provincial theatres were very ill-equipped and the scenery, which the companies toured with them, often only just fitted on to the stage. Athene Seyler remembers one night when all the set doors jammed:

The door stuck and we couldn't push it off or on stage. We couldn't get off at the prompt corner because it was built in; it was a very old-fashioned theatre in the provinces. Somebody tried to get on to do a scene with me and couldn't move the door. In the middle of the stage there was a wardrobe. It was a bedroom scene and the wardrobe was never opened so it had no back – it went straight onto the back of the stage. To my surprise – I was watching the door – the wardrobe opened and the actor came in. Throughout the whole of the rest of the act, we went on and off through the wardrobe. I must say we did laugh. I think the audience did too.[12]

The hazards of touring were not confined to the stage. Lena Ashwell, who began her career in 1891 and became an actress-manager, was just one of the many young actresses who found staying in strange digs a lonely and frightening experience:

It was the first time that I had been quite alone on tour, entirely on my own and the rooms in which I found myself filled me with terror. As there was no key or lock, I barricaded the door every night with all the furniture I was strong enough to move, and then I was afraid to sleep. Manchester is a grim city unless one knows the way to get out of it.[13]

Gradually the actresses adapted to their nomadic existence, staying in a succession of theatrical lodgings where the menu was always the same and it was advisable, in case of damp bedding, to put a mirror between the sheets and wear flannel. They maintained contact with their friends in the profession through the visitor's book at their lodgings. Cicely Hamilton explains:

> It was the custom, moreover, when you signed your testimonial, to add to your signature the title of the piece you were playing in, and sometimes the name of the part; which meant that the book was a source of information with regard to professional activities. From its pages you discovered that the girl you had known as a Shakespearian understudy had changed over into musical comedy, and that the low comedian in your last melodrama had recently appeared as the Dame in *Aladdin*, or the Uncle in *Babes in the Wood*.[14]

Touring the industrial cities of the North of England and Glasgow made a lasting impression on many young actresses, who had never seen slums or the effects of poverty before. For some, like Cicely Hamilton, it was the beginning of a political awareness which led to their involvement in the women's rights movement:

> It was verging on winter when I took up my quarters for the week in these two little rooms, and morning by morning, long before it was light, I would hear my landlady shuffling downstairs and out into the street, for a couple of hours hard cleaning and scrubbing of office floors before she came back to give the children their breakfast and pack the elder ones off to school. ... A little hunted woman, who so far as one could see, never, from morning till evening, had a moment of rest and good comfort.[15]

A similar experience was recorded by the music hall actress, Kitty Marion, who became a militant suffragette and a leading figure in the American birth control movement:

> Whenever I went on tour in the provinces ... I seemed to gravitate for my sight-seeing expeditions to the slums. All through the cities and towns of England and Scotland and Ireland and Wales whenever I and the other girls of the company went out together they would warn me: 'None of your slumming trips, now.' But sooner or later I found myself in the poorest parts of the city. I

learned the tragedy of the unwanted child, the tragedy of the parents who have nothing to give their children.[16]

Apart from dealing with the shock of seeing barefoot children in winter begging for food, the actresses had to deal with a problem that was far less easily articulated. Although their parents had been horrified at their choice of career, they had not explained the basis of their puritan revulsion. Sex was a taboo subject in the Victorian home and it was a common belief that girls should only learn the facts of life when they married. But in the eyes of their audience, young actresses were sexually sophisticated and therefore fair game for the stage-door johnnies. In the more established companies, the actor-managers, realising the impossible position that young actresses found themselves in, provided chaperones. When Eva Moore joined John Toole's summer touring company in the late 1880s she was accompanied by an elderly lady called Eliza Johnston:

> She dragooned me effectively: young men who showed any tendency to gather round stage doors, or gaze at one in the street, were sternly discouraged. At Cambridge, I remember, I had a passionate love letter from some undergrad who said he refrained from signing his name, as his 'trust had been broken before', but, if I returned his affection, would I reply in the 'agony column' of The Times to 'Fido'. I did nothing of the kind naturally; but so definite were the feelings of Eliza Johnston as to 'things of that kind', that she told me she could 'not help feeling that I was in some measure to blame'.[17]

Eva Moore found Fido's advances amusing, but one of her friends was the victim of a series of obscene postcards from an 'admirer'; while May Whitty, who had no Eliza to protect her, was accosted by a man who accused her of being 'A female cad. You're nothing but a female cad. And I have no time for female cads.'[18] The contradiction between their own sexual ignorance and the prevalent belief that they were promiscuous often encouraged the actresses into early marriages. Eva Moore married a young actor called Henry Esmond with the money they had won on a horse in the Liverpool Cup. After the wedding they both went to their respective theatres for the evening performance and Henry, who was working at Terry's Theatre, was presented with two books by his employer – Dr Chavasse's Advice to a Wife and Dr Chavasse's Advice to Mothers.

Having achieved a degree of respectability as a married woman and permanent protection from unwanted admirers, Eva then had to deal with the additional problem of her husband's sexual possessiveness:

> It was in *Little Christopher Columbus* that I wore 'boy's clothes'. ... But, behold the *deus ex machina*, in the person of my husband! He came to the dress rehearsal, and later we rode home to our little flat in Chelsea on the top of a bus, discussing the play. Suddenly, as if struck by a bright thought he turned to me and said: 'Don't you think you'd look awfully well in a cloak?' I felt dubious, and said so, but that did not shake him. 'I do,' he said and added: 'Your legs are much too pretty to show! I'll see about it in the morning.'[19]

Although the desire for respectability encouraged actresses to marry, if they were committed to their career they were not prepared to honour and obey a husband who expected them to be a conventional wife. Marriages between actresses and men who were not involved in theatre frequently proved disastrous as Marie Tempest, who was married three times, discovered. 'My young husband wished me to be both Patti (the famous Victorian singer) and Mrs Beeton. He liked the glamour of my little success at the academy, but this was not enough! Oh no! He wished me to throw my career aside and mend socks and fuss about food when I came home.'[20]

In order to disentangle themselves from unhappy marriages the actresses had to go through the divorce courts. This proved a tortuous business because of the expense and the laws which dictated that, though a husband could divorce his wife for adultery, a wife had to prove adultery as well as cruelty or desertion of two years. Lena Ashwell, who married an alcoholic, had to wait years before she was legally separated from her husband. 'A struggle for freedom is always difficult,' she wrote, 'and mine was desperate. There is no doubt that in my misery and despair, I might have taken to drink, like many other women condemned to a life of torture and desperation; but I was saved by two friends that came to my rescue.'[21]

Once an actress had suffered the ordeal of the divorce courts, she could continue her career with no fear of discrimination. Eva Moore's husband, Henry Esmond, who was a playwright as well as an actor, summed up the liberal attitude of the theatrical profession towards the private lives of actresses, in a letter to a moralistic friend:

If authors in engaging artists for plays allowed themselves to be biased by the private lives of each artist, I fear many theatres would close and many deserving people would starve. If Miss Smith, Jones or Robinson suits the requirements of a play, it is not my business, or the manager's, to enquire whether or no she murdered her mother. Is she the right person for the play? — that's all one can consider.[22]

The theatre-going public proved equally tolerant, as Eva Moore's story about two women who were watching her perform shortly after Henry's death illustrates:

'I think Eva Moore's good, don't you?'
'Very good.'
'She lorst 'er 'usband lately, poor thing. Very 'ard for 'er. Though mind yer, its a pleasant change, in one way: most of these 'ere actresses only mislay theirs.'[23]

Actresses with successful marriages tended to be married to actors who did not expect them to conform to the conventional role of wife and mother. Traditionally, in the theatre an actress was not expected to give up her career to look after her children. Ellen Terry, who came from a theatrical family, toured the country with her parents and every theatre they visited had the equivalent of a nursery in the green room where children could sleep or play during rehearsals and performances. By the end of the Victorian era, most successful actresses employed nannies and sent their children to boarding schools. When Sybil Thorndike gave birth to her first child, John, she immediately went on a year's tour with her husband, Lewis Casson:

We came back after a year and a month, and of course John didn't know us. He was the most entrancing baby with golden curls. He was really beautiful! He was rather shy and didn't like me very much. Mother had looked after him so wonderfully, and he had that nice little nurse called Alice, and when he'd been with me for a few minutes he'd say 'Want Alice'. It was awful.[24]

However awful Sybil Thorndike felt, she was never criticised for leaving her children. In fact the day after her fourth child was born, Lilian Baylis (the manager of the Old Vic theatre) walked into her room and demanded, 'Well, when can you start Hamlet?' Ironically, it was an actress who adopted a child, Lena Ashwell, whose suitability as a mother was most questioned by her colleagues:

> Adopting children was not usual as it is now. Heaps of women now, both married and single, adopt a child or two. But last century such an action was regarded as most suspicious: it must hide some commandment broken and there seemed to be only one of any importance. Without a doubt the child was mine and I was ashamed to own her! Even some who knew me well were convinced that I was concealing the facts, though why on earth I should I can't imagine.[25]

However unconventional their family lives or shortlived their relationships, most actresses at the turn of the century defined themselves as married women. Only a few who were sufficiently successful on the stage to be financially secure chose to live outside conventional marriage ties. Ellen Terry, who became the first Dame of the British theatre, was married three times: her first marriage (when she was sixteen) to the forty-six-year-old painter George Frederick Watts lasted less than a year, and her two subsequent marriages to Charles Kelly and James Carew lasted five and two years respectively. None of these husbands played as important a part in her life as two of her lovers: Edward Godwin, the father of her two children, Edith and Edward Gordon Craig, and Henry Irving, with whom she worked at the Lyceum Theatre. Although Ellen wrote an autobiography, she never expressed her views on marriage or spoke about her lovers. This English reticence was not shared by foreign actresses visiting London, who were often amazed by the plethora of supposedly respectable theatre marriages. Simone La Borge was so astounded by this phenomenon, that she declared that in France 'C'est impossible'; whereas Isadora Duncan openly attacked the hypocrisy of the actresses' marriages:

> I was against marriage with every intelligent force of my being. I believed it then, and still believe it to be an absurd and enslaving institution, leading, especially with artists, inevitably to the divorce courts and preposterous and vulgar lawsuits.[26]

The popular press had a field day with these unconventional foreigners; it was particularly vindictive towards Sarah Bernhardt:

It was said for a shilling anyone might see me dressed as a man, that I smoked huge cigars, leaning on the balcony of my house; that at the various receptions where I gave my one act plays I took my maid with me to play a small part; that I practised fencing in my garden, dressed as Pierrot in white, and that when taking boxing lessons I had broken two teeth of my unfortunate professor.[27]

The implications of homosexuality that were levelled at actresses who refused to conform to the role of wife and mother, together with accounts of actresses dressing as men, or dancing with women at theatrical parties, suggest that some women took advantage of their sexual freedom as actresses to build lesbian relationships. Hence the following hysterical outburst by Violet Vanbrugh in her book for young, would-be actresses, *Dare to be Wise*:

I must write a word of warning against those whose instinct is abnormal and perverted. Those poor wretches – unnatural and morally unhealthy themselves – they contaminate all who come within their influence. You must shun their companionship. Their principles and practices are vile. If ever through your own folly or by some misadventure you should find yourself in such a set, or even on its outskirts, don't hesitate or delay. Cut yourself adrift. Never be blackmailed by promises of advancement, or threats of damage to your reputation, into having anything to do with them. At all costs you must get clear of their influence and fight your way back to decent, sane companionship. People who have any standards of right – however far short they may fall in living up to it – will not tolerate sex perverts.[28]

The reverberations in the theatre of the Oscar Wilde trial prevented any open acknowledgement of homosexuality among actresses. But its existence was a reflection of the gradual breakdown of the rigidity of official sex roles that had characterised the mid-Victorian period. This relaxation found an expression, surprisingly enough, on the music hall stage. In the late nineteenth century there was a vogue in the halls for male impersonators. The roots of this art were in seventeenth-century breeches parts, which were considered erotic because they exposed women's legs. But the music hall actresses did not seek to increase their femininity by assuming male clothing. Instead they observed men of different classes and professions and tried to represent them on the stage.

Vesta Tilley, the most successful of the male impersonators, began her career in 1868 at the age of three and created the famous songs, *Burlington Bertie* and *Piccadilly Johnny with the Glass Eye*. She always researched her character sketches with great care and, when touring America, visited the New York Stock Exchange in search of a particular type of man to satirise:

> It was truly a sense of excitement — perspiring men in their shirt-sleeves pushing their way through crowds, waving arms, and stentorian voices; here and there a well-dressed man, very bedraggled, but all from broker to office boy carried away in the excitement of buying or selling shares. I carried the scene in my mind, and incidentally visualised what the New York stock broker at the height of his day's business would look like on stage. I called in Mr. W. Jerome, an American author who had many clever songs to his credit, and together we evolved the song, 'The Man who Broke the Brokers'. I produced the song ... and it was a great success.[29]

Vesta Tilley never risked alienating the men in her audience, but it was the women who were her real fans. Not because she gently satirised male behaviour, but because they found her attractive. She, however, refused to see any homosexual implication in the devotion of her fans:

> It may be because I generally appeared on the stage as a young man that a big percentage of my admirers were women. Girls of all ages would wait in crowds to see me enter or leave the theatre, and each post brought me piles of letters varying from impassioned declarations of undying love to a request for an autograph, or photograph, or a simple flower, or a piece of ribbon I had worn. To illustrate the impression I made upon at least one of my girl admirers, I have in my possession now a complete diary of a young girl, covering a period of some ten years, in which she records the first time she saw me, her journeys to see me in various towns at which I appeared, her opinion of the many new songs I had introduced during the time, all punctuated with expressions of lasting love and devotion.[30]

In the late nineteenth-century theatre, as opposed to the music hall, there were no equivalent androgynous figures, except the occasional female Hamlet. In fact, the majority of women in popular plays could be sub-divided into romantic heroines, dutiful wives and mothers, and repentant or depraved divorcées. Many actresses, who no doubt had accepted these stereotypes as accurate representations of their sex when they visited the theatre in their childhood, began seriously to question the characters they were employed to portray. Once they started to look more critically at their roles on the stage, they began to realise that the equality they had imagined behind the footlights was non-existent. Their wages were half those of the actors in the company – despite the fact that the first equal pay case in the theatre had been fought and won at the beginning of the nineteenth century.

In 1826, an opera singer, Velluti, sent a letter to his chorus promising them an extra pound if they sang well at his benefit evening, but after the performance he gave only the men the bonus. The women sued Velluti, who claimed in his defence that he had addressed the letter, 'Signori Coristi', in other words, 'Gentlemen Choristers'. It was contested on behalf of the women that the phrase, 'Signori Coristi' meant all the chorus and the judge decided in their favour. The success of the Velluti case had absolutely no effect on the wages of ordinary performers and the myth of equal pay in the Victorian era, as in the present day, was based on the salaries of the stars, who were paid according to their popularity, not their sex.

Although the actresses were irritated by the inequality of their wages, the real roots of their dissatisfaction lay in the artistic tyranny practised by the Victorian actor-managers. The main criterion by which a play was chosen for production was the size and dramatic possibilities of the central male character. The arrogance of the great actor-managers knew no bounds: when the early Victorian actress, Madame Vestris, asked Macready to produce her play *Woman*, he replied that he would only do so if the major speeches of the leading lady were given to the leading man. The casting of the female roles was equally subject to the control of the managers. 'Twice in the course of my life,' wrote Cicely Hamilton, 'I was thrown out of work to make room for a manager's mistress; no fault was found with the playing of my part, but it was wanted for other than professional reasons and therefore I had to go.'[31] Even as established an actress as Marie Tempest was cast according to the whims of the managers; she made her name in modern comedies and in her whole career never attempted classical or tragic parts. When she was about to retire an interviewer asked her why she had never played Shakespeare's Beatrice or Katherine:

> I have never been allowed to play what I have wished. You don't
> seem to realise that actresses are the victims of managers. I have
> never been allowed to leave that one peak. It was Frohman's fault.
> When I succeeded in comedies, he kept me in comedies and would
> never let me break new ground. Of course I wanted to play Beatrice
> and even some of the more dramatic parts, but the chance has never
> come my way.[32]

Ellen Terry, unlike Marie Tempest, was permitted to play Beatrice by
her manager, Henry Irving, but according to his interpretation:

> Owing to Henry's rather finicky deliberate method as Benedict, I
> could never put the right pace into my part. I was also feeling
> unhappy about it because I had been compelled to give way about a
> traditional 'gag' in the church scene, with which we ended the
> fourth act. ... When I was told that we were to descend to the
> buffoonery of:
>
> BEATRICE: Benedict, kill him – kill him if you can.
> BENEDICT: As sure as I'm alive, I will.
>
> I protested, and implored Henry not to do it. He said it was
> necessary: otherwise the 'curtain' would be received in dead
> silence. ... After holding out for a week, I gave in. 'It is my duty to
> obey your orders and do it,' I said, 'but I do it under protest.'[33]

The actresses were not alone in their dissatisfaction with the actor-
managers' regime. In 1889, William Archer, the critic in the *Fortnightly
Review*, challenged playwrights to say

> whether they have not again and again found themselves
> consciously sacrificing artistic considerations to the necessity of
> conciliating the masses. Have they not altogether rejected powerful
> and interesting themes, which for one reason or another, could not
> be treated in accordance with established formulas.[34]

The belief that theatre should challenge rather than reinforce an
audience's preconceptions was particularly prevalent in the socialist
circle surrounding Eleanor Marx, the youngest daughter of Karl Marx,
and her common-law husband Dr Aveling. They were both fascinated
by the theatre – Aveling had written plays and Eleanor Marx had

contemplated becoming an actress. In their search for a drama that could satisfy them politically and artistically they discovered the plays of Henrik Ibsen. He became their prophet of the 'new drama', and they championed him both as a poet and as a propagandist.

In 1886, they arranged a private reading of *A Doll's House*, which Ibsen had written seven years before. The play had been performed in Russia in 1884 and in Germany in 1880. Ibsen was forced to rewrite the final scene for the latter production so that the ending was more palatable. In the original version, Nora, having realised that she is just as much a dependent child in her husband's house as she was in her father's, leaves her husband and children in order to become a self-determining adult. In the German version she never leaves; her husband forces her to look at their sleeping children and she relents. A similarly mutilated version of the play, entitled, *The Breaking of a Butterfly*, was performed in England in 1884. Harley Granville Barker, the actor and playwright, saw the production and wrote afterwards:

> Burlesque could do no more. Torvald-Humphrey behaves like the pasteboard hero of Nora's doll's house dream: he does strike his chest and say: 'I am the guilty one!' And Nora-Flora cries that she is a poor weak foolish girl, '... no wife for a man like you. You are a thousand times too good for me', and never wakes up and walks out of her doll's house at all.[35]

Three years after the private reading organised by Marx and Aveling, an actress, Janet Achurch, and her husband, Charles Charrington (both of whom were connected with the Marx-Aveling circle) performed the original version of the play to a select audience of Ibsenites. Of this production Granville Barker wrote:

> The play was talked of and written about mainly abusively, it is true — as no play has been for years. The performances were extended from seven to twenty-four. The takings were apt to be between £35 and £45 a night. Charrington lost only £70. This was not bad for an epoch-making venture in the high drama.[36]

Shaw defended the play in his review for the *Manchester Guardian*, but most of the reviewers were horrified. Clement Scott wrote in *Theatre*, 'The atmosphere is hideous ... it is all self, self, self ... a congregation of men and women without one spark of nobility in their nature, men without conscience and women without affection, an unlovable, unlovely and detestable crew.'[37] Whereas the *Standard* felt, 'it would be a misfortune were such a morbid and unwholesome play to gain the favour of the public' and the *Referee* concluded that the play was 'of no use – as far as England's stage is concerned'.[38]

In the heated debate over the relationship between theatre and politics which followed, Ibsen was accused of being a preacher not a playwright, that what he preached was untrue, and finally, that he overstepped the bounds of artistic propriety. In reply to the latter criticism, Eleanor Marx, in a lecture to the Playgoers entitled *Morality and the Stage*, argued that 'all subjects were fit for the stage if artistically treated, including religion and politics. What, indeed, did we in England mean by "morality". Like the word "virtue", it was applied to only one special quality, and referred to sexual relations.'[39]

The impact of Ibsen's work reverberated throughout the theatre, but the actresses who saw the first performance of *A Doll's House* were more excited by the possibility of portraying his characters than in the ideological importance of his plays. This 'glorious actable stuff', as Elizabeth Robins, a young American actress, described it, converted her into an Ibsenite:

> What you won't be able to imagine (unless you are an actress in your twenties) is the joy of having in our hands ... free hands ... such glorious actable stuff. If we had been thinking politically, concerning ourselves about the emancipation of women, we would not have given the Ibsen plays the particular kind of whole-hearted, enchanted devotion we did give. We were actresses ... actresses who wouldn't for a kingdom be anything else. We got over that; but I am talking about '89-'91. ... Ibsen taught us something we were never to unlearn. The lesson had nothing to do with the New Woman; it had everything to do with our particular business ... with the art of acting.[40]

The chasm which separated an actress like Elizabeth Robins from her predecessors was graphically illustrated a few months after the production of *A Doll's House*, at a matinée of another of Ibsen's plays, *Pillars of Society*. Mrs Beringer, the novelist and playwright, who had arranged the performance, was terrified that the audience would neither understand nor appreciate the play and asked Mrs Kendal, who had made her name playing romantic heroines, to finish the matinée with a comic monologue. Shaw, who was in the audience, described the bizarre result:

> She walked round the house at the back of the circle ... an entrancing vision, and presently appeared on the stage and recited. ... She felt, I think, that she was producing a tremendous effect; but she did not know what sort of effect, and does not, probably, to this day. It was as if some good natured pagan, coming into a cathedral at high mass, and seeing a number of people looking very grave, had with the best intentions tried to cheer them up with a comic song.[41]

Mrs Kendal's response to the Ibsen 'cathedral' was echoed by the actor-managers. They could see no reason for performing such contentious and unpleasant plays. Tree, the only manager who even considered producing an Ibsen play, said he would do *The Master Builder* if Solness were a sculptor instead of a builder and if the play were set in England. It became increasingly clear to the Ibsenites that the actor-managers would play no part in the development of the new drama; that all productions of interesting contemporary plays would have to be mounted by private theatre societies. In France, Ibsen's plays had been performed by an amateur society, the Théâtre Libre. After the French company had visited England in 1889, George Moore made the following plea in *The Hawk*:

> Why have we not a Théâtre Libre? Surely there should be no difficulty in finding a thousand persons interested in art and letters willing to subscribe five pounds a year for twelve representations of twelve interesting plays. I think such a number of enthusiasts exist in London.[42]

A private society as Moore outlined, though financially precarious, had the advantage of immunity from official censorship because it performed to a preselected audience. Every play that was publicly advertised had to be licensed by the Lord Chamberlain's office. The censor from 1895 was G. A. Redford who regarded religion, sex and politics as unsuitable subjects for drama. Among the many plays he refused to license were the *Oberammergau Passion Play*, *Oedipus Tyrannus* and *The Mikado*.

England's first 'Théâtre Libre', created in 1891 by the Dutchman J. T. Grein and called the Independent Theatre, capitalised on its freedom from censorship by choosing Ibsen's *Ghosts* as the first production. The critics were outraged by the play, particularly Clement Scott, who wrote:

> If people like the discussion of such nasty subjects on the stage, if they care to make the theatre a closed borough and not a free place of assembly, if it is desirable to drive decent-minded women out of the playhouse, and to use the auditorium as a hospital-ward or dissecting-room, let it be so. Whatever the people desire they will have, and no talking in the world will prevent it. But in our hurry to dramatize the Contagious Diseases Act let us first set about writing a good play.[43]

The idea that Ibsen's plays would alienate women appeared laughable to those actresses who perceived how little the female stereotypes of the West End stage related to their everyday lives. Their belief that Ibsen's characters could speak to all women inspired them to devote their energies to productions of his plays.

Of the half-dozen actresses who pioneered the work of the Norwegian dramatist, Janet Achurch was the most fanatical; apparently she persuaded Henry Irving to give her money to stage a comedy *Clever Alice*, and then used it for the 1889 production of *A Doll's House*. Shaw felt this production was, 'the decisive blow for Ibsen – perhaps the only one that ... really got home in England.'[44] His judgement was based not only on the London performance but also on the provincial tour organised by Janet Achurch in conjunction with the Independent Theatre. Achurch was adamant that the play should be seen by as many people as possible and endlessly traversed England and Scotland in what Shaw described as 'a pretty miserable tour'. The psychological and physical stresses of this work contributed to Achurch's addiction to morphine, from which she eventually died in 1913.

In 1891, the same year as the Independent Theatre's production of *Ghosts*, Florence Farr produced and played Rebecca in *Rosmersholm*. She had given up acting some years before, after a disastrous marriage with an actor, and had studied embroidery under William Morris's daughter, May. Through her connection with the socialist circle surrounding Morris, she encountered the work of Ibsen, which revived her interest in the theatre, and met George Bernard Shaw. He wrote of her: 'She set no bounds to her relationship with men who she liked ... she was in violent reactions against Victorian morals especially sexual and domestic morals.'[45] Florence Farr's production of *Rosmersholm* – which was financed out of a small legacy she had been left by her father – was performed at the Vaudeville Theatre. Although praised by Ibsenites, the performance was totally overshadowed by a production, a few months later at the same theatre, of *Hedda Gabler*.

The English performing rights to *Hedda Gabler* had been secured by Elizabeth Robins and another American actress, Marion Lea. They compared the meeting in 1891 at which they cast the play to 'choosing a Cabinet in a national crisis'.[46] Hedda encapsulated for them all the frustrations of middle-class women who had been denied the opportunity of developing their potential. She is an anti-heroine whose energy and intellect have been converted into negativity and destructiveness, yet at no time does she express remorse or guilt for her actions. Elizabeth Robins, who played Hedda, described her as 'a bundle of unused possibilities, educated to fear life; too much opportunity to develop her weaknesses'.[47] The two actresses were aware that the critics and many of the men in their audience would interpret Hedda's sadism and her ultimate suicide as mere melodrama, but as they pointed out:

> Mr. Clement Scott understands Hedda? Any man except that wizard Ibsen really understand her? Of course not. That was the tremendous part of it. How should men understand Hedda on the stage when they didn't understand her in the persons of their wives, their daughters, their women friends? One lady of our acquaintance, married and not noticeably unhappy, said laughingly, 'Hedda is all of us!'[48]

Contrary to their expectations the production, which had been planned for only five matinées, was so successful that it ran for five weeks. Robins and Lea were praised for their performances as Hedda and Thea, and for their courage as managers in the face of opposition scarcely short of persecution. Their achievement proved that a short run of an Ibsen play could be financially successful and, together with Florence Farr and Janet Achurch, they showed that actresses, though they might be dependent on the actor-managers for their everyday living, could organise their own productions.

Having staged three Ibsen plays between 1889–91, the Ibsenite actresses found themselves in the same dilemma as the Independent Theatre: if the private productions of new drama were to continue, it was essential to find a British playwright who could follow the work of the Norwegian dramatist. After his production of *Ghosts*, J. T. Grein approached authors who had been reluctant to work for the commercial stage and asked them to write plays for the Independent Theatre. His challenge was taken up by Shaw, whose first play, *Widowers' Houses*, was presented in 1892. As well as assuming the role of the British Ibsen, Shaw declared that he could provide the actresses with characters that were as demanding and stimulating to play as Nora or Hedda. He created Blanche Sartorius, the heroine of *Widowers' Houses* (who was played by Florence Farr), as a direct attack upon the female stereotypes of the commerical stage:

> The horrible artificiality of that impudent sham the Victorian womanly woman ... had become more and more irksome to the best actresses, I mean those who had awakeningly truthful minds as well as engaging personalities. I had so little taste for the Victorian womanly woman that in my first play I made my heroine throttle the parlour maid.[49]

Shaw was fascinated by actresses and conducted numerous literary and, occasionally, sexual affairs with them. He wrote:

> As to personal relations with actresses, the affectionate freemasonry of the profession makes it very difficult to let the public see it without misleading them absurdly. Morals and emotions are not the same on both sides of the footlights.[50]

For the most part, Shaw's affairs were theatrical courtships during which he flattered actresses into performing his plays. He claimed to have been inspired to write plays for, amongst others, Janet Achurch, Ellen Terry, and Florence Farr, but the extent of his manipulation only becomes clear when his letters to various actresses are compared.

In his celebrated correspondence with Ellen Terry he wrote:

> My conscience was so burdened with the infamy of having written plays for ... other people about whom I don't care a straw (thank my stars they can't act them) and made no play for you, that it had to be done. Now it is done – the only thing on earth in my power to do for you.[51]

But when Ellen asked for the rights to 'her' play, *Captain Brassbound's Conversion*, Shaw prevaricated. Apparently he wanted Ada Rehan to produce the play and wrote to her friend Lady Barrington:

> A nice time I shall have of it with Ellen. Your Ada, though she has no respect for really first rate plays and great dramatists, can at all events sit still and look noble. Ellen will fidget and flounce all about the place until I freeze her with mere terror; and then she'll forget every word of her part.[52]

Ellen Terry neither flounced nor forgot her lines as Lady Cicely Waynflete, but Shaw took all the credit for her performance: 'Ellen's skin does not fit her body more closely than Lady Cicely Waynflete fits her, for I am a first class ladies tailor, and I love Ellen and Ellen loves me.'[53]

A similar pattern of flattery and criticism emerges in the *Major Barbara* correspondence. While publicly praising Annie Russell's performance in the title role, he wrote to Eleanor Robson saying:

> between ourselves, the play, especially in the last act is a mere ghost; at least so it seems to me. This is no doubt your fault to some extent; I see you in the part; I love you in the part; I was inspired to write the part so that when the Word became Flesh (these old religious catchwords are the plainest common sense to me) the flesh should be yours.[54]

Elizabeth Robins was one of the few actresses who refused to allow Shaw to patronise her. Apparently when he made a pass at her, he was 'flung out of the vehicle into the mud with wheels flying over me this way and that and horses dancing and stumbling on my countenance.'[55] He took his revenge by refusing her the performing rights of *Candida*:

> It so happens accidentally that a single play of mine, *Candida*, presents to her three people who have read all the books she has read, who speak touchingly in her dialect, and conduct a moving drama. The relationship to, say, *The Philanderer*, is no more forced upon her than the implications of *The Master Builder*, which she plays without understanding, by poetic infection.[56]

By accepting Shaw's adulation, the actresses, by implication, accepted his intellectual patronage. He saw them as intuitive beings, 'whose work requires constant physical training, an unblunted nervous sensibility and fastidious refinement and self-control',[57] but he had little respect for their intelligence. While analysing the effect of Ibsen on the theatre he wrote:

he lifted them [the actresses] from being doll-sweethearts, with no influence except the influence of those pretty faces, into serious and sometimes heroic figures, exercising moral influences and religious influences, responding to these influences from others; and struggling with all the currents of the thoughts of their day.[58]

Shaw saw himself as one of the creators of these currents of thoughts that the actresses were struggling to comprehend. He could not accept that an actress, who displayed her emotions on stage with what he perceived to be a childlike lack of inhibition, was capable of analytic thought.

Although Shaw carefully manipulated his actresses, the women he created for them manipulated all the other characters on the stage. In *Candida* – which he claimed 'won the hearts of women, because it turned Ibsen's *Doll's House* upside down by showing the doll in the house was not the woman but the man'[59] – the central character treats her husband and lover as though they were children in an infant school. She allows her husband to indulge in politics and her lover in poetry, but they can only function if she is there to build their egos. This battle between the sexes which underlies many of Shaw's comedies finds its clearest expression in his play *Man and Superman*, in which the behaviour of the two central characters, Ann Wingfield and John Tanner, appears biologically determined. She represents the life-force in all women, without which the species would die out; he, though fatally attracted to this force, attempts to escape his drone role and use his intellectual energies to further civilisation. This reactionary delineation of sex roles, though an underlying theme in Shaw's plays, was overshadowed by his belief in the necessity of legal equality for women. He used his plays as a platform to attack the marriage laws and prostitution, and spoke in favour of women's suffrage and against the forcible feeding of suffrage hunger strikers, on numerous occasions. In 1910, he conducted a personal battle with the taxation office over the assumption that a husband was legally obliged to declare his wife's income as his own. He claimed that he could not force his wife to disclose her income to him and, in an article to *The Times*, hypothesised as to the consequences should the courts insist that he do so:

I am unable to obey the injunction, because no man can tell what he doesn't know. I go to my wife and tell her that I shall be put in prison if she does not tell me her income. She replies that many women have gone to prison for the cause, and it is time that the men should take their turn. Am I to languish in gaol, to the delight of the whole suffragist movement, because I cannot perform impossibilities? Take the obvious alternative. Suppose the courts enjoin my wife to disclose her exact income to me. She refuses. She is sent to prison. She promptly resorts to the hunger strike. Mr. Lloyd George and Mr. Winston Churchill have then either forcibly to feed her ... or else surrender at discretion.[60]

Not only actresses, but also, in later years, the suffrage movement, were confused by Shaw's creations. One critic in The Suffragette[61] acclaimed his Lady Cicely Waynflete – who is merely an older version of Ann Wingfield subduing bandits and savages with her sewing basket and first-aid kit – as the most 'advanced lady' ever 'conceived of by man'. Whether or not Shaw's heroines were as advanced as this critic believed, they were, nevertheless, exciting and challenging roles and Janet Achurch, Florence Farr, Ellen Terry and Mrs Patrick Campbell all staged their own productions of his work.

2. DRAMATIC JOAN OF ARCS

The actresses who played the Ibsen and Shaw heroines in the 1890s achieved a certain independence and notoriety. Nevertheless, in order to earn their living they still had to work on the commercial stage. Once they had been branded as an actress of the 'new drama', they found it increasingly difficult to find an actor-manager who would cast them as a conventional heroine. Their predicament was summed up by Shaw in *Our Theatre in the Nineties*:

> These able and energetic women who pioneered the new movement have had, so far, little to repay them except unlimited opportunities of looking on at fashionable dramas, in which placidly pretty and pleasant actresses enjoyed a heyday of popular success by exhibiting themselves in expensive frocks and going through half a dozen tricks which they probably amuse themselves by teaching to their poodles when they are at a loss for something.[1]

At first it must have seemed to these pioneering actresses that they had ruined their careers. But in the 1890s there was a dramatic change; a new heroine appeared on the commercial stage who had her roots in Ibsen's dramas. In 1893, George Alexander, the actor-manager who had achieved striking successes with Wilde's plays at the St James' Theatre, agreed to produce a play by Pinero entitled *The Second Mrs Tanqueray*.[2] He was risking his reputation with the play — because Paula Tanqueray, the central character, was little more than a prostitute.

The 'woman with a past' was no stranger to the St James' stage. She was one of the stock characters that had been imported with French drama, but usually as a secondary character who simply added a little spice to the plot. Wilde had made use of her in his society dramas. In *Lady Windermere's Fan*[3] she is a mother who left her husband and child for another man and returns to prevent her daughter repeating her own mistakes. In *A Woman of No Importance*,[4] she is, once again, a mother.

Her illegitimate son is offered a government post by his unknown father. She reveals the son to the father and the father to the son and the play ends with the son renouncing the society that made an outcast of his mother while condoning the actions of his father. Despite the apparent message in this play, Wilde was as interested in satirising the morals and manners of the upper classes as in examining the position of an outcast woman. His contempt for the bourgeois preoccupation with the sexual double standard reached its clearest expression in *The Importance of Being Earnest*,[5] when Jack thinks he has discovered that the governess, Miss Prism, is his long lost mother.

In contrast to Wilde's women with a past – peripheral and distanced figures – Pinero placed Paula Tanqueray in the centre of his drama and demanded that the audience identify with her tragedy. The role was considered so controversial that Alexander had difficulty persuading a West End star to play it; eventually he approached three Ibsen actresses, Elizabeth Robins, Mrs Patrick Campbell and Janet Achurch, all of whom had appeared together on stage in a production of *Little Eyolf*.[6] The part was finally accepted by Mrs Patrick Campbell.

The 'past' of the second Mrs Tanqueray, considered so shocking in the 1890s, was as the mistress of countless wealthy men. When she meets Tanqueray he refuses to exploit her and offers her marriage and a home. He knows that this marriage will alienate him from his friends and that, like Paula, he will become a social outcast, but hopes that in time they will both be reabsorbed into respectable society. After their marriage his daughter, who had previously decided to become a nun, returns home unexpectedly. To Tanqueray she is the personification of youth and purity and he is terrified that Paula, who has been irretrievably corrupted by her past life, will destroy her innocence. Paula tries desperately to win Ellean's love but fails and the young girl is sent away to stay with her dead mother's closest friend. She returns to tell her father that she has fallen in love, only to discover that her fiancé is one of Paula's ex-lovers. Although she is prepared to forgive her fiancé, she refuses to forgive her stepmother and Paula, realising that she can never escape her past, commits suicide. In the final scene, before she kills herself, she confronts Tanqueray:

> PAULA: You'll see me then, at last, with other people's eyes;
> you'll see me just as your daughter does now, as all wholesome
> folks see women like me. And I shall have no weapon to fight

with — not one serviceable little bit of prettiness left me to defend myself with! A worn-out creature — broken up, very likely, some time before I ought to be, my hair bright, my eyes dull, my body too thin or too stout, my cheeks raddled and ruddled — a ghost, a wreck, a caricature, a candle that gutters, call such an end what you like! Oh, Aubrey, what shall I be able to say to you then? And this future you talk about! I know it — I know it.[7]

The audiences flocked to see *The Second Mrs Tanqueray*. They saw it as a searing attack on the sexual double standard. In effect it merely reinforced conventional morality. Although Paula is a pathetic victim of sexual hypocrisy, her soul has been destroyed by her sexual exploits; the audience inevitably agrees with Tanqueray that she is not a suitable companion for their children. Her recognition of the consequences of her fall leads to a self-hatred so intense that death is the only solution. Thus she vindicates the audience's judgement.

Following the success of *The Second Mrs Tanqueray* a number of *risqué* heroines appeared on the stage in what came to be known as the 'New Woman' plays of the 1890s. All these women live for love and their greatest tragedy is growing old and unattractive. If they step outside the bounds of conventional morality they suffer and accept their fate as just punishment. The most invidious of these plays was Pinero's *The Notorious Mrs Ebbsmith*.[8] The central character, again played by Mrs Patrick Campbell, was based on what Shaw described as 'a woman of the type of George Eliot, Miss Josephine Butler, (or) Mrs Besant'. Mrs Ebbsmith is the daughter of a secularist agitator. When her husband dies she takes up her father's work as a platform speaker, but poverty forces her to give up this career and become a nurse. She falls in love with one of her patients who is unhappily married and realising that her love for him is more important than her work, or her ideas, puts on a low-cut gown and attempts to seduce him. In the final scene, she is about to succeed when a clergyman arrives and presents her with a Bible: she throws it into the fire and then thrusts her hands into the flames to retrieve it.

It is significant that when the 'New Woman' plays were in vogue in the 1890s, the suffrage campaign was making little headway in parliament, the Tories were against votes for women on principle and the Liberals would not support a limited form of enfranchisement if it meant more votes for Tories. This situation was aggravated by the press, which imposed a virtual boycott on the question; though in 1899, they did publish a Protest Against Women's Suffrage which had been signed by, amongst others, Mrs Humphrey Ward, Mrs Creighton and Mrs Sidney Webb, part of which read: 'We believe the emancipatory process has now reached the limit fixed by the physical constitution of women.' The new woman plays reflected this reaction against the women's rights movement by showing women struggling for sexual freedom, not legal equality. Only Mrs Ebbsmith has a glimmer of political independence and this she readily gives up for love. To actresses working in a profession where husbands and lovers could be exchanged without much guilt or retribution, the anxieties of Paula Tanqueray and her successors must have appeared absurd. But in contrast to the romantic heroines of contemporary musical comedies, these female characters were startlingly real. In 1896 Marie Tempest had caused a sensation in *The Geisha Girl* at Daly's Theatre, playing O Mimosa San, the geisha girl who was in love with a British naval officer. The lyrics to one of her songs ran:

> A goldfish swam in a big glass bowl,
> As dear little goldfish do,
> But she loved with the whole of her heart and soul
> An officer brave from the ocean wave
> And she thought that he loved her too!
> Her small inside he daily fed
> With crumbs of the best digestive bread.
> 'This kind attention proves', said she,
> 'How exceedingly fond he is of me.'[9]

Elizabeth Robins, who turned down the part of Paula Tanqueray, wrote, 'Events after Hedda emphasised for us the kind of life that stretched in front of the women condemned to the "hack work" of the stage. That was what we called playing even the best parts selected by the actor-managers.'[10] The only way to escape the tyranny of the actor-managers, as Elizabeth Robins realised, was to set up independent managements run by women:

> The further result of the reception given to *Hedda Gabler* was to encourage Miss Lea and me in a hope that haunted our dreams before we ever heard of Hedda — a hope of escape from the need to accept the conditions of the existing Theatre. We had come to

realize how essential to success some freedom of judgement and
action are to the actor. The strangulation of this role and that
through arbitrary stage management, was an experience we had
shared with men. But we had further seen how freedom in the
practice of our art, how the bare opportunity to practise it at all,
depended, for the actress, on considerations humiliatingly different
from those that confronted the actor. The stage career of an actress
was inextricably involved in the fact that she was a woman and that
those who were masters of the theatre were men. These
considerations did not belong to art; they stultified art. We dreamed
of an escape, through hard work, and through deliberate
abandonment of the idea of making money ... beyond what would
give us the wages of going on. We would organize a season ...
leading up to future seasons ... of that Lea-Robins joint
management, so dear to our hearts, that had already seen Hedda
through.[11]

Elizabeth Robins' idea of the actress-manager was not new. Madame
Vestris claimed to be the first English actress to run a company when
she leased the Olympic Theatre in 1830, and, to draw attention to this
fact on the opening night of her season, she had recited the following
prologue:

> Noble and gentle – matrons – patrons – friends!
> Before you here a venturous woman bends!
> A warrior woman – that in strife embarks
> The first of all dramatic Joan of Arcs.
> Cheer on the enterprise that dared by me!
> The first that ever led a company.[12]

Madame Vestris was an actress who had made her name in 1817
playing Giovanni in a burlesque of Mozart's opera. She was renowned
for playing breeches parts, in particular Captain Macheath in *The
Beggar's Opera*, which won her critical acclaim for her singing and
turned her into a Georgian sex symbol:

> What a breast – what an eye! What a foot, leg and
>   thigh!
> What wonderful things she has shown us.
> Round hips, swelling sides, masculine strides –
> Proclaim her an English Adonis.[13]

The debate over the perfections of her body reached such a pitch that the critic from *The Age* wrote that he:

> knew as much of the fair proportions of the fair Vestris's legs as any man breathing – we have a cast of one of Madame's legs in our possession, and in comparison with the Medicean Venus we pronounce that of the living Venus to be faultless![14]

Although Vestris was frequently irritated by the attention of the press, the publicity boosted her popularity to such an extent that her salary reached thirty guineas a week. With the money she made as an actress, Madame Vestris employed her own company and set out to eradicate from her theatre the very qualities that had led to her success as an actress. She forced her fellow actors and the public to respect her art rather than her legs. According to a contemporary critic, 'she has banished vulgarity, coarse manners, double entendre, and impertinence from the boards on which she presides, and in their place has evoked the benefits that flow from a dramatic interpretation of polished manners, refinement and politeness.'[15]

A few Victorian stars followed Madame Vestris' example and managed theatres for limited seasons, but usually they did so in conjunction with actor-husbands, and their productions differed little from those of the actor-managers. However, in the provinces, Sarah Thorne, who knew she would never succeed on the West End stage, did manage to develop a thriving touring company in the late nineteenth century. Violet Vanbrugh worked with her for three years:

> Miss Thorne was an exceedingly good actress, and knew her business from A–Z. She seldom in these plays acted herself, having given it up except for special performances a few years before I joined her. She had an important reputation as an actress in the country, but as she used to say herself – 'My dear, I know I can act, but I am very plain, and I don't look the parts; that is why I shall never be a leading actress.'[16]

In contrast to their predecessors, Elizabeth Robins and Marion Lea had a vision of a new kind of theatre developed under their management. They had no desire to mimic the long runs of the commercial stage, but were determined to produce a repertoire of plays that were both artistically and economically viable. They chose *Karin*,[17] a play by the Norwegian woman playwright Alfhild Agrell, for their first production at the Vaudeville Theatre in 1892. The play, written in the Ibsen mould, was about a young woman who becomes increasingly angry and resentful towards her husband as he fritters away their money on his many mistresses. She is terrified that her child will be deprived of any education or financial support, so in order to safeguard his future, she borrows some money from a family friend. Her husband finds out about the loan and he demands it to pay back the money he has embezzled from his employers. When she refuses, he abducts the child and denies her access to him until she gives him the money. The exchange in the final scene has a tragic ending. Karin is given the dead body of her child, who has died of an infantile disease.

Karin was followed by a production, in 1893, at the Trafalgar Square Theatre of *The Master Builder*.[18] Elizabeth had persuaded Ibsen to give her the performing rights of the play while it was still being written. She received it, an act at a time, through the post. The central relationship in the play — between Solness, the master builder, and the young woman, Hilda Wangel — appeared to Elizabeth as a reflection of her own artistic involvement with Ibsen. After reading the play, she declared 'Hilda Wangel is me'. Solness, the male artist, ruthlessly exploits people for his work, but lives in fear of retribution which he sees personified by youth. When youth does 'knock on his door', it is in the unexpected form of a young woman, Hilda, who instead of destroying him, demands that he creates her 'castles in the air'. She has no creative expression herself, except through his art, but the intensity of her inspiration ultimately kills him. Elizabeth's identification with the part was so strong that years later she wrote, 'It was in my part as Hilda Wangel in *The Master Builder* that I suppose I scored my greatest triumph. I certainly remember that as the crowning pleasure of my theatrical career.'[19]

Despite Elizabeth's vision of a permanent actress-manager's theatre, her work with Marion Lea was still restricted to occasional productions and, in that sense, was little different from the Independent Theatre. The problem was capital. If they were to secure a long lease on a theatre they had to find a patron, or rather a patroness of the arts. This they failed to do, but Florence Farr, who had produced *Rosmersholm*, [20] met with more success. In 1894 she leased the Avenue Theatre for a season of three plays; the money for this venture had been provided by Annie Horniman, the daughter of a wealthy Victorian tea merchant. Although she had no knowledge of theatre and had trained at the Slade,

Annie Horniman had seen Ibsen's plays performed in Germany and, on returning to England, became involved in the Ibsen movement. Together with Florence Farr, she shared Elizabeth Robins' vision of an actress-manager's theatre that could develop the new drama. Their season at the Avenue Theatre consisted of *The Comedy of Sighs* by Dr John Todhunter, W. B. Yeats' *The Land of Heart's Desire* and Shaw's *Arms and the Man*. The plays were financially disastrous, particularly Shaw's, which averaged in box office takings between 21 April and 7 July, £22 3s. 5d. a performance. In the 1890s, seat prices in West End theatres ranged from 1s. in the pit to half a guinea in the stalls, and a large musical comedy theatre like Daly's expected box office takings of £3,000 a week in order to break even. Annie Horniman was not discouraged by the figures. She considered the venture a 'fruitful failure' because it contributed to the growth of the repertory movement by providing a limited season of contrasting plays in an age when the norm was to play a single production for as long as the demand lasted. It was also the first production of a Shaw play outside the private theatre societies and the posters were designed by an unknown artist, Aubrey Beardsley.

Shortly after the Avenue season, Florence Farr, who was seriously ill, became a student of theosophy and travelled to South-East Asia, where she died. Annie Horniman, who determined to continue subsidising the new drama, offered her assistance to W. B. Yeats. Although she was not a performer, her career as a manager is worth pursuing because she shared the ideals of the Ibsen actresses. She built the Abbey Theatre in Dublin for Yeats at her own expense and provided it with an annual subsidy. In return she expected some influence over the artistic policy, but she was an Englishwoman in an Irish nationalist theatre and was relegated to the position of a distant patroness. Eventually she decided to create an equivalent theatre in England. There were no suitable theatres for lease in London, so together with the artistic director, Iden Payne, she established the Gaiety Theatre in Manchester. In 1907, the following announcement advertising her new company was placed in the Manchester papers:

> We shall seek to produce good new plays, to revive old masterpieces and to present translations of the best works of foreign authors. We have chosen Manchester because we feel that of all towns it is the one most ready for such an undertaking, and that there, if

anywhere, there will be the necessary support for our scheme.[21]

An impression of Annie Horniman from the early Gaiety years survives in a letter written by a young actress in the company, Sybil Thorndike, to her brother Russell:

> I like her awfully on first acquaintance. She looks as if she stepped out of a mid-Victorian picture — tall and dignified and I think just a beautiful face, and she wears the most wonderful clothes, all made in the same mid-Victorian style of the loveliest materials — Beautiful stuff that you'd only think of for curtains, and are surprised to see how well it furnished the human body. She makes a real picture. I like seeing people as if they'd been painted by someone — Miss Horniman looks like that. She is a very enterprising woman. She spends most of her money on theatre and lives very simply herself in a sort of bachelor way. I admire her, I would like to do what she is doing.[22]

At the Gaiety, Annie Horniman once again exercised the artistic control that she had had in the Avenue venture. She encouraged new playwrights, women as well as men, read all their scripts and advised as to possible production. Although she was not actively involved in the women's rights movement, the Gaiety had a bias towards plays concerned with the position of women and which provided actresses with satisfying roles. One of the Theatre's most successful productions was Stanley Houghton's *Hindle Wakes*.[23] Whereas the new woman dramas had restricted sex to the marriage bed, this play asserted that extra-marital sex could be as enjoyable for women as it was for men. Fanny Hawthorn, the central character, is a mill girl who goes to Llandudno for a holiday weekend with Alan, her employer's son. When she returns, her parents demand that Alan marry her, but Fanny is appalled. As far as she is concerned, the weekend had been just 'a lark' and hardly the basis on which to build a marriage. The play ends with Fanny leaving home, confident that while she has the security of her trade, she will never be forced to conform to her parents' morality. By linking Fanny's demand for sexual freedom to her economic independence as a mill girl, Stanley Houghton succeeded in taking the sexual struggle out of the middle-class drawing rooms.

In the same year that Annie Horniman created the Gaiety, Lena Ashwell attempted a similar scheme in London. Her venture was also financed by two wealthy women, referred to in her autobiography[24] as Jane and Lady Caroline. Apparently the latter was infatuated with Lena and persuaded Jane to finance her scheme for a co-operative company dedicated to producing new plays. Lena signed a ninety-nine year lease for Penley's Theatre and renamed it the Kingsway. Athene Seyler remembers it as a charming theatre:

> The Kingsway was so beautifully run. All the programmes and the chocolate boxes and the aprons of the maids were pink striped – pale pink and deep pink. The whole thing was so feminine. It looked so pretty when your programme matched the box of chocolates and the apron of the girl who gave it to you.[25]

The first season was a financial disaster. Lena had never intended her theatre to be commercially viable and assumed Jane would continue to subsidise her. Unfortunately, Lady Caroline, who was central to the scheme, was jealous of Lena's relationship with her future husband, Dr Henry Simpson, and the money was withdrawn. Consequently Lena lost all her savings, while still legally responsible for a financially crippling lease on the Kingsway. She was forced to abandon her co-operative scheme and agreed to share the theatre with another manager, Mr Otho Stuart.

Despite the abortive nature of Lena's venture, it did succeed in pioneering the way for other women to secure financial backing for independent managements. By 1912 there were four actresses running London theatres and, more importantly, at the Victoria Music Hall in Waterloo Road, the young manager, Lilian Bayliss, had secured a theatre licence from the Lord Chamberlain's office. Just as Annie Horniman laid the foundations of the modern repertory movement at the Gaiety, Lilian Bayliss was to lay the foundation of the National Theatre at the Old Vic.

By securing their own theatres, even for limited seasons, Elizabeth Robins, Florence Farr and Lena Ashwell broke their dependency on the actor-managers. But the new drama they chose to produce, though frequently concerned with women's rights, was still written by Ibsen and Shaw. Elizabeth Robins, who perceived the irony of their position, wrote:

> Whether for purposes of jest or earnest, it is clear that intelligent representation of women cannot be left to men who, however

modern they think themselves, have as regards women the medieval mind – where that order of mind attempts to deal with women, the spirit of true comedy takes flight as George Meredith long ago pointed out.[26]

In the nineteenth century there had been little opportunity for women to write for a male-dominated theatre. Rather than struggle to get plays accepted for production by actor-managers who were more concerned with spectacle than language, women writers concentrated on novels which could be written in the isolation of their own homes. The actress-managers had little success in persuading these novelists, who had no practical knowledge of theatre, to write drama – so inevitably the actresses, in particular Elizabeth Robins and Cicely Hamilton, began writing their own plays.

Elizabeth Robins' first play was written in collaboration with the novelist and playwright Lady Bell, who had translated the Norwegian play *Karin*, by Alfhild Agrell, for the Vaudeville season. Dramatised from the Norwegian short story *Befriad*, by Elin Armeen, the play was relocated in the north of England and entitled *Alan's Wife*.[27] Jean Creyke, Alan's wife, has chosen to marry a beautiful, sensual miner, rather than a 'book-learned' minister. She describes Alan as 'a man who is my master as well as other folks; who loves the hills and the heather, and loves to feel the strong wind blowing in his face and the blood rushing through his veins.' In the opening scene, she appears content with her role of housewife and expectant mother and defends her choice of husband by implying that she prefers sexual to intellectual fulfilment. The scene ends with Alan's body being carried on stage; he has been killed in a pit accident. The second scene takes place a few months later, after Jean has given birth to a deformed child. Her mother is appalled by her apparent rejection of the baby, but when Jean is left alone she reveals her fear that her son's future will be a lifetime of suffering. She baptises the child and smothers it. In the final scene she has been tried and convicted of murder. Her family and friends try and persuade her to claim temporary insanity or, at very least, to beg for forgiveness; but Jean tells them she is quite sane and goes willingly to her death.

The play, which was performed by the Independent Theatre in 1893, caused an uproar. The establishment critics found the theme of *Alan's Wife* as disgusting and unacceptable as that of *Ghosts*; whereas Shaw ridiculed the play because he found the central character too heroic for a working-class woman. In contrast, William Archer, a close friend of Elizabeth Robins, described the play as 'a life tragedy, not a great one, but Jean Creyke has this in common with Orestes, that she is placed in one of those agonising dilemmas where it seems equally possible, equally human, to act or to refrain.'[28]

In the context of the late nineteenth century, the play appeared to challenge conventional attitudes to both female sexuality and motherhood. However, Jean's decision to smother her child is not only based on a refusal to accept her role as mother and nurturer, but also intricately connected with her decision to marry Alan, whom she describes as if he were a member of a master race. Ultimately, she is asserting that the life of a crippled child, or for that matter a 'weakling minister', is inferior to that of a physically beautiful, natural leader of men.

Although Elizabeth Robins played Jean Creyke, she and Lady Bell did not reveal that they had written the play. They were concerned that *Alan's Wife* should not be patronised as the work of women writers. Their fears were based on the fate of women novelists, who were perpetually compared to each other as though they were an inferior sub-section of authors. Cicely Hamilton, who had begun her theatrical career as an actress in touring companies, also wrote her first play in the 1890s and had the same experience:

> Otho Stuart warned me it was advisable to conceal the sex of its author until after the notices were out, as plays which were known to be written by women were apt to get a bad press. My name, therefore, appeared on the programme in the indeterminate abbreviated form of C. Hamilton.[29]

Cicely Hamilton could disguise her sex from the critics, but not from the managers – she had to wait until Lena Ashwell took over the Kingsway before one of her full-length plays was produced. *Diana of Dobson's*,[30] a comedy about an impecunious middle-class shop assistant, was the only successful production mounted by the Kingsway co-operative company. Set in the bleak girl's dormitory of Dobson's drapery firm, the play begins with Diana, the rebel, complaining to her friend Kit 'I wish I could see anything at all humorous about Messrs. Dobson's high class drapery emporium. Grind and squalor and tyranny and overwork, I can see plenty of those – but I fail to detect where the

humour comes in.' She is about to be sacked when a letter arrives, like a
deus ex machina, saying that she has inherited £300. Instead of deciding
to live sensibly off the income of her inheritance, Diana travels to
Switzerland, posing as a wealthy widow. She finds herself staying in the
same hotel as one of her ex-employers. Of course, he does not recognise
her, so she decides to confront him over the 'secret of his success':

DIANA: The question is – how do you manage to give them a
            half-penny cheaper than anyone else?
SIR JABEZ: That's the secret – organisation – keep down working
            expenses.
DIANA: Working expenses – that means wages, doesn't it?
SIR JABEZ: Wages is one item.
DIANA: And generally the first to be kept down. Oh that's the
            way to make money – to get other people to work for you for as
            little as they can be got to take, and put the proceeds into your
            pockets. I sometimes wonder if success is worth buying on those
            terms.[31]

Just as she is about to leave for England, having spent all her money,
one of the guests, Captain Bretherton, asks her to marry him. When
she reveals her true identity and occupation, he withdraws his proposal.
Diana, aware that he considers a woman who earns her own living his
social inferior, challenges him to try to survive without his private
income for six months. The play ends on the Thames Embankment,
where Bretherton, who has failed to qualify for a single job, is sleeping
rough. By chance he meets Diana, admits his failure and once again
asks her to marry him.

Diana of Dobson's was a critical and financial success. The profits
from the play went into the Kingsway co-operative, so Cicely
Hamilton only received £20, but there were other compensations:

In the morning there were notices, favourable notices, which I read
with a feeling that they couldn't be real – all this praise and
encouragement and kindliness couldn't really be written about me!
... And in the afternoon I got a bus and went all the way to
Liverpool Street; for this reason only, that my chosen bus had
Diana of Dobson's by Cicely Hamilton advertised along the top.
'Cicely Hamilton' was writ very small, and in all probability few
who saw the advertisement noticed it; but I noticed it, and it was
that that mattered.[32]

In essence, Cicely Hamilton's play is a traditional sentimental romance in which the poverty-stricken heroine marries a wealthy young aristocrat; within this structure she manages to expose the exploitation of shop girls, though at the expense of the racialist stereotype of a Jewish capitalist, Sir Jabez. This technique of manipulating a popular theatrical form to provide a platform for the demands of the women's rights movement was used with even greater success by Elizabeth Robins in her second play *Votes for Women!*,[33] which was performed at the Court Theatre in 1907.

Instead of a sentimental comedy, Elizabeth Robins chose to write a subtle pastiche on Paula Tanqueray. Vida Levering is a suffragette who had an illegitimate child that died at birth; the father of the child was a member of parliament, George Stonor. Ten years later, Vida meets Jane Dunbarton, Stonor's fiancée, and persuades her to join the cause. Eventually, Jane discovers that Stonor deserted Vida and demands that he marry her, but Vida refuses and tells Stonor that he can repay his debt, not to her, but to all women by supporting votes for women in the House. The most successful part of the play is a suffragette rally in Trafalgar Square at which Vida is speaking. The political speeches are sheer propaganda for the Cause, but Elizabeth Robins maintains the dramatic tension by incorporating a recognition scene between Stonor and Vida.

Elizabeth Robins' play heralded the beginning of a suffrage theatre that was to go far beyond the individual efforts of the Ibsenite actresses, actress-managers, and women playwrights of the late nineteenth century. Through their involvement with the women's rights movement and their dissatisfaction with a male-dominated theatre, these women had begun to develop a drama that could express the reality of women's lives, but they were still working in comparative isolation. With the emergence of the mass suffrage movement in the Edwardian era, over a thousand actresses were thrust into the fight for votes for women. Out of their struggle the first women's theatre movement of the twentieth century was born.

Part Two

THE ACTRESSES' FRANCHISE LEAGUE

'That women should possess the vote is the merest justice. All the political philosophies that man has invented have as yet produced no sensible argument against woman's claim to say what shall be the nature of those laws to which she shall conform. ... There is a fashionable belief prevalent among the opponents of women's suffrage that – so the formula goes – all intelligence in women is but a reflection of the intelligence of men. The simple logic of this proposition must be that if man did not exist, women would possess no intelligence whatsoever.' – *Sarah Bernhardt*[1]

3. KISSES OR VOTES: THE AFL
1908–10

On a cold mid-December afternoon in 1908 the first public meeting of the Actresses' Franchise League was held at the Criterion Restaurant, London. It was a glittering affair as the stars of the West End stage arrived surrounded by hordes of fans and autograph hunters. Ellen Terry, the Shakespearean heroine of the Lyceum Theatre, and the delightful comedienne, Mrs Kendal, both in their 60s and close to retirement, arrived and were met by the Edwardian stars Violet Vanbrugh, Eva and Decima Moore. Inside the restaurant 400 actresses, actors and dramatists listened to telegrams of support from Madame Sarah Grand, Arthur Wing Pinero, J. K. Jerome and Henry Neville. The meeting began at three o'clock, but despite the large number of women present and the exclusively female membership of the League, the chair was taken by the actor-manager, Mr Forbes Robertson. The two speakers were both women: Evelyn Sharp spoke about the problems facing women industrial workers, and Cicely Hamilton told an amusing story about a speaker at an anti-suffragist meeting who had argued that women should not be given the vote because it was their duty to stay at home and console their husbands. As the journalist from the *Stage* reported:

> Miss Hamilton failed to see why a husband should need consoling, and thought too, that there might be difficulty in the way of some women fulfilling this mission in life as a consoler, should they happen not to possess a husband waiting at home to be consoled.[1]

After a short debate in which various celebrities declared, in a more or less theatrical manner, their support for the women's cause, the following resolution was passed:

> This meeting of actresses calls upon the Government immediately to extend the franchise to women; that women claim the franchise as a necessary protection for the workers under modern industrial

conditions, and maintains that by their labour they have earned the right to this defence.[2]

Next day the newspapers were filled with the names of the West End stars who had publicly demanded the vote. Among those not mentioned was an unknown actress, Jane Comfort, who also joined the League. She was at the very beginning of her career in 1908, but when I interviewed her some seventy years later she still remembered the meeting:

> Gertrude Forbes Robertson came to collect my aunt, the dramatist Madeline Lucette Ryley, to take her to the meeting, and I was dragged along because wherever my aunt went in those days I went too. I had just left school and I was studying for the stage. I remember on the way home in the car I was terribly excited about all I had heard, and what a wonderful thing it was, and how I wished I could join the Actresses' Franchise League. My aunt said, 'You're not eligible to join; you're not an actress!' But Gertrude, who was always ready to help, said, 'Why don't you come and walk on in *The High Bid* at Her Majesty's Theatre.' And so I went on in one of the crowd scenes for a guinea a week, and provided my own costume. That was my first appearance on the London stage and as soon as I could say I was an actress I became a member of the League.
>
> The League grew and grew until nearly every actress in the business joined. We had an office on the ground floor in the Adelphi. There were three windows. Somebody bought some material for blinds, I suppose it was my aunt, and I embroidered the letters ACTRESSES FRANCHISE LEAGUE in black letters about four inches high to hang in the windows. That was my contribution. The office was always open, but we had regular meetings there one day a week with tea and buns. That again was my job and as a novelty, I used to charge them for their cups of tea. I suppose it was a penny, and the buns were free – the little farthing buns, dear little things about the size of a scone. People didn't quite take to the idea, so we charged for the buns and let the tea be free.[3]

The most immediate issue for discussion at the League's first meetings, apart from the payment of refreshments, was whether the actresses should support the National Union of Women's Suffrage Societies,

NUWSS, or the Women's Social and Political Union, WSPU.

The NUWSS was created out of the independent suffrage societies of Manchester, Bristol, London and Edinburgh in 1897 and continued their tradition of constitutional agitation for the vote, 'on the same terms as it is or may be granted to men.' In the closing years of the nineteenth century it organised a nationwide petition which gathered over a quarter of a million signatures. This inspired the Manchester Women's Trade and Labour Council to organise a further petition of women textile workers in Lancashire, Cheshire and Yorkshire in the early 1900s. As well as collecting signatures these Manchester suffragists took the fight for the vote into trade union branches, trades councils, labour clubs and socialist societies. Central to this campaign was their insistence that working women needed the vote in order to improve wages and conditions of employment. According to Jane Comfort it was the demand for equal pay that initially galvanised the actresses into action:

> There was a public-spirited actress called Adeline Bourne, who was interested in the suffrage question and had attended some meetings. As one of the planks in the suffragists' platform was the question of equality of payment for men and women – My God, just as it is today – Adeline said we ought to support them, because in the theatre a leading lady gets the same salary as a leading man; she may get more, it all depends on the part. Adeline canvassed all the actresses she knew, leading ones and lesser ones with this idea that we should band together and support the suffragists. Then she went to see Mr Forbes Robertson, the manager of the company she was with – he was her boss – and asked him to support the organisation and he said yes, he would.[4]

Adeline found recruiting for her Actresses' Franchise League comparatively easy. Many of the leading actresses of the day had already been converted to the cause by the Women's Social and Political Union. The WSPU had been formed in 1903, by Mrs Pankhurst and her daughter Christabel, to win the support of the Labour movement for the early enfranchisement of women. The WSPU became increasingly distanced from its Labour roots after the 1906 general election. Of the twenty-nine Labour members who were returned to parliament, only Keir Hardie considered votes for women a legislative priority. The majority were more concerned with the possibility of a Right to Work Bill and the necessity of reversing the Taff Vale Judgement which had limited the power of the unions. They felt that if the franchise were reformed it should result in universal suffrage and not a limited form of enfranchisement for women. Christabel could not accept this policy, so the WSPU concentrated its energies on the new Liberal Government. She encouraged influential women to join the union because, as she remarked, somewhat acidly, 'the House of Commons, and even its Labour members, are more impressed by the demonstrations of the feminine bourgeoisie than the female proletariat.'

The WSPU or suffragettes, as they were nicknamed by the press, differed dramatically from the NUWSS. The Pankhursts were cynical about the effectiveness of the National Union's constitutional methods which after fifty years had brought no results. In contrast they developed a hierarchal organisation which gradually became more and more militant. Their conviction that the Liberal Government would not respond to polite deputations and petitions was strengthened in 1908, when a Women's Franchise Bill was deliberately killed by the Government. The Bill, proposed by H. Y. Stanger, had won a place in the private members' ballot and was put down for a second reading. Although it was carried by 271 votes to 92, the Government, through a skilful manipulation of parliamentary procedure, prevented a third and final reading.

In the course of the debate in the House the Home Secretary, Herbert Gladstone, had said:

On the question of Women's Suffrage, experience shows that predominance of argument alone, and I believe that this has been attained, is not enough to win the political day. ... Then comes the time when political·dynamics are far more important than political argument. ... Men have learned this lesson, and know the necessity for demonstrating the greatness of their movements, and for establishing that force majeure which actuates and arms a government for effective work. That is the task before the · supporters of this great movement. ...

Looking back at the great political crises in the 'thirties, and the 'sixties and the 'eighties it will be found that people ... assembled in their tens of thousands all over the country. ... Of course it cannot be expected that women can assemble in such masses, but power belongs to the masses, and through this power a government can be influenced into more effective action than a government will be likely to take under present conditions.[5]

Taking him at his word, the WSPU organised a mass demonstration for Midsummer's Day, 1908. The suffragettes, who were transported to London by thirty special trains, were instructed to wear white dresses and carry banners in the WSPU colours of purple, white and green. Seven processions, each headed by a well-known personality in a four-in-hand coach (one of whom was the actress Lillah McCarthy), marched through the city to converge in Hyde Park. A quarter of a mile of railings had been removed to facilitate easy access to the twenty speakers' platforms. Thousands of women and men filled the Park, among them Israel Zangwill, Mrs H. G. Wells, Mrs Thomas Hardy, Sarah Grand, Bernard Shaw and Keir Hardie. When the speeches ended and the bugles sounded a great shout of 'Votes for women!' was repeated three times. The correspondent from *The Times* was suitably impressed:

> Its organisers had counted on an audience of 250,000. That expectation was certainly fulfilled; probably it was doubled; it would be difficult to contradict anyone who asserted that it was trebled. Like the distance and the numbers of the stars, the facts were beyond the threshold of perception.[6]

A few months after this demonstration, when the actresses met at the Criterion Restaurant, a number of them were already members of either the WSPU or the NUWSS. To prevent an internal split within their franchise league, the actresses offered their support to all the suffrage societies and declared themselves impartial over the question of tactics. Eva Moore, a vice-president of the AFL, explains: 'It was non-party and non-political. Though it did not advocate extreme measures, it did not condemn them, its policy was "the aim is everything".'[7] However, it soon became apparent that the majority of the League's members did identify with the militant wing of the movement. Psychologically the actresses were inevitably attracted to the more theatrical methods of the WSPU and the Women's Freedom League (WFL), which was created in 1907 by members of the WSPU who split from the Pankhursts over the lack of internal democracy in the union – Mrs Despard was their first president. In the spring of 1909, a member of the WFL had sailed over the House of Commons in a balloon painted with the slogan 'Votes for Women'; followers of Mrs Pankhurst drove around London in a prison van marked EP (her initials) and dispatched themselves as human letters to 10 Downing Street. Actresses were encouraged to sell *Votes for Women*, the suffrage newspaper originally published by the Pethick-Lawrences; in 1908, when the paper was self-supporting through sales and advertisements, they had given it to the union and by 1910, it had a circulation of 40,000. Mrs Pankhurst and Mrs Pethick-Lawrence were guest speakers at the Actresses' Franchise League meetings in February 1909, and in April, when the latter was released after a month in Holloway Prison, the AFL headed her victory procession to the Aldwych Theatre.

For the actresses in the League who supported the NUWSS the contradiction between the avowed aims of the AFL and the obvious tendency towards militancy of the majority of its members became intolerable. After a particularly traumatic meeting at Drury Lane a number of them resigned; Irene Vanbrugh, the leading lady of the West End stage in 1909, who had agreed to become a vice-president of the League on condition that it was going to fight on the non-militant side, was one of the speakers at that meeting:

I was asked to speak in favour of the vote at a big rally in Drury Lane Theatre organised by the Actresses' Franchise League to bring the importance of the movement home to a wider circle of the dramatic profession. I consented only under the definite assurance that it was on constitutional lines that the meeting would be held and that under that assurance Mrs Henry Fawcett and other prominent members of the right wing had consented to be on the stage with us. This seemed to preclude any speeches being made in favour of militant methods.

Drury Lane was packed to suffocation. The meeting opened more or less quietly when, to my consternation, two speakers with militant leanings stirred up a tremendous amount of enthusiasm and shouting from an audience which I gathered must have been almost entirely composed of those in favour of any form of attack. When my turn came to speak I knew that I was bound to encounter opposition, but I had made up my mind to make my position clear and I also felt in honour bound to our guests who had obviously come, as I had, under false pretences. It came quickly, for no sooner

had they realised the attitude I was taking in the matter than there
were shouts of 'sit down', 'why did she come?' etc., etc. However,
by this time all cowardice had left me. I finished my say and was
followed by Lena Ashwell, a very prominent member of the
movement, who said that while she appreciated my wishing to
clarify my own attitude it was not possible for the AFL to dissociate
themselves from either side of the campaign. In these circumstances
our guests left the stage.

I felt very bewildered by what had happened and was mobbed by
a large number of women who begged me to form a separate party
in which they would enrol themselves and would follow my
leadership. However, this was quite outside what I had proposed to
tackle and I eventually got home, shattered by my experiences but
still glad to have faced it out.[8]

While the actresses were arguing about the internal policy of their
League, the battle between the Government and the suffragettes was
escalating. Coinciding with the opening of parliament on 29 July 1909,
the WSPU, as usual, held their own women's parliament at Caxton
Hall; it concluded with a deputation to the House of Commons, led by
Mrs Pankhurst. When the women arrived in Parliament Square, they
were informed that Asquith, who had taken over from Campbell
Bannerman as prime minister in 1908, would not receive them. During
the inevitable clash between the suffragettes and the police which
followed windows in a number of government offices were smashed.
This was the first time that the militants had deliberately attacked
government property and they took suitably ladylike precautions to
avoid human injury: the stones were wrapped in paper, tied with
string, tapped against the glass and dropped through the holes.

In the coming months, finding themselves effectively banned from
political meetings organised by the Liberal Party, the suffragettes
resorted to similar tactics – breaking windows and ripping the slates off
the roofs of public buildings in which the meetings were being held.
Arrests and imprisonments followed; the women demanded the right to
be treated as political prisoners rather than common criminals and
when this was refused, they retaliated with hunger strikes. By
September, thirty-seven women had succeeded in terminating their
prison sentences after four to six days of self-imposed starvation. Then
on 24 September, the Home Secretary, Herbert Gladstone, instructed

the authorities to forcibly feed all hunger strikers. His decision was greeted with a wave of protest: in parliament, where Keir Hardie described forcible feeding as 'a horrible beastly outrage'; in the *British Medical Journal*, where Gladstone's conduct was described as 'contemptible'; and in the letter columns of *The Times*, *Manchester Guardian* and the *Observer*.

Eva Moore was among the public figures in the entertainments industry who criticised the Government's decision:

> At a time when forcible feeding was being resorted to very much, two girls, who were suffragists, were presented at court. They were both of very good social position, and very charming. One of them on being presented to the King said, 'Your Majesty, won't you stop forcible feeding?' She was promptly hustled out of the presence, and the press the following day were full of 'the insult offered to the King'. It may have been, probably was, the wrong time to do it; it was probably the wrong way to attempt to do it; but I did feel, and still feel, that the girl must have called up every ounce of courage she possessed to say what she did. At a meeting next day I ventured to say just what I have written here, ending with: 'Whatever one may feel about the wisdom or propriety of her action, you must take off your hat to the girl for her courage.' Then the storm burst. That evening I found headlines in the papers: 'Eva Moore takes off her hat to the woman who insulted the King', and so on, it was astonishing. The result was rather dreadful; men I had never seen wrote to me, wrote the most abusive, indecent letters I have ever read or ever dreamed could be written, letters which left me gasping that people who could write at all should descend to using such epithets and expressions. Had I not already been a suffragist those letters would have made me one! However it came to an end, and I survived, though I admit at the time it distressed me very much indeed.[9]

Although the majority of the AFL's membership, like Eva Moore, supported the WSPU and sympathised with the hunger strikers, only a few were directly involved in militant action. Like most working women in the suffrage movement, they could not afford the luxury of a debilitating month in prison. Even one night in a cell, resulting in one missed performance, was sufficient to damage their chances of future employment. In fact Kitty Marion, the one member of the AFL who was repeatedly arrested and imprisoned, was forced to give up her theatrical career. She was of German origin, arrived in England at the age of fifteen and began her career in the chorus of *Robinson Crusoe* in 1889. Subsequently she toured the music halls of England, Scotland and Ireland billed as a 'refined comedienne and vocalist'. Eventually she made her name in a musical comedy entitled *Kitty Grey*, playing an immoral actress who, after madly flirting with a succession of earls and barons, sings:

> My little head they are all bent on turning—
> But, no thanks! Kitty's not built that way.[10]

Unlike successful actresses in the 'legitimate' theatre, Kitty Marion had little opportunity to play anything other than principal boys and *risqué* heroines. The closest she came to a new woman drama was a burlesque on Ibsen's plays entitled *Madcap Maws*. Although her portrayals on stage did little for the women's rights movement, she won a reputation as a feminist for her backstage campaign against the 'kiss your agent' method of getting work. In 1909, after listening to a speech by Mrs Pankhurst, she was inspired to join the suffragettes.

In the following six years Kitty was arrested for taking part in suffrage demonstrations, breaking Post Office windows, throwing bricks and setting fire to a race track grandstand. During one of her many prison sentences she conducted a secret correspondence on prison toilet paper with a fellow suffragette prisoner whom she addressed as RP. Their correspondence has been preserved at the London Museum. RP's letters are a mixture of mysticism and fan mail. She writes:

> Mars gives energy and enables you to be a good fighter — also it gives you your red hair, which by the by I thought was golden, but which ever it is, I know it is gloriously beautiful, for that much I have seen of you from the window. I expect you are very pretty really — apart from the make up and the foot lights. I wonder now. I expect you have blue eyes — very bright ones — particularly so at night, that would be Venus. Mine are when I am outside but in here they are quite dull. Venus gives a nice complexion too as a rule and a nice figure albeit a tendency to plumpness. But what is best about beloved Venus is she gives us love.[11]

In reply to this sexually ambiguous epistle Kitty is both practical and provocative:

You are quite right about my eyes, but my lashes and brows are too light for beauty and really, my greatest enemy could not accuse me of being pretty, especially now. ... I am enclosing a lock of my hair, my own relations always called it red, Father hated it, others call it golden, carrots or ginger. ... I have appeared much as a boy in tights and the general opinion is that I have a beautiful figure. If they saw me more they'd say 'You're from a barnyard', and yet, anyone seeing one for the first time would not call me thin. ... Yes, I suppose I have gained love in my life for I seem to get on with most people, though my love affairs are not a success. Most men seem to have a funny idea about love. Thank goodness men are not the only pebbles on the beach to love, though they think they are.[12]

Unfortunately the identity of RP and the outcome of this correspondence is unknown. But Kitty's letters to RP and another imprisoned suffragette, MR, continue in the form of a prison diary in which she describes her hunger strike and forcible feedings:

Well by the time they had me in position I was just panting and gasping and the gag was in and the tube down before I knew what had happened. I had expected the nasal, they have always started with that on me before and the second or third time it won't go down but comes out of the mouth, then they use the other tube. I can't describe what it felt like, but my uppermost thought was 'protest', pain seemed to have left me for the time. I got up, dressed and smashed every bit of glass I could reach, the glass over the gas and the jug and the basin, and hot water ran all over the cell. Then they came in and said they hoped I felt better now and I told them I did. In the afternoon I barricaded and it took some time to get in, a man with a crowbar forced the door and the furniture rose up in the middle and so gave way. ... Fearful struggle and of course inexpressible pain, feeding seemed to take ages and I was on my feet like a shot, on the bed, screaming with all my might ... and trying to get to the broken window, with several wardresses holding me back. It was such a blessed relief to exercise my lungs and throat after that fearful sensation of being held in a vice and suffocating and choking. Gradually I calmed down and my eyes fell on the unprotected gas and ... I fired the bed, it smouldered and smoked fearfully, the smoke penetrated through the cracks of the door and they came to the rescue with buckets of water, a fearful mess, after which ... I was left in the dark though I told them they could leave the light on as I had no intention of doing any more that night. In fact I didn't do any more, it seemed all so trivial and made unnecessary work for the women who had to clear things away.[13]

At the outbreak of war in 1914, Kitty's German origins caused her some unpleasantness. She wrote later that she had been accused of being a spy. In 1915 she left England and emigrated to America, where she met Margaret Sanger and joined the birth control movement. She never attempted to work in American vaudeville, perhaps because the images she would have portrayed would have negated her feminist politics. But Kitty never lost her affection for the stage and for fifteen years she sold the *Birth Control Review* outside the theatres on Broadway.

The majority of the actresses in the AFL worked in the legitimate theatre rather than the music halls. The contradiction they experienced between their work on the stage and their work in the women's rights movement was less severe than Kitty's and they were not prepared to follow her example and jeopardise their careers. But having ruled out the possibility of militancy, they had no idea what kind of political action the League could take. A solution to their dilemma was provided by women from the other suffrage societies who wrote to the League asking the actresses to speak at meetings all over the country. Edwardian women, with the exception of those involved in the trade union movement, had no experience of speaking in public and the performance skills of the actresses were in great demand. So the AFL decided that initially it would assist the political work of other societies rather than instigate independent campaigns.

Eventually in 1913 the League set up special speakers' classes for women in the suffrage movement, but in the interim they tried to fulfil as many engagements as possible. Actresses were asked to send their touring lists to the AFL secretary who tried to arrange political meetings before their evening shows or, as in the case of Decima Moore, during the interval. 'The first time I appeared on a suffrage platform was in Manchester. I slipped out to a meeting between the two "houses" of the hall where I was acting.'[14] Decima Moore's sister Eva remembered her first speech for very different reasons:

My first speech was made at the Queen's Hall. They rang me up at very short notice to ask if I would 'say a few words'. Rather fearful as to my powers of oratory, I went. I remember Christabel

Pankhurst was in the chair. I began to speak, and a small blood vessel broke in my lip. I stood there speaking and between sentences mopping up the small but persistent stream of blood. When my handkerchief was no longer of any use, Christabel passed me another. By the time I had finished my speech a small pile of gory looking handkerchiefs lay at my feet, and not a woman on the platform had a handkerchief left. It was a horrible experience for a 'raw hand'.[15]

As well as political speeches, some of the actresses prepared suffrage poems to recite at meetings; Jane Comfort was one of them:

One Friday my dear old uncle was coming home from lunch when a leaflet was thrust into his hand with my name on it, saying I was appearing at the Women's Social and Political Union meeting at the Queen's Hall, Upper Regent Street. He was always interested in what I was doing so he toddled along to the meeting and sat at the back of the hall to see what I was up to. Well I recited my little bit, a prologue by Laurence Housman. It began:

No cause is great that is not hard to gain
No right so clear as not to be denied.
Else in the past no martyrs had been slain,
No prophets stoned, no saints by torture tried.

It went very well and Christabel Pankhurst who was in the chair passed word along the platform: 'Did I have an encore; did I know the poem *Woman This and Woman That*?' I was horrified because Decima Moore always recited *Woman This and Woman That* and I thought it was sacrilege for anyone else to perform it. So I felt very foolish and said, terribly sorry, I didn't. After the meeting I sneaked out and went home for tea, and as I put my key in the door, I heard my uncle say, 'You silly juggins, why didn't you take a call?' That was the actor speaking, so I said, 'How could I take a call? It was a political meeting, and anyway Christabel Pankhurst is the star of the thing.'[16]

The technique of breaking the monotony of political meetings with a song, dance or poem was not original to the AFL. Many late nineteenth-century political gatherings had included an element of performance: Christabel Pankhurst, in her childhood, performed dances at Independent Labour Party functions and, in 1889, her mother arranged musical interludes for meetings of the Women's Franchise League. However, the actresses, encouraged by the success of their poems, did begin to develop original forms of one-woman political theatre, in particular character monologues. Specially written for suffrage meetings, the monologues required strong performances, costumes, props and all the trappings of conventional theatre. They were structured like fables and demonstrated how a woman, frequently working class, converted her husband or friends to the cause. As the char in *Showin' Samyel*,[17] by Evelyn Glover, explains, 'The men are right enough. When I 'ear some women goin' on against 'em I always says to myself, "You 'av'n't took the right way with 'em. What they want is showin' – that's all!" ' Samyel, her husband, has been persuaded by an anti-suffragist that women should keep well clear of politics and be a silent influence in the home. Instead of arguing with him, she agrees – and then refuses to cook breakfast because of the taxes on tea and sugar, or to take the children to school because the visits of the school inspector prove that parliament passes laws on education. Finally she stops charring and sits by the fire being a 'silent inflooence'. Samyel, who is no match for these guerilla tactics, admits his mistake and joins the suffragettes.

Jim, an equally misguided husband, is taught a similar lesson by his wife in L. S. Phibb's monologue *Jim's Leg*.[18] For years Esther has listened to Jim telling her that women's work is easy: 'You can jest sit at 'ome and amoose yerself, lookin' after the kiddies and cleanin' up. Why that's only play, that is. Where's your responsibilities? And 'oo's you to 'ave a vote? Thinkin' yourselves on a level with us men.' Then one day Jim is run over by a bus and loses a leg. Esther takes over his job as a bottle washer at the brewery and Jim stays at home to mind the children. After a week as a housewife Jim is a changed man, 'Esther,' he says, 'I'm a goin' to be a suffragette myself. ... One 'as to be an 'ole man to be up to them women, and you did ought to 'ave a vote, Esther. Bottle washin' 's play to byby mindin' and 'ome work what ain't never over.'

Although the day-to-day details of working-class life may be described fairly accurately in these monologues, the characters and the dialect writing have more in common with the comic servants in Bernard Shaw's plays than with contemporary cockneys. In their desire to show why working women needed the vote, the middle-class actresses unintentionally parodied East End life. Not surprisingly, the monologues which characterised middle-class women were far better observed. In *The Other Side*,[19] by H. M. Paull, Miss De Lacey, a scatty provincial debutante, attempts to convince her audience that women should not be given the vote. She tells them about the one and only meeting of the Little Pendleton Anti-Suffragist Society, 'None of the ladies would speak, they thought it would be unladylike, so Lady Bellamy said that they must appoint a secretary and to my horror she proposed me, and so Mama accepted for me; I couldn't speak, I was blushing so.' By repeating the facile arguments that she heard at that meeting she unconsciously condemns the anti-suffragist cause. Her final plea for recruits ends, 'it's one's duty to do something useful in the world even if it does mean a lot of strain on one's brain, isn't it?'

As an indictment of the Anti-Suffrage Society of Women formed in 1908, *The Other Side* was far more effective than a conventional political speech. The antis were notorious for their negative platform and had tried to improve their image by demanding that women should be more active in local government. The suffrage societies were quick to realise that the contradictions of the antis' policy were ridiculed far more effectively by theatrical satire than tub-thumping oratory.

As the demand for suffrage entertainments increased, the AFL responded by setting up a separate play department run by an actress called Inez Bensusan. Born in Sydney, Bensusan had acted professionally in Australia before emigrating to England. As well as working in the theatre, she published numerous articles on the suffrage issue and several short stories. Initially she must have felt overwhelmed by the problems involved in creating a repertoire of suffrage drama; particularly as the audiences were spread throughout the country and were demanding plays which could be performed anywhere from a drawing room to a civic hall. Ideally, a permanent AFL touring company was needed, but with no financial backing Bensusan was forced to persuade and cajole actresses into rehearsing in their spare time and performing on Sundays, during the day, or when they were unemployed. The other major difficulty was finding suitable plays. Bensusan approached sympathetic male dramatists as well as women writers and any actress she could find who would put pen to paper, and bullied them into writing a monologue, duologue or one-act play.

The first of the AFL's purpose-made plays were performed at a suffrage exhibition at the Prince's Skating Rink in Knightsbridge in

1909. The exhibition was organised by the WSPU to publicise the cause, win recruits and raise money — it was also a glorious holiday from the strains and stresses of militancy for Mrs Pankhurst and her followers. Like most of the WSPU's mass events, it was spectacular — the journalist from the *Christian Commonwealth* observed, 'Purple, white and green everywhere, from the first moment that you catch sight of the Prince's Skating Rink in the distance, and everyone in your omnibus cranes forward to see "whatever are those suffragettes doing now".'[20] Inside the enormous hall, magnificent murals, designed by Sylvia Pankhurst, covered the walls. Over the entrance was a colossal figure of a woman sowing grain and facing her, at the far end of the hall, stood a woman bearing corn bathed in bright summer sunshine. A photographic display charted the history of the militant movement, while life-sized models depicted life in a prison cell and suffragettes in a court room. The stalls, which were run by local branches of the union, sold hats, dresses, flowers, books, poultry, Yorkshire pickles and lamp and candle shades. The advertised refreshments included a soda fountain bar, where 'Mrs Baille Guthrie and her daughters are to dispense American iced beverages at moderate prices.'[21]

The exhibition lasted a week and every day the AFL provided entertainments at 3.15, 4.30, 5.45, 8.00 and 9.15. Eighteen different acts were presented to appreciative audiences, who contributed £369 19s. 6d. towards the WSPU funds. Every show was different: like a variety bill it offered a mixture of songs, dancing, recitations, sketches or short plays. Although Inez Bensusan organised the programmes, she exercised little control over the content of individual items. One play, performed by Eva Moore, caused quite a stir in the League.

My husband wrote a one-act play, called *Her Vote*, the story of a 'fluffy' young woman who, after persuading everyone she meets that is is 'their duty' to attend a big suffrage meeting, does not go herself, because her 'young man' had taken tickets for a fashionable ball. That, roughly, was the story. I played the sketch, and it really was very funny. Two days later, at a meeting of the League, 'someone' got up and stated that they had seen the sketch, and that evidently, 'Eva Moore preferred kisses to votes', and suggested that I should be told not to play the sketch again, or resign. I resigned. I felt that one could work as well for a cause outside a society as in one. I must say I was asked to go back, which I did, still reserving the right to myself to play *any* play, without the assumption that I was working on anti-suffrage propaganda. That line, 'Prefers kisses to votes', has always struck me as so very excellent, it should be used in a play.[22]

The row over *Her Vote* forced Bensusan into the role of Lord Chamberlain for the AFL. As the policy of the League was to serve rather than lead the other suffrage societies, the department had no alternative but to provide non-controversial plays. The reviewer for *Votes for Women* summed up the successful plays at the exhibition by saying:

From different points of view they all tell the same story, and all point to the same moral, but though they are propagandist in their character, they are full of life and reality, and will be quite sure to keep any audience fully interested from beginning to end.[23]

In the following year, Bensusan organised performances of these and other plays in Reigate, Redhill, Loughton, Saffron Walden, Newport, Sevenoaks, Southampton, Portsmouth, Glasgow, Eastbourne and most of the London boroughs. The majority of these bookings came from the NUWSS (which by 1910 had sixty branches) and these audiences expected plays which reflected the demand for the vote, 'on the same terms as it is, or may be granted to men', and the belief that men and women should fight together through constitutional means for this great reform. The AFL also performed for the members of the WSPU who preferred plays which advocated militancy. To satisfy both audiences, Bensusan carefully selected the programme for each venue from a diverse repertoire. The plays were written by novelists like Beatrice Harraden, women playwrights such as Gertrude Jennings, Madeline Lucette Ryley, George Paston, Josephine Preston Peabody and Cicely Hamilton, and women like Vera Wentworth and Rita Milman who were writing for the first time. The male playwrights included Lawrence Housman, J. M. Barrie, Shaw and Arncliffe-Sennett.

One result of this self-imposed censorship was that *Lady Geraldine's Speech*,[24] by Beatrice Harraden, which had been popular with audiences at the WSPU exhibition, was never performed to the NUWSS. The plot was not particularly controversial: Dr Alice Romney is holding a professional women's suffrage meeting in her home. Just before her guests arrive an old schoolfriend pays her a surprise visit. Lady Geraldine, the schoolfriend, has got herself 'into the most fearful scrape'; she has been chosen to speak at a mass meeting of the Anti-Suffrage League and has no idea what to say. At first Dr Alice refuses to write her a speech that attacks votes for women, but loyalty to her friend makes her relent. While she is constructing a brilliant diatribe against women's enfranchisement, her four suffragette friends arrive. The first, an eminent painter, talks about her suffrage painting 'for next year's Academy'; the second, a professor of literature, quotes Shakespeare and Chaucer; the third, a musician, dashes to the piano and plays Brahms' First Intermezzo; and the last, a shorthand typist, sells the others copies of *Votes for Women*. Lady Geraldine is so impressed by Dr Alice's friends that she becomes a suffragette. As they settle down to their meeting, the maid — whose work does not qualify her for this select gathering — brings in the tea. It was not the unconscious irony of the maid's role that Bensusan believed the NUWSS members would object to, but the fact that Dr Alice and her friends were supporters of the WSPU.

The plays that were popular throughout the suffrage movement and which provided the basis for the AFL repertoire kept well clear of specific suffrage party politics and concentrated on the generalised sexual inequalities of Edwardian society. They illustrated the need for the vote in an agitational form and were essentially of political but not literary value. The theatrical style of these plays was derived from the social dramas of Granville Barker and Shaw, which attempted to expose social ills in an ultra-naturalistic form. Their influence can be seen quite clearly in Bensusan's own play, *The Apple*,[25] which she described as 'an episode of today'. Set in a suburban villa, it tells the story of Helen, a typist, and her fight for equality within her family. She has two sisters: Ann, who at twenty-seven is already old and tired from waiting on her father and brother, and Norah, whose youth and looks are quickly fading through the drudgery of her job as a nursery governess. The three sisters, with a stoicism reminiscent of Chekhov's play, struggle for their livelihood and independence, while their brother, Cyril, the apple of their father's eye, has the meagre financial resources of the family lavished upon him. The play begins with Helen coming home early from the office. Her boss, Nigel Dean, has asked her to become his mistress and rather than accept his offer she has handed in her notice. In desperation she decides to emigrate and begin a new life in Canada. Unfortunately, Cyril has already persuaded their father to mortgage the family estate and buy him a partnership, so there is no money for Helen's fare. She is furious with Cyril and attacks him for his selfishness:

HELEN: And what about my happiness? My future? My chances?
CYRIL: Girls don't want chances. They only want husbands. If you'd stay at home like a decent young woman, some decent man might want to marry you, but while you prefer —
HELEN: I don't want your decent husband. I want a little pleasure, a glimpse of life, a taste of joy of living, a few pence in my pocket, my rights as an individual —[26]

Cyril, the apple of his father's eye, wins the fight and Dean persuades Helen to return to the office — whether as his mistress or secretary is unclear. The play gives a vivid picture of the sexism inherent within middle-class family life, but it is weakened by the romanticism of Helen's relationship with Dean. What is impressive is the skill with which Bensusan creates the story with only four characters: Helen, Ann, Cyril and Dean. Her experience as the secretary of the play department had taught her the technical limitations involved in performing in church halls.

Although serious dramas, like *The Apple*, dominated the early AFL repertoire, the League's first smash hit was a play that was steeped in the nineteenth-century tradition of farce. Originally a short story by Cicely Hamilton, the play was adapted by the author and produced for the WSPU exhibition in May 1909, by Ellen Terry's daughter, Edy Craig, a woman who matched Inez Bensusan in energy and inventiveness. She had begun her career as an actress in Henry Irving's Lyceum company, several years later became his costume designer and finally, in 1911, established her own theatre company, the Pioneer Players.

The farce, *How the Vote Was Won*, opens on the first day of a women's general strike; tired of being denied political power, the women of England have stopped work and are demanding that their nearest male relative supports them. The catastrophic effect of the strike is felt: in 10 Downing Street where the prime minister is forced to make his own bed; in the House of Commons where blackleg chars are provided by the Navy; and in the Brixton home of a clerk named

Horace Cole where the play takes place. One by one Cole's female relatives arrive at his house – first his sister, then his wife's sister, then his aunt and finally a whole string of distant cousins. Desperate to be rid of them he is miraculously transformed into an ardent suffragist.

According to *The Times*, 'The audience were delighted. How could they help it? ... The denouement, conceived and carried out in the finest spirit of farce, reflects the highest credit on the authors.' Performing *How the Vote Was Won*[27] was apparently as enjoyable as watching it; Jane Comfort was in the original production:

> Edy roped in all her friends to act in the play, we were ready to do anything she suggested. We rehearsed on Sundays, as everyone was working in the evenings, and performed it twice at the exhibition and in the West End at the Royalty Theatre. It was like a continuous review, I remember Marie Lloyd coming on and Auriol Lee and Maud Hoffman. The man was played by Nigel Playfair and his neighbour O. P. Heggie. I was the youngest, a journalist who simply chucked up my job and came to live with Uncle Horace.[28]

Inez Bensusan organised a further twelve performances of the play at suffrage meetings all over the country, but as most of the original cast were performing in West End shows, Edy had to re-cast for virtually every performance. Allan Wade, a close friend of Ellen Terry and Edy Craig, played Horace Cole on several occasions. He remembers:

> playing it in all sorts of places and with a variety of different casts. I cannot now recall exactly the working out of the plot, but I seem to remember the climax came with the entrance of a maiden aunt of the husband or wife; this part was played by Edy who made a tremendous entrance looking like a drawing by Leech or Charles Keene, and carrying either a cat in a basket or a parrot in a cage.[29]

Apart from a few rather vague reminiscences from actors and actresses there is very little information about suffrage plays performed by the AFL outside London. The local newspapers were far more interested in the antics of the militant suffragettes in their High Street than in the performance of a play in a nearby church hall. When the AFL appeared in Croydon at the Pembroke Hall on 11 November 1909 there was no mention of the performance in the local press. That same week the *Croydon Advertiser* ran a story about a woman who protested outside the Empire Music Hall over a sketch which ridiculed the suffragettes.

Apparently she threatened to 'fight' the performers, but the crowd told her that, 'she should stop at home and mind the baby, which was the proper place for a woman'.[30] In Reigate two weeks later the local newspapers again ignored the AFL, but found space for a review of *Modern Women and How To Manage Them*, a book 'mere men may get a good deal of entertainment from'.[31] Judging from these two stories, even if the local press had reviewed the plays their reactions were likely to have been hostile.

The only play toured by the AFL in 1909 which did attract the widespread attention of the press was Bernard Shaw's *Press Cuttings*.[32] Originally written for the West End stage, and first performed at the Court Theatre on 9 July 1909, the play was refused a licence by the Lord Chamberlain's office on the grounds that Shaw's characters, Balsquith (Balfour/Asquith) and Mitchener (Lord Robert Kitchener) contravened the ruling that 'no representation of living persons is to be permitted on the stage'. Set in the War Office, the play begins with the arrival of Balsquith, the prime minister, in drag. He has been forced to assume the disguise in order to escape the armed suffragettes in the streets. Together with the Army Chief of Staff, Mitchener, he plans to defeat the suffragette urban guerillas by enforcing a woman-free zone for two miles around Westminster. They are interrupted by the arrival of two anti-suffragists: Mrs Banger, a middle-aged tyrant, who believes that women should run the armed forces, and Lady Corinthia Fanshawe, a typical Shavian beauty, who manipulates men through feminine wiles. The play ends with Balsquith deciding that a military dictatorship controlled by these two women would be infinitely more terrifying than votes for women.

Although *Press Cuttings* is apparently about women's suffrage, it is in fact more concerned with the issue of compulsory military service and the contemporary hysteria over the build-up of armaments in Germany. Shaw makes his audience consider these issues while providing comic relief in his caricatures. However, there is a marked difference in his treatment of the sexes: the men are ludicrous because of their political prejudices while the women are ridiculed for being ugly, aggressive predators.

Soon after the production at the Court Theatre, the play was licensed and Shaw was approached by a number of amateur drama groups, theatres and suffrage societies, including the AFL, about the performing rights. One of the actresses interested in producing the play was Bertha

Newcombe; in reply to her request for the rights, Shaw wrote on 30 August 1909:

> I understand that Redford has licensed the play. It now goes into the machine with my other plays as I told you it would; and the machine is hardly more under my control than under yours. Miss Edith Craig says she is going to tour through the villages and small places where they are giving performances in schoolrooms with fit-ups and she has asked if she may have P.C. for the cause. If you will undertake that enterprise, you have first call; but you won't and can't. Miss Horniman is to produce the play in Manchester on or about the 13th September. You cannot get beforehand with her, as the only theatre you could now get would be her own. In short you should have booked dates 'in pencil' for a tour the day after the Court performance and submitted it to me if you really meant to follow the thing up and make use of your privilege. That was not possible. ... I should have told you if I thought you could do anything. There was nothing in it for you but the first big bite. Edy Craig is not likely to make twopence out of it either for herself or her society (which infuriated Charlotte by writing Votes for Women in an indelible smear of butter and black lead on our doorstep). She will be lucky if she does not loose every rap she possesses. ...[33]

Although the press persistently ignored the majority of the play department's touring work, the national newspapers all reviewed their next production. This spectacular event, which involved the stars of the West End stage, was entitled *A Pageant of Great Women*.[34] It was performed on 10 November 1909, in the Scala Theatre, two months after Gladstone had instructed the prison doctors to forcibly feed suffragette hunger strikers. The main character in the Pageant is Woman, who demands freedom from Justice, while Prejudice, a man, argues against her. Prejudice's objection to Woman's case is that her innate stupidity makes her incapable of mature thought. This is how Woman answers:

> Oh well, indeed, well does this come from you
> Who held the body as all, the spirit as nought.
> For you who saw us only as a sex!
> Who praised a dimple far above a brain!

> So we were trained to simper, not to think,
> So were we bred for dimples not for brains![135]

The language may be unduly formal but the message is clear: if you treat women as sex objects that is what they become. But the Pageant is primarily an excuse to introduce women warriors, artists, scholars, monarchs and saints, who demonstrate the physical, intellectual, creative and ethical strengths of women. Written by Cicely Hamilton and directed by Edy Craig, the Pageant gave fifty-two actresses the opportunity to express on stage their support for the suffrage cause in an endless stream of positive images of women. They had little opportunity to project similar images on the West End stage. Only a month before a reviewer in *Votes for Women* had written:

> There is not one play on the London stage at the present time which takes any account of women except on the level of housekeeping machines or bridge players – the actual or potential property of some man, valuable or worthless as the case may be. It is strange to go out of the world where women are fighting for freedom, into the theatre, where the dramatist appears unaffected by this new Renaissance. Strange, indeed, it is too, when 'King Lear' at the Haymarket seems more modern, more of the stuff of which Winson Green prisoners are made than any heroine imagined by Pinero or Maugham.[36]

Jane Comfort, the actress in the Pageant who played Saint Hilda, remembers the performance as a spectacular affair:

> Edy got them into groups, all the women in history she could think of. There was a group of saints, I was in that; she wanted my aunt for Saint Theresa and told me, 'You'd better be Saint Hilda, because you'll be in the same group and you can look after your aunt and help with her costume.' There was a group of nurses and Marion Terry was Florence Nightingale; Edy always roped in her family as much as she could. There was a group of soldiers, women who had dressed up as men and joined the army and weren't discovered to be women until they were wounded. There were the painters, Angelica Kauffman and Rosa Bonheur, which she played herself in a wonderful costume. Then, of course, there were a group of actresses and there she had to bring on her mother, Ellen Terry. Adeline Bourne, who was playing the Woman, introduced all the

other characters, but Ellen Terry came on and said:

> 'By your leave,
> I'll speak my message for myself,
> If you, Sir Prejudice, had had your way
> The stage would now be dull as 'tis merry,
> No Oldfield, Woofington or Ellen Terry.'

And off she went. Lillah McCarthy played Justice and was seated upstage on a throne with a bandage over her eyes, sword in one hand, scales in the other. Poor darling, she had to sit there all through the performance. Everybody in the theatre was in the Pageant, with the exception of Irene Vanbrugh. She was the principal leading lady in London at that time, but her husband, Dion Boucicault, disapproved of the suffrage movement.[37]

The audience at the Scala Theatre, according to *The Times*, 'were in sympathy with the cause. But even its opponents must have been struck by the intense earnestness and absolute good taste with which these ideas were presented.' The Pageant proved so popular that suffrage societies all over the country performed it. Edy, who wanted to encourage women to express themselves through theatre, directed local productions in Eastbourne, Southport and Bristol. The Actresses' Franchise League provided the costumes and leading performers and the Great Women were cast from the local suffragists which, as Cicely Hamilton explains, often caused problems:

> The secretary of the local suffrage movement was furnished beforehand with a list of types required for the various parts; the list I should add was marked 'strictly confidential' — as well it might, considering it contained such items as 'need not be good looking' and, in the case of one character whose face was all but concealed beneath her head-dress, 'any old thing will do'. The extreme popularity of Joan of Arc was on more than one occasion a source of real unpleasantness, when Edy had to deal firmly with some lady of entirely unsuitable appearance who, by sheer determination or the pulling of strings, had got herself cast for the part.[38]

Encouraged by the success of the Pageant, the local suffrage societies, many of whom had already invited the AFL to perform agitational plays at their meetings, decided to rehearse their own plays. At first they relied on the AFL for scripts (Inez Bensusan had persuaded the play department to publish five plays from the League's repertoire), but gradually they began to write their own material. The most ambitious of these productions was a musical comedy written and performed by the employees of Selfridges at the Court Theatre in 1911. Entitled *The Suffrage Girl*, it was set in a country where women have the vote. In the final scene the fate of two of the candidates in the general election is decided by the heroine's casting vote.

The tradition of drawing-room amateur theatre, which dated from the late Victorian era, made it comparatively easy for the AFL to persuade women to produce their own suffrage plays. The League also succeeded in breaking down the delineation between amateur and professional theatre. It became the policy of the AFL to provide theatre groups, whenever possible, with scripts and expert assistance in the form of a director. By 1911, amateur performances had multiplied so much that the entertainments at suffrage fairs and exhibitions were provided partly by the AFL and partly by the local suffragists.

4. CHINA TEA-CUPS 1911–18

By 1910, the suffrage theatre was flourishing. In parliament the Government, led by Asquith, directed their energies to the restriction of the legislative power of the House of Lords and to Lloyd George's People's Budget. Meanwhile, a Conciliation Committee of members from all the parties had been created to promote yet another women's suffrage bill. The committee had been set up by H. N. Brailsford, the author and liberal journalist and Lord Lytton, MP. As a result, the militants were persuaded to call a truce from militancy so that the Government would have no excuse to block the Bill.

Before the Conciliation Bill reached its first reading, the parliamentary session was disrupted, on 7 May, by the death of Edward VII. Christabel Pankhurst, together with the other suffrage leaders, expressed their devotion to the throne. After a month's delay, on 14 June, the Conciliation Committee introduced their proposals to the House of Commons. Four days later, on 18 June, the WSPU led a demonstration of all the suffrage societies, including the NUWSS in support of the Bill. Ten thousand women, dressed in white, marched in a two-mile long procession from the embankment to the Albert Hall. The AFL played a prominent part. The actresses, dressed in fashionable gowns and elegant wide-brimmed, white hats, marched behind a banner embroidered with the linked comedy and tragedy masks. Lena Ashwell was one of the contingent:

> long before the last woman had left Cleopatra's Needle, we heard of the orderly and well-drilled army, carrying banners and flags of different societies, which arrived at Albert Hall. In the windows of the clubs and along the crowded streets were curious and contemptuous people. Well-dressed men, with ridicule in their eyes and the smile of superiority on their sneering lips, stared as we

passed along. It was really infuriating, and now it seems quite unbelievable.

Lots of funny things happened to cheer us on that exhausting walk in the dust and heat of the roadway. Everyone was in mourning for King Edward VII, but for this procession we asked to wear white dresses. Owing to a rush of work, I had no time to change, so there I was, conspicuous in black among all the white dresses. As we passed through Piccadilly there was a hold-up for a few minutes, and I heard a man say to his neighbour, 'You see 'er, that there in the black? That there is the bad girl of the family.'[1]

Three days later, Lena Ashwell found herself representing the AFL again, this time at 10 Downing Street.

When the Women's Suffrage Deputation was received in Downing Street, as I was the only woman then in management, I was asked to represent our society. The whole affair was irresistibly comic because it was so tragic. We were just a very ordinary little group of women, received by the flunkeys as if we had a strange odour and had been temporarily released from the zoo. We were ushered into a room where rows of chairs faced a door at the end. As we sat patiently waiting, a head was thrust round the edge of the door and stared contemptuously at us; then the door was shut, but presently the other door, by which we had entered, was opened and again this hostile person surveyed us – Mrs Asquith, the wife of the Prime Minister!

I had a place in the front row of the deputation and was not only able to hear well all the speeches made by the different leaders of the movement, but to watch the effect on the ministers. The speech that Mrs Despard made seemed to move Mr Lloyd George the most, though all were listened to with attention and each was admirable. But Mr Asquith was not interested, for he had made up his mind. His expression made me think of that iron curtain which descends in the theatre to ensure that the stage is completely shut off from the auditorium. When the speeches were ended, after a few polite phrases he said that so long as he was Prime Minister he would give no facilities for the discussion of the Bill. A clear voice from the back of the room called, 'Then you must be moved.' With his thumbs in the armholes of his waistcoat and a spreading of his chest and abdomen, his head thrown back, he said firmly, I will not say defiantly, 'Move me'. And like a gentle refrain of the Litany, the deputation replied, 'We will'.[2]

Another actress who visited 10 Downing Street in a slightly different capacity was Lillah McCarthy; she had been invited to give a private performance there before the king and queen. At the rehearsal she found herself alone in the Cabinet Room:

> There were the baskets of papers and there was the blotting paper, the austere, solid ornaments of the Prime Minister's desk. Fervour for the cause took hold of me. I felt like a Joan of Arc of the ballot-box. Martyrdom or not, the occasion must be seized. I opened my box of grease paints, took out the reddest stick I could find, and wrote across the blotting paper 'Votes for Women'. I went out of the room exultant. When the rehearsal for which I had gone to Downing Street was over, Mr Asquith came to me. We had tea together. He asked: 'Why do you think women should have the vote?' By Heavens, I told him! I poured out arguments in no unstinted measure. He greeted them with a quizzical smile which, whilst it did not discourage me, forced me to wonder whether the weight of my arguments was as great as their volume.[3]

The intimacy with which Lillah McCarthy writes of Asquith in her autobiography implies that they were lovers, an impression which is confirmed in a letter written by Virginia Woolf to her sister Vanessa describing a party in 1916, at which she saw Asquith 'carried to bed drunk by Lillah McCarthy'.[4]

July 11 and 12 were set aside for the second reading of the Conciliation Bill. Although it was passed with a majority of 110 votes in favour, the Government prevented any further discussion of the Bill by dissolving parliament, whereupon the suffragettes broke their truce in protest. But their militancy was shortlived. They entered into another truce for a further nine months to enable the Conciliation Committee to draft a second bill.

While the battle over the Conciliation Bill was being waged in parliament, the Actresses' Franchise League's attention was turned to the political education of its members. Since its inauguration the League had occasionally invited speakers to address informal meetings but, from 1910, a lecture or debate was organised every month at the Criterion Restaurant for members and their friends. The lectures covered a wide range of subjects including: Old Chinese Philosophy and its Relation to Women's Emancipation, Actresses in Molière's Day, Women under the Poor Law, The Ethics of Rebellion, French Women in the Seventeenth Century and The Influence of the Women of the Fronde, Parliamentary Procedure, and Sweated Women Workers. Initially, the debates were concerned with the immediate problems of the Conciliation Bill in parliament — at the November meeting the resolution, which was passed with a large majority, was 'That the policy of opposing the government is the only effectual one for the suffragists'. A week before the debate the WSPU had staged a demonstration to force the Cabinet to provide time in the autumn session for the Bill, and while the suffragettes were fighting with the police in Parliament Square the actresses had performed *A Pageant of Great Women* at the Aldwych Theatre. Despite their combined efforts, the Cabinet refused to support the Bill in its original form.

During the truce in the winter of 1910–11, the League's monthly meetings were consistently well attended and one debate, held at the Caxton Hall on 24 February 1911, proved so popular that the actresses had to be turned away at the door. Although the resolution for that afternoon's debate was not directly connected with the demand for votes, it was of intense interest to the League's members. It read 'That equality in the marriage laws will be desirable for the progress of the community'. Most Edwardian actresses had greater sexual freedom than their contemporaries, largely because of their financial independence and social mobility, but many of them had suffered through the inequalities of the divorce laws. Until 1923, when the law was changed, a husband could divorce his wife if she committed adultery, but a wife could only divorce her husband if he committed adultery and was also guilty of gross cruelty or desertion. Despite the large number of actresses present at the debate, not one voted against the resolution. In fact, they enjoyed discussing the question so much that a further debate about the marriage laws was arranged in May.

The actresses were almost as enthusiastic about two debates on the relationship between their work in the women's movement and their work on the commercial stage. The first, 'That the stage conception of women is conventional and inadequate', was passed unanimously after a discussion in which most of the audience agreed that 'It would be well for dramatists to study modern women in their workshops, studios and factories, if they wish to find the true feminist spirit.'[5] In the second,

'That an interest in politics is not injurious to dramatic art', Mr Antony Ellis, who opposed the resolution, asserted that 'emotion pure and simple was the fundamental necessity of an actress's equipment and that politics, requiring deep and serious study, would detract from the time and thought that should be devoted to drama'.[6] Only three of the audience agreed with him, and the rest, according to the report in *Votes for Women*, on 27 January 1911, felt, 'that an interest in politics was a vital necessity for the truthful interpretation of the drama of life.'

These debates stimulated a growing awareness amongst actresses of the discrimination within their own profession. In the spring of 1911 an incident occurred which led them to confront the theatrical establishment. Lena Ashwell explains:

> At the time of the coronation of King George and Queen Mary a gala performance was arranged to take place at His Majesty's Theatre. The arrangements were advertised, a programme of plays in which all the leading actors of the day could take part with just two or three women needed to support them. I appealed to Sir Charles Wyndham that it would be a matter for discussion for the Manager's Association, out of courtesy, to include a play in which all the women might appear. Nothing was done, however, so I composed a letter to Her Majesty the Queen expressing the regret of the actresses that we were excluded. I submitted a copy to Sir Charles with a note saying that, unless something was done, I should most certainly send the letter. Sir Charles told me that the association had decided to do nothing. The meeting had, indeed, broken up when he said that it would be as well for them to hear the letter which I was sending, and they all hastily sat down to review the situation. I was given twenty-four hours to get the approval of the actresses and find a suitable play in which they could appear. Both these obstacles were easily overcome as everyone wanted to be included and I had already produced *The Vision of Delight* by Ben Johnson for the benefit performance at the Kingsway and had had special music written for it. On that memorable night this little masque ended the programme.[7]

On 5 May the re-drafted Conciliation Bill had its first reading in the House of Commons and was passed with a large majority. All the suffrage societies organised processions and meetings in anticipation of victory and the AFL, after a winter of introspective debates, initiated its first propaganda campaign outside the theatrical profession. During the previous two years, the actresses had performed at countless meetings organised by the NUWSS and the WSPU, but in March they set up a special campaign fund to finance a series of their own meetings in the East End, 'for the poor working women whose lives held so little pleasure'.

On a fine April evening in 1911, the actresses held their first meeting at Bow Bath Hall. They arrived early, arranged the few pieces of furniture necessary for the play and waited. The hall was soon filled with local people who, according to the reviewer from *Votes for Women*,[8] listened with 'eager interest and attention' to the speeches made by Miss Brackenbury and Mr Lansbury, the labour MP for Bow and Bromley, and 'vociferously applauded' the songs and recitations. The evening ended with the performance of a play by Mr Arncliffe-Sennett, entitled *An Englishwoman's Home*.[9] The central theme of the play was the artificial division between women's and men's work. In the years immediately preceding the First World War, inflation and unemployment forced women who were married to skilled workers into part-time work to supplement their family's declining income. But there was a resistance on the part of the men to help with the housework and childcare. Consequently, many women who had two jobs, one in the home and one outside the home, and who were sympathetic to the suffrage cause, found it impossible to find the time to be politically active. Hannah Mitchell, a working-class suffragist, graphically describes this situation in her autobiography. 'No cause can be won between dinner and tea,' she wrote bitterly, 'and most of us who were married had to work with one hand tied behind us.' Arncliffe-Sennett's play, with its punch-line 'Home is the place for men', dealt with precisely this dilemma.

Set in the East End home of Maria and John Jenkins, the play opens with Maria hard at work in her kitchen. It is early evening, she has given the lodger his tea and put the children to bed. Outside a couple of drunken men sing 'Rule Britannia'. Maria recognises John's voice and as he staggers into the house she introduces him to the audience as her 'purtector'. In the ensuing scene the conflict between husband and wife becomes apparent – John, who is a master carpenter, has been unemployed for over a year, during which time Maria has supported the family by charring, taking in washing and looking after the lodger.

Although he realises that she is overworked, John, as an unemployed man, already feels emasculated and refuses to do 'women's work, cleaning grates, scrubbing floors'.

While Maria goes out to buy an egg for the lodger's breakfast, John explains his position to the audience and bemoans the fact that women have no sense of humour. The lodger, who is washing his hair, calls out for some hot water. While John is at the stove the baby starts to cry. Incapable of doing two things at once, John panics, drops the kettle, burns his hand and loses his temper. The lodger, John, and the baby are all screaming when a suffragette arrives at the door. She helps to restore peace only to be shouted at by John for bringing 'votes for women' into his house. Maria reappears with the egg and reminds John that she pays the rent and the rates. Suddenly the lights go out. No one has any money except the suffragette. She gives Maria a penny, and persuades her to go to a suffrage meeting at the local hall. Furious, John demands that Maria do her duty and stay at home, but she replies that he can look after the house, clean the lodger's boots and have a go at the washing.

Alone and bored, John slumps into a chair; in the background the lodger can be heard singing, 'Put me among the girls/The ones with the curly curls.' 'Put him among the girls,' groans John, 'put him among the suffragettes more likely.' He convinces himself and the audience that the lodger can look after the house while he goes for a drink. Hearing John leave, the lodger (whose name is Bates) enters from his room covered in shampoo and, turning to the audience, says: 'Blow me if he ain't bally well been an' done it! Lef' me in charge! This is comin' a bit thick!' Slowly but insistently, the baby begins to cry. Terrified, the lodger dashes to the cot and calms her with music hall songs. He is about to pack his belongings and leave when the suffragette returns. She persuades him to stay and embarks on a nonsense conversation about the relative values of the words 'fat' and 'thick', which is interrupted by the return of John and Maria:

(Enter John, excitedly, holding dirty handkerchief to his face)
JOHN: A woman what leaves 'er washin' ain't fit to 'ave a vote.
(Enter Mrs Jenkins)
MARIA: An' a man as disgraces 'isself ain't fit to 'ave one either.
SUFFRAGETTE: What has happened? What's the matter?
JOHN: I tell ye I were doin' nothin'.
BATES: Yus, but 'ow did ye do it?

JOHN: I jest asked to see my wife.

MARIA: An' pushed yer way through an' made a dreadfu' row.

JOHN: Nothin' o' the sort, I tell ye I was shoved. An' when I shoved back, I got landed one in the eye an' thrown out o' the 'all. An' ye call yersels *women*!!!

While John bathes his eye in the washing, Maria tells the others what was said at the meeting:

MARIA: That tall 'aughty lookin' lady was speakin', and O' my, didn't she let 'em 'ave it. It was splendid.

BATES: What did she say?

SUFFRAGETTE: Yes, what was it?

MARIA: She said – *Home* was the *place* – for *men*![10]

The curtain falls on a tableau: Bates watching John bathing his eye at the wash tub and Maria shaking hands with the suffragette and laughing.

The play is a mixture of styles. The opening scene with its serious look at the effects of poverty on Maria's and John's relationship is contrasted with the monologues, in which each character appeals to the audience for sympathy, and with the slapstick elements, which demonstrate the inability of the men to deal with the 'women's work' they consider so degrading. The tendency in the play for the men to be comical while the women are serious is counter-balanced by Maria's opening monologue in which she appears warm and humorous, and by the parody of the suffragette's middle-class evangelism. During her conversation with John she asks, 'You don't believe then, that what is sauce for the goose is sauce for the gander?' To which he replies, 'I dunno nothin' about goose's sauce, 'cos we don't have none.'[11]

According to the suffrage press, the play 'achieved a firm hold in the minds of the audience'[12] at Bow and was enthusiastically received at Poplar and Stratford East. Unfortunately, none of the actors recorded their impressions of the performances. Yet it must have been the first time that any of them had performed to an exclusively working-class audience, and meeting the people on whom their cockney stereotypes of the West End stage were supposedly based no doubt affected their characterisations in the play.

Throughout the summer of 1911 the actresses continued their work in the East End, performing at women's clubs and settlements.

However, the League's activities were not restricted to London: in Edinburgh, Glasgow, Liverpool and Eastbourne local offices were set up to organise meetings for touring actresses and plays for provincial suffrage groups. With five regional offices, the AFL was contacting a broad audience. In three years the membership had grown to 550, but almost all these actresses worked in the straight theatre. Little attempt was made by the League to recruit popular performers, or to introduce propaganda sketches to the music hall stage. Although there was no equivalent suffrage society for music hall artists, individual singers and comedians did incorporate suffrage material into their acts. Edith Hutson, a singer who performed in music halls in the north of England before the First World War, told her granddaughter about a troupe called Manchester Musical Mountebanks, which she joined in 1912. The granddaughter recalls:

> There were six people in the group: four men and two women. My grandmother was a mezzo soprano. The other woman also sang. One of the men played the piano, two sang and the other, Joseph Bridgford, who was my grandfather (grandma married him after the war), was the comic. The troupe played concert parties, at social evenings and on the local music hall circuit. They were part-timers and had day jobs. Grandma was a supporter of the WSPU and persuaded the others to include material about the struggle for the vote in their act, usually one song and perhaps a short sketch. I think this got the political message over fairly well as, together with all their 'normal' material, it was acceptable to a fairly wide audience.[13]

The AFL's lack of interest in music hall was not matched by a reluctance to move into cinematography. In June, Inez Bensusan approached Mr Barker of Barker's Motion Photography and persuaded him to make a film called *True Womanhood*. Bensusan wrote the script and played the principal character, a sweated woman worker who, together with her husband, is about to be sent to the workhouse. They are saved by their fairy godmother, played by Decima Moore, who appears in the guise of a suffragette. There are no surviving prints of the film, but the reviews indicate that with the exception of two scenes – a poster parade advertising a suffrage procession and an election meeting at which a leading politician is interrupted by suffragettes – it was merely a photographic record of a stage play. The film was advertised in

Votes for Women and readers were encouraged to visit their local cinematograph theatre and persuade the manager to buy a print from Barker's.

As autumn approached the suffragists became increasingly confident that the Conciliation Bill would become law. So confident were they that on 27 October the actresses held a Grand Matinée at the Lyceum Theatre to celebrate the coming victory. The climax of the performance was a new pageant which depicted the historic struggle for the vote. All the suffrage societies were represented: the pioneers of the 1860s led the way followed by the NUWSS carrying torches of green, white and red and the warrior maidens of the WSPU and the WFL; next there were the artists, writers, teachers, tax resisters, Irish and Welsh suffragists; and bringing up the rear were the actresses, symbolised by Comedy, Tragedy, Music and Dance.

Less than two weeks after this pageant was performed, the suffragists' hopes were destroyed: on 7 November Asquith announced, of all things, a bill to further enfranchise men. The suffragettes were flabbergasted; Mrs Bernard Shaw said that Asquith's speech filled her with an impulse of 'blind rage'. She felt she had been personally insulted and that he had said to her in effect, 'that the vilest male wretch who can contrive to keep a house of ill-fame shall have a vote, and that the noblest woman in England shall not have one because she is female'. In fact Asquith had said he would consider an amendment to the Manhood Suffrage Bill which would include votes for women. But the suffragists knew that such an amendment would have to be introduced by a private member and they had learned from long experience that only a government-sponsored bill stood the least chance of success.

The suffragists felt they had been tricked out of a limited form of franchise by a vague promise of a wider measure. The militants immediately broke their truce and organised a stone-throwing raid on the windows of shops and government offices, which resulted in 223 arrests. Asquith was besieged with suffrage deputations. Resolutions condemning the Government were sent to the House of Commons, including one from the AFL, part of which read:

> The AFL expresses its profound indignation at the manner in which this great imperial question is being handled by the Prime Minister and the Chancellor of the Exchequer. It demands ... that women, as equal human beings as men, of equal importance to the state and

equal supporters of the state, shall be given equal rights and dignities
incorporated by the Government in the coming Reform Bill on
equal terms with men.[14]

Despite persistent pressure from the suffrage movement the
Government refused to give any assurance that women would be
included in the original draft of the Reform Bill and the suffragettes,
who were highly suspicious of Asquith's promised amendment,
resorted to 'arguments of stone'. After a mass window-smashing raid
in March, the leaders of the WSPU, with the exception of Christabel
Pankhurst who escaped to France, were charged with conspiracy. Eva
Moore was one of the many witnesses at their trial:

> A disagreeable experience was when I was called to give evidence in
> the case of 'Pankhurst and Pethick-Lawrence v. The Crown'. ... I
> was to give evidence for Mrs Pankhurst. I was instructed not to
> answer too quickly, not to answer too slowly, and no first night has
> brought such a torture of nerves as did that cross examination at the
> Old Bailey. I remember very little about it all, except the grim air
> which seemed to brood over everything, and the fear that I might
> 'say something wrong'. Sir Rufus Isaacs was for the Crown, and I
> was in the witness box. I remember after some time he said: '— and
> so you suggest so-and-so, Miss Moore?' It was a question very like
> the old story, 'Do you still beat your wife?' — whichever way you
> answered, you were wrong. I admit frankly I was paralysed with
> fright; I tried to collect my wits, tried to think of some really telling
> answer; no inspiration came. At last I said with what dignity I
> could muster, 'I suggest nothing,' and heard him say the most
> welcome words which I think have ever struck my ears, 'You may
> stand down!'[15]

The defendants were all found guilty and sentenced to nine months'
imprisonment. On hearing the verdict, they began a hunger strike and
within a fortnight were released, but not before the Pethick-Lawrences
had been forcibly fed. The suffragettes, outraged at the treatment of
their leaders, protested both inside and outside Holloway Gaol. The
AFL supported them indirectly by sending a memorial to Asquith
demanding that the Government immediately 'introduce and carry
through a women's suffrage bill', and by taking part in a series of mass
meetings in Manchester and London. The most spectacular of these

demonstrations was held in Hyde Park on 14 July. This date was chosen because it was the anniversary of the storming of the Bastille and Mrs Pankhurst's birthday. The Park was filled with highly coloured flags and banners, many of which had been designed by Sylvia Pankhurst and made by WSPU volunteers. Each society had banners in its own colours: purple, white and green for the WSPU, orange and green for the Irish, black and brown for the Tax Resisters and white and red for Labour. According to Sylvia none of the societies were so difficult to please as the AFL:

> What a hunt for the white bullion fringe for the pink, white and green banners of the Actresses' Franchise League, who fiercely refused to accept a trimming of the traditional yellow! After half of London had been searched for it, the desired white fringe was found in John Barker's hire department, left over from the Queen's funeral.[16]

The change in the political climate of the suffrage movement which followed the defeat of the Conciliation Bill not only influenced the political activities of the League, it also affected the work of the play department. During the previous three years, as well as arranging propaganda tours, Inez Bensusan had tried to find new women playwrights. She never considered limiting the AFL productions to plays written by women, in fact nearly one-third of the plays performed by the League were written by men. But she was concerned that women who were writing experimental drama should be encouraged. Instead of relying on the tradition of naturalistic social drama, some of these women had been influenced by the poetic symbolism of the late Ibsen and Yeats. Among them was Vera Wentworth, a militant suffragette who played the big drum in the WSPU band, who wrote a play called *Allegory*[17]. The play takes place on the Road of Progress which runs between the City of Soul's Bondage and the City of Freedom: it is narrow, dusty, covered with sharp stones and brambles. Man enters, tall and strong, walks unhindered down the road. He is followed by Woman, who is in chains, tattered clothes and has bleeding feet. Prejudice and Fear block her path and try to persuade her to return to the City of Soul's Bondage. She pleads that man cannot walk on the Road of Progress alone and, with the help of Courage she breaks her chains and fights her way past them. Man, tired and weary, returns to beg Woman to help him on his journey; they are about to leave when the Slave Woman enters. She is covered in jewelled chains and laughs at the unadorned Woman:

SLAVE WOMAN: What shall thy sisters say, who see thee without chains? Thou shameless one. Thinkest thou that I would lose my chains, which are set with precious stones?

WOMAN: All women's chains are not jewelled, sister. Some are chains of iron, which drag upon their limbs until they die, because they cannot bear their constant weight. I am in haste to reach my journey's end that I may help them. Wilt thou not follow?[18]

At first Slave Woman refuses, but as Man, Woman and Courage walk into the distance, she stretches out her hand and follows.

The first performance of *Allegory* was given at the Rehearsal Theatre in April 1911. Although the critic from *Votes for Women*[19] thought it was 'Beautifully played, this little piece, so direct, so true', the play was not kept in the repertoire. Most of the suffragists wanted naturalistic plays for their campaigns. If the second Conciliation Bill had been passed and Bensusan had set up an experimental women's theatre, Vera Wentworth might have produced more than one play. But when the Bill was, in Lloyd George's words, torpedoed, she gave up writing and re-joined her suffragette sisters fighting on the streets.

After the winter of 1911 Bensusan tended to concentrate on plays which were popular with the whole suffrage movement. Between 1909-11 forty-three plays had been performed by the League; in the two-and-a-half years prior to the outbreak of war the number was cut to fifteen, but these plays were performed far more frequently to more diverse audiences. In the spring of 1912 Bensusan organised a series of matinées at the Rehearsal Theatre, Maiden Lane, at which the new plays were performed before invited audiences, which included representatives from suffrage societies who were interested in booking the plays. In the following year, as well as performing for the local branches of the NUWSS and the WSPU, the League took plays to professional women's groups such as the Sanitary Inspectors and Health Visitors, and to specialised societies like the Women's Aerial League – an organisation which existed not to train pilots, but to 'secure and maintain for the Empire the same supremacy in the air as it now enjoys on the seas'.

There was now a shift in the emphasis of both the form and the content in the League's propaganda repertoire. The actresses and playwrights felt more confident about confronting the political issues which dominated the suffrage movement. Instead of portraying the generalised sexual inequalities of pre-war society, they concentrated on more detailed examinations of the specific arguments surrounding the suffrage question. Consequently, the positive images of the *Pageant* and the satire in *How the Vote Was Won* were replaced by complex characterisations. In form the plays were still predominantly naturalistic, but Bensusan had found the administrative problems involved in booking plays with large casts almost insurmountable and now encouraged the dramatists to write duologues. In order to incorporate the necessary political content within a two-hander, the writers were forced to engineer a confrontation between a suffragist and an anti-suffragist. Without resorting to a third character the dramatist had to invent plausible curcumstantial reasons why two characters with totally opposing viewpoints would converse with each other for half an hour.

In *The Maid and the Magistrate*[20] the writer, Graham Moffat, solved this problem by combining romantic love and suffrage militancy. The play begins with a man and woman in evening dress escaping into a quiet, empty room from an adjacent ballroom. The man, Mr Potter, is a middle-aged magistrate who is desperately in love with the woman, whose name is Phyllis. Recently he has noticed a new life and vitality about her and fears that she is engaged to be married. Phyllis explains to him that there are more exciting things in life than to be 'left to wither in matrimonial cold water', and asks if he has ever tried a woman for a crime. The magistrate replies that the very next morning he intends to sentence some suffragettes to three months' imprisonment. 'Not the women who were arrested at Downing Street today?' gasps Phyllis. 'Yes, but how did you know?' replies Potter. Phyllis reveals herself to be one of the arrested women and Potter decides to change the sentence to two weeks in the first division, which allowed for many privileges. She declares her love for him and he asks when they shall be married. Phyllis hesitates:

SHE: Perhaps you'd better ask –
HE: I'll ask your father of course.
SHE: On no – not Dad – you should ask Mr Asquith.
HE: Indeed – why should I?

SHE: Because it is a government question. Until women gain
their freedom I have better work to do than get married. My
mind is fully made up – I remain a spinster till we get the vote.
(They exit arm in arm – he protesting)[21]

Ultimately, the situation comedy in *The Maid and the Magistrate* is
developed at the expense of the politics. In contrast, Evelyn Glover's
duologue, *A Chat with Mrs Chicky*[22], develops the politics at the expense
of the characters. Mrs Chicky, a char, is busy cleaning her employer's
study when she is interrupted by his sister, Mrs Holbrook, who asks if
she may have 'a little chat'. Amazed that a 'lady' wishes to talk to her,
Mrs Chicky reluctantly agrees. Mrs Holbrook launches forth on a long
monologue about how she is collecting signatures for a petition to prove
that women do not want the vote. When Mrs Chicky questions the
usefulness of such a survey, she is sharply reprimanded and told to
continue her work. The class difference between the two women makes
it impossible for Mrs Chicky either to disagree with Mrs Holbrook or
leave the room; she must suffer in silence while her employer's sister,
who has no intention of leaving without a signature on her petition,
recites anti-suffragist propaganda. Slowly Mrs Chicky begins to
undermine Mrs Holbrook's confidence by relating all the anti-
suffragist arguments to the daily experience of working women in the
slums of London. When Mrs Holbrook is reflecting on the joys and
wonders of motherhood, Mrs Chicky points out that a mother has no
legal rights over her child, 'the lor don't give 'er no voice in 'er child's
schoolin' nor religin' nor vaccinatin' nor such like'. Mrs Holbrook is
astounded by these and other facts revealed by Mrs Chicky and she
becomes increasingly disorientated, particularly when the char, in a
broad cockney accent, claims to be French. As Mrs Chicky cleans the
grate she explains to Mrs Holbrook that as her dead husband was
French, that is now her nationality. Mrs Holbrook is confused:

MRS HOLBROOK: That does seem rather peculiar, certainly.
MRS CHICKY: Yes 'm. I don't feel French!
MRS HOLBROOK: Of course not – of course not. Of course if one
thinks a moment one sees the beautiful idea at the back of it. A
husband and wife are one, you know.
MRS CHICKY: Yes 'm. Which one?[23]

For a brief moment it seems as if Mrs Holbrook may become a

suffragist, but she regains her confidence and prepares to leave. As she reaches the door, she informs Mrs Chicky that her name will be added to the petition. 'Then can I arsk you somethin' 'm?' enquires Mrs Chicky, 'Speakin' straight as one lady to another, an' no offence meant or taken?' Hesitantly, Mrs Holbrook agrees. Suddenly the power relationship is reversed: it is now Mrs Chicky who talks and Mrs Holbrook who listens. Mrs Chicky reveals that she is a suffragist; she explains why women should have the vote and, losing her temper, accuses Mrs Holbrook and the anti-suffragists of sitting in drawing-rooms pontificating about the wonderful way women's interests are protected by men, while having no conception of the way in which ordinary women are exploited in the factories and on the streets. Finally, her anger spent, she admits that the vote will not solve everything, but she tries to make Mrs Holbrook see that, 'You 'ave to be a woman yourself to know where things 'urt women!' Defeated, but not converted, Mrs Holbrook leaves the room.

Evelyn Glover incorporates every major suffrage argument into her play. But Mrs Holbrook and Mrs Chicky are not two-dimensional political mouthpieces, they are clearly drawn characters. The audience is never allowed to forget that the root of their conflict lies in their differing social classes because, throughout the play, Mrs Holbrook insists that Mrs Chicky continue to clean the room. In order to contradict her employer's sister, Mrs Chicky assumes the guise of an ignorant, stupid woman who is unaware of the implications of her anecdotes. Occasionally, the delineation between what is assumed and what is real in the character is blurred and Mrs Chicky sinks into a stereotyped char. Despite this weakness the conflict between the two women is sustained until the last five minutes of the half-hour play, at which point the realism of the characters falters because there is no reason for Mrs Holbrook to listen to Mrs Chicky's insults. By overwriting Mrs Chicky's final speeches, Evelyn Glover weakens the dramatic structure of an otherwise dynamic play.

Of the eighty performances organised by the play department between the summer of 1912 and 1914, a large proportion were of *A Chat with Mrs Chicky*, and in the annual report of the AFL for 1913–14, the play is mentioned as the most popular piece in the League's repertoire. Its success was partly attributable to the ease with which a play with two characters, table and chair, could be toured, and partly to the political clarity, and the sex, of the playwright. Evelyn Glover was just one of the many women who, due to the growth in the women's movement and the possibility of a production by the AFL or an amateur suffrage group, was encouraged to write plays. Whereas the men wrote suffrage plays to demonstrate their support of the movement, the women were stimulated by the movement to express themselves in a creative form hitherto denied them. A few, like Evelyn Glover (whose first play *Miss Appleyard's Awakening*[24] was produced by the AFL in 1911), continued to work as dramatists after the vote had been won.

As the date approached for the debate on the women's suffrage amendments to the Reform Bill, the executive of the AFL, not content with merely supporting the other suffrage societies, initiated their own parliamentary campaign. They sent a memorial to the Speaker and members of the House of Commons in which they requested permission to plead for women's suffrage before the Bar of the House.

> We the undersigned beg to address you as follows. While adding to the gaiety of the nation the actresses have themselves been suffering from great wrongs arising out of sex disability. The broad expansive view of life which the actresses' calling engenders has revealed to them the state of society in Great Britain which they, as patriotic women, can no longer support. Debarred by sex disability from the exercise of the franchise to right these wrongs, repudiated by the government of the day, unprotected by any party machinery, the actresses, representing a very large and important faction of working women, do appeal to the highest tribunal in the land, the House of Commons, and ask to be allowed to stand before the Bar of the House and lay before the Commons at first hand their reasons for claiming equality with men in the state. ...[25]

As the League only received a formal acknowledgement in response to their memorial, a second letter was sent to the prime minister and the Speaker. It pointed out that the actresses were asking no more than had been granted to the Lord Mayor of Dublin who had been admitted to the Bar of the House on 12 May 1910 to lay the views of the Dublin Corporation on women's suffrage before parliament. Asquith replied that he was of the opinion, 'that the question of Women's Suffrage can be fully and adequately dealt with in the ordinary course of debate in the House of Commons'. But the Speaker added that it was the members of the House, not the Government, who were empowered to give the necessary permission. The AFL published their original memorial and the subsequent correspondence in the suffrage papers and asked all the franchise leagues to sign a petition requesting the members of parliament to pass a resolution calling upon the actresses to plead their case in the House.

On Monday, 18 January 1913, while signatures were still being collected for the petition, the debate on the amendments to the Reform Bill was held in the Commons. The League organised a peaceful picket outside the Houses of Parliament from noon on the Monday; it was to have continued until the House voted, but after two days the picket was abandoned. During the debate, the Speaker had made it clear that in his opinion the adoption of any women's suffrage amendment would so alter the nature of the Bill as to necessitate its re-introduction to the House as a new measure. Consequently, Asquith, who claimed to have no prior knowledge of the Speaker's decision, felt obliged to withdraw the Bill before the final vote. The suffragettes and the suffragists were furious. They demanded an immediate Government Bill to enfranchise women, but the Liberal Government offered nothing more than parliamentary time for a Private Member's Bill.

Depressed and disenchanted, the suffragists embarked on yet another series of campaigns designed to force the Government to change its mind – or to change the Government. The wording of the AFL petition was altered so that representatives of the whole suffrage movement, not merely the actresses, requested the right to plead for the women's cause in the Commons. The petition, signed by thirty suffrage societies, representing over 100,000 women, was presented on 22 April 1913. Needless to say, the women's request was denied. Despite the failure of the petition, the actresses were so delighted by their success at organising a nationwide campaign that they set up a parliamentary 'Lobbying Committee'. They also joined the Federated Council of Suffrage Societies, an association committed to pressurising for a Government Bill on women's suffrage and to opposing the Liberal Party at all elections.

The actresses continued to support the militant suffragettes, but the special relationship which had existed between the AFL and the WSPU in 1909-10 had disappeared by the time the League joined the Federation. After the defeat of the Reform Bill, the suffragettes launched a new attack on government and private property. They poured acid into pillar boxes, cut telegraph wires, set fire to empty houses, slashed paintings in public art galleries, destroyed golf courses and broke streetlamps. They experimented in the area of psychological warfare, painting out the numbers of houses and persuading old ladies to take out gun licences. Although Kitty Marion was the only member of the League who was directly involved in these guerilla activities, the actresses did try to offer some assistance. In the spring of 1913, a young suffragette called Grace Roe found herself temporarily in charge of the WSPU London headquarters – the Pethick-Lawrences had left the union, Christabel was still in France and Mrs Pankhurst was recovering from a hunger strike. Grace knew that the police had a warrant out for her arrest, but with a little help from the AFL, she managed to evade them:

> Next day, two members of the Actresses' Franchise League came to give me a new disguise. This time I was dressed as an elderly lady and I had to remember that all my movements must be slow.
>
> I moved to Hampstead but felt in danger all the time. Just as things were at a pitch, Mrs Mansel turned up. When she saw me she went into peals of laughter – I looked so odd in my disguise. ... It seemed an interminable time but it must have been only a few days before I found myself in a quiet upstairs flat in an old house in Earls Court. ...
>
> Before I went into this flat, the Actresses' Franchise League came to the rescue and I was redisguised as a chorus girl. Charlie Marsh, who did much secret work for me, had a similar disguise. My transformation was golden and her wig was black. We certainly made a striking pair, but it was a very good disguise indeed. Our costumes were so cleverly designed that only the wrong type of man looked at us! We called ourselves 'The Sisters Blackamore'.[26]

The transformation skills of the actresses were increasingly in demand after the Prisoners' Temporary Discharge Act, otherwise known as the Cat and Mouse Act, was passed in March 1913. The Act empowered the prison authorities to release a prisoner whose health was endangered by hunger strikes and forcible feeding for a short period of recuperation. Of course, once the women were released, they went into hiding, but several were re-arrested. As all the leaders of the WSPU were supposedly serving prison sentences, they had to be smuggled in and out of suffrage meetings in a variety of disguises, some of which were provided by the AFL. When the police attempted to arrest the speakers during a meeting, they had to contend with suffragette bodyguards.

These women literally fought the police with their bare hands; some of them had learned the basic elements of self-defence from an AFL play entitled *Physical Force*,[27] which featured a jujitsu display.

The AFL never withdrew its support from the WSPU, but politically the two organisations grew further and further apart. The Union's policy of violent protest necessitated an underground organisation, which gradually lost contact with the rest of the suffrage movement. The suffragettes also became increasingly separatist in outlook, particularly after Christabel Pankhurst wrote *The Great Scourge* in which she claimed that over 70 per cent of men were infected with venereal disease and recommended 'Votes for Women and Chastity for Men'. In contrast, the AFL strengthened its contact with the NUWSS, continued its work in the East End of London and allied itself with the Men's League for Women's Suffrage, a militant organisation which frequently broke up meetings held by Liberal statesmen. By 1913, not only were there 901 members of the AFL, but there was also a men's group for actors and dramatists.

From its inception the League had devoted virtually all its energies to securing the franchise and improving the position of women outside the theatre world. The actresses had learnt a great deal from performing to suffrage audiences all over the country and had given women playwrights a chance to see their plays performed, but they were still earning their living in the male-dominated theatre. In 1913, the actresses turned their attention to their own profession.

A degree of equality had always existed on the stage; the discrimination which did exist related more to the size, number and nature of the women's roles than to the conditions in rehearsal and performance. However, off-stage the theatre was controlled almost exclusively by men. The play department had given women the opportunity to stage-manage, administrate and design, but this was only part-time, unpaid work. Instead of convincing the actor-managers and major theatre companies to employ these women, the League decided to set up an independent Women's Theatre Company. Inez Bensusan, who was the driving force behind the scheme, announced her plans in *Votes for Women* on 23 May:

> I want it to be run entirely by women. The whole business management and control will be in the hands of women, I mean there will be women business and stage-managers, producers and so

on. Actors and authors will naturally be drawn from both sexes and so will (at present) the scenic artists. My ultimate hope is to establish a Women's Theatrical Agency in connection with the Women's Theatre.[28]

Despite Bensusan's vision, the plans for the first Women's Theatre season were comparatively modest: the play department organised the production of two full-length plays, which were performed in repertoire for one week at the Coronet Theatre in London in December. To pay the salaries, production expenses and rent of the theatre, Inez set up 'a great co-operative scheme extending to all branches of the women's movement, even to those not especially occupied in furthering women's suffrage'. The initial capital was provided firstly by individual women who were persuaded to buy £1 shares in the company and, secondly, through Bensusan's advance booking system. After five years of organising propaganda tours, she was in contact with women's groups all over the country. She wrote to each society asking it to buy tickets for the season which could either be used by its members or sold locally at a profit – the ticket prices varied from a seat in the stalls at 10s. 6d. to one in the gallery at 1s. The response from the suffrage movement was overwhelming; the box office receipts for the week were £522, the net profit for the season was £442, and each share-holder received 11s. 6d. in the pound, in other words 57$\frac{1}{2}$ per cent.

Financially the season was a resounding success and proved that women could manage a theatre on their own, but the artistic side of the venture proved more controversial. Although the two plays, *A Gauntlet* and *Woman On Her Own (La Femme Seule)*, examined the position of women in the late nineteenth century, they were written by men. The dramatist, Cicely Hamilton, defended this choice of plays, somewhat inadequately, in the season's souvenir programme. She wrote:

in order to present the Women's Point of View to the best advantage, an opening choice has fallen upon the work of two male dramatists. Possibly the choice may have been accidental and possibly it may have been Hobson's; but whatever it was, I consider it wise and fortunate.[29]

Underlying this choice was the desire of the actresses to work on plays which contained more demanding roles than those found within the League's propaganda repertoire. Most of the new women dramatists were concentrating on one-act, small cast plays. Consequently, the actresses were forced to rely on plays that were about women, even if they were not written by them. In her article Cicely Hamilton made a fairly sarcastic apology for the inevitably conventional nature of the productions:

> In order to avoid disappointment it will be better to state at once that we have no unusual views on the presentment or production of plays. We have been influenced neither by the Russian Ballet nor by Reinhardt [the Austrian actor-director]: we make our exits into the wings instead of into the stalls and I have not heard of any particular struggles to attain that ideal of nobody acting better than anybody else which is frequently admired as 'ensemble'. ... We feel these admissions may be damaging; but we plead, in excuse for our deficiencies, that we are only beginning our enterprise. Later on, perhaps, we shall put out the footlights and tinker with the building and go in for Really High Art.[30]

A Gauntlet,[31] by the Norwegian playwright Bjornstjerne Bjornson, proved the more popular of the two plays. It was written in 1883 and challenged the notion that a women must have an irreproachable past in order to be fit for marriage, whereas a man may be totally debauched and suffer no recriminations. The play tells the story of Svava, a young provincial girl, who is engaged to Alfred, the son of a wealthy and influential businessman. When Svava is told that Alfred has had an affair with a married women, she breaks off the engagement. Her parents attempt to change her mind, particularly after Alfred's father has threatened to reveal a scandal involving Svava's family. At first she is confused by her parents' behaviour, but later she discovers that her father is involved in an extra-marital affair. The play ends with Svava feeling totally distraught. Betrayed by her father's deceit and her mother's silence, she finds comfort in her friendship with Alfred, who has learned to question the double standard of sexual morality.

Although the play is essentially a comedy in which Svava's principled stand confounds and terrifies her family and friends, Bjornson was a serious campaigner for equal political and moral rights for women. He lectured throughout Norway, and wrote a pamphlet on the subject which sold 80,000 copies. The fight for the vote in Norway began in earnest in 1885, two years after *The Gauntlet* was written, but it met with considerably more success than the English campaign. In

1901, Norwegian women were given the municipal vote and in 1907, all women taxpayers and all women married to men with taxable incomes of not less than £20 a year were given the parliamentary vote.

When *A Gauntlet* was performed in Norway, it was said that hundreds of contemplated marriages were broken off; but in England the suffrage theatre critics, while praising the production, adopted a faintly superior attitude to the theme:

> We of the progressive women's movement have come to regard almost as commonplace the woman's right to claim that a man's past shall be as 'clean' as that of the woman he asks in marriage. But in spite of the immense progress that has been made in the last six or seven years in this respect, a large proportion of the public does not yet regard the matter in this light, and the women's movement therefore owes a good deal to the Women's Theatre for having chosen *A Gauntlet* as one of the two plays to be produced by them in their inaugural week.[32]

The reactions to Brieux's play, *La Femme Seule*,[33] were less favourable. In the play, translated by Charlotte Shaw as *Woman on Her Own*, an upper-class woman tries to maintain her independence by earning her own living in a society which offers no opportunity to women outside the home. She gets a job in a book-binding factory and, in her spare time, works on the staff of a 'feminist' paper. But ultimately, her experiment fails and she is forced to return to Paris as her former lover's mistress. In the programme notes, Shaw, who believed Brieux to be the greatest French playwright since Molière, compared the play to his own *Mrs Warren's Profession*:

> Brieux deals with this horror much more disturbingly than I did, because whereas I was content to shew how society brings about and supports prostitution by paying poor girls better and treating them better as prostitutes than in the sweated trades which are the sole alternative for them, Brieux shews how educated, refined and high-spirited women are not allowed even this alternative, because their attempt to support themselves brings them into competition with men in the labour market, and the men thereupon deliberately drive them out of the market and force them into marriage or prostitution without any alternative at all.[34]

Shaw's view of the play was not endorsed by the theatre critics of the suffrage press who found Brieux's work depressing and unrealistic. According to *Votes for Women*,[35] the only laugh in the play came 'when one of the paper's staff says to a "manlike", cigarette smoking colleague, "I've some good news for you," and she replies, "Are all the men – dead?" ' The writer in *The Suffragette* was even more critical:

> With all M. Brieux's earnestness and high ideals, I cannot look upon such a false and pessimistic presentment of women in the labour-market as desirable propaganda for the Feminist cause. ... It is very good of M. Brieux and others to champion the women's cause, but I wish they would do it in a more optimistic spirit, and be a little less lavish of their pity. 'Loneliness is bad for a man, it is much worse for a woman', 'the lonely little room', 'the empty arms', and so on. Loneliness is bad for everyone, but woman is better able to cope with it than man. An unmarried woman with a small salary can make herself a cosy little home and cook a dainty meal with her own hands. ...
>
> I wish some woman would write a play showing the real spirit of the Suffragette. It has never been done yet, and I do not believe that a male dramatist will ever do it.[36]

The response of the suffrage critics to Brieux's play raised fundamental questions in the play department about the nature of political theatre. In effect, the suffrage movement was demanding plays in which the last act portrayed women as happy, independent and victorious, rather than lonely and defeated. The implication of this demand was that theatre should serve the political aims of the movement by posing an ideal to which its audience could aspire, instead of realistically depicting the oppression of women. But the actresses had not developed a theatrical style which could portray this ideal in a satisfactory way. They had been trained to create three-dimensional characters for a naturalistic theatre and in the short propaganda plays – when a character was given a political as opposed to an emotional justification – they had been dissatisfied with the two-dimensional result. The dilemma they faced was whether to pursue the tradition of social drama which, by depicting victims, shamed the audience into political action, or develop a new form of theatre which could successfully represent an alternative. Unfortunately, the outcome of this debate within the League will never be known. The Women's Theatre Company's second season, which was planned for November the following year, never took place; by that time England was at war with Germany.

As soon as war was declared on 4 August, Mrs Pankhurst told the Government that not only would the WSPU suspend militant action, but they would also join the war effort until Germany was defeated. Six days later all the suffragette prisoners were unconditionally released. The actresses were as eager as the members of the WSPU to prove that they were prepared to fight for their country. Their decision is not surprising if viewed against the background of patriotism in late Edwardian England. The AFL's memorials and resolutions had always referred to the actresses as 'patriotic women' who were fighting for 'this great imperial question', and the propaganda plays were full of militaristic references — Mrs Chicky speaks with pride of her brother in the army, the Pageant had a contingent of women fighters and Joan of Arc appeared in virtually every suffrage procession. To the actresses, the war was an opportunity to demonstrate that they were 'equal supporters of the State'.

Within two weeks the AFL had joined together with the Women's Freedom League and the Tax Resisters' League to form the Women's Emergency Corps, which established a register of women who were qualified and willing to help with the war effort. The Government was as uninterested in the actresses' corps as it had been in their franchise league and when Lena Ashwell went to Whitehall to suggest a scheme for the training of 'intelligent and educated women' for work on the land, she was sent to Beatrice and Sidney Webb. 'They were very courteous and rather sorry for me,' wrote Lena, 'expressing their appreciation for my efforts, which, however, were quite unnecessary since the war would be over before Christmas — this in October, 1914.'[37]

By the end of October the actresses had begun work on a project that was acceptable to both the Government and the Army. In camps all over the country enlisted men were waiting to be transported to France and there had been a public request for volunteers to organise troops' entertainment. Lena Ashwell immediately approached the Army Council and pointed out that it was unfair to ask professional artists to volunteer to work for nothing and unfair to the troops if the volunteers were amateurs. She suggested that the AFL organise fifty travelling companies to play three nights in rotation at each of the fifty Army bases. Her proposals were accepted and by mid-November the actresses were performing at Aldershot and Colchester and by the following spring at Grantham, Purfleet, Newhaven and Dover.

As the troops moved out of England, Lena Ashwell organised concert parties to follow them to the front. Each party – consisting of a soprano, contralto, tenor, baritone or bass, an accompanist and an instrumentalist and an entertainer – was allocated a particular geographical area and billeted by the YMCA. Cicely Hamilton was based at Abbeville:

> The huts run by the YMCA were the usual scene of entertainment for the troops. ... The 'camp followers' of the YMCA were quartered for the most part in hostels – houses leased for the purpose from their French owners – and we of the entertainment business had a good sized hostel to ourselves. ... Conveyance of the parties to the various destinations was by car, usually of the lorry type, into which were packed a party, its properties and makeshift effects. Make-up and dressing, so far as possible, would be got through before starting since dressing accommodation at huts and hangars was not always extensive or convenient.[38]

Initially, the actresses were kept well clear of the front line and performed to large numbers of new recruits. In contrast, the all-male parties spent most of their time performing under fire and for the wounded. A nurse, writing from a hospital at Wimereux, remembered one of these parties giving a concert in the orderly room:

> the men were too bad for us to have a concert in the hospital itself, but afterwards those kind people came into each ward and sang softly, without any accompaniment, to the men who were well enough to listen, and the little Canadian story-teller went round and told his stories to each man in turn as they were having their dressings done, the result being, that instead of a mass suffering of humanity having their wounds dressed, the men were happy during that time that is usually so awful.[39]

As the war dragged on, the actresses began performing plays with the help of the actors in 'khaki'. The only disadvantage of this was that the leading man was liable to disappear without warning to the front. Their repertoire bore little relation to the AFL's earlier work; the average programme consisted of scenes from Shakespeare, Barrie, Sheridan or Shaw. The only play that the actresses performed to both the suffragists and the troops was Barrie's *The Twelve Pound Look*[40] — a domestic comedy about a man's chance meeting with his first wife and his discovery that she had left him for a typewriter. The inability of the actresses to incorporate their suffrage consciousness into the troops' entertainments is indicative of the effect the war had on the whole of the women's movement. The suffragettes and suffragists who joined the war effort, particularly those that went to France, were so appalled by the slaughter and bloodshed they witnessed that the cause of women's enfranchisement suddenly seemed unimportant.

By 1917 most of the men in the concert parties had joined up, so the actresses were providing virtually all the troops' entertainments in France, Malta, Egypt and Palestine. In one of his war poems, Siegfried Sassoon described a troupe of entertainers in the desert:

> Jaded and gay, the ladies sing; and the chap in brown
> Tilts his grey hat; jaunty and lean and pale,
> He rattles the keys ... Some actor bloke from town ...
> 'God send you home'; and then 'A long, long trail',
> 'I hear you calling me', and 'Dixieland' ...
> Sing slowly ... now the chorus ... one by one.
> We hear them, drink them; till the concert's done.
> Silent I watch the shadowy mass of soldiers' stand,
> Silent they drift away over the glimmering sand.

By the time of the armistice there were twenty-five parties in France alone, giving approximately 1,400 performances a month. But the actresses' role had subtly changed from entertainers to unobtainable sex-objects. Lena Ashwell encouraged them to assume this guise:

> When it was impossible to find men, the parties were composed entirely of women. One YMCA leader complained at the selection we had made. I was persistent, so finally he asked if I realised that there was not a single member whom the men did not long to kiss, and he was petrified with horror when I said that that was just why they were chosen. Even a china tea-cup, a coloured cloth, a coloured stone, a flower, was a gift to those thousands starved of all beauty, all loveliness. ...[41]

The experiment proved a tremendous success, because the chivalry of everyone was immediately aroused at the sight of these 'helpless' women, and throughout, touring parties of women only were the most successful, which can easily be understood if one can realise that it was an intense joy, as one man said to me, 'to see a pair of slippers'; and the girl who at the beginning of the war always dressed in rather serviceable clothes, soon found out that the brightest colours and the prettiest frocks gave the greatest pleasure to the men. ...[42]

After their years of struggle before the war to represent the reality of women's lives, the actresses were back in their time-worn roles – an image of beauty like a china tea-cup with sexual overtones.

In 1917, when the Government announced that franchise was to be granted to women above the age of thirty, the apocalyptic carnage of the war had overshadowed for many suffragists the importance of the vote. Cicely Hamilton was still in France when she heard the news:

I remember – how well I remember – receiving the official intimation that my name had been placed on the register of the Chelsea electorate! I was in Abbeville at the time, and, as the post arrived, a battery of Archies, somewhere on the hill, began to thud; an enemy airplane was over, taking photographs. I remember thinking, as I read the notice, of all that the suffrage had meant to us, a year or two before! How we had marched for the suffrage and held meetings and had been shouted at; and how friends of mine, filled with the spirit of the martyr, had hurled themselves at policemen – and broken windows – and starved themselves in prison; and that now, at this moment of achieved enfranchisement, what really interested me was not the thought of voting at the next election, but the puff of smoke that the Archies sent after the escaping plane. Truth to tell, at that moment I didn't care a button for my vote; and, rightly or wrongly, I have always imagined that the Government gave it to me in much the same mood as I received it.[43]

However disillusioned Cicely Hamilton may have felt about the importance of the franchise, on returning to England she once again became active in the women's movement. Only now the emphasis was on how to use the vote wisely. A series of campaigns was begun to repeal laws discriminating against women, such as divorce, guardianship of children, widows' pensions, maternity services and equal pay. Within ten years, due to these pressure groups, no less than twenty-eight laws were passed of special concern to women and children. Although a few actresses were involved in these campaigns they made no attempt to revive the AFL, or to use theatre to propagandise their aims.

In the 1920s, it was the Labour movement rather than the women's rights movement that developed its own agitational theatre. Drama groups were set up all over the country, which eventually merged to form the Worker's Theatre Movement. A number of early plays performed by these groups were by dramatists who had written for the suffrage movement. In fact one of the first plays performed by the Hackney Labour Dramatic Group in the early 1920s was Barrie's *The Twelve Pound Look*. The Worker's Theatre Movement developed a sophisticated agit-prop theatre which rejected naturalism for didactic realism − an X-ray picture of society and social forces − nevertheless some of the roots of their theatre are to be found in the play department of the AFL.

Part Three

EDY AND HER PIONEERS

At first sight it would seem that women's theatre died with the AFL; however, the Pioneer Players, a women's company that grew out of the League's work, survived until the 1920s. The company was formed in 1911 by Edith Craig who, at the age of forty, found in the suffrage movement the catalyst she needed to galvanise her theatrical skills into those of a director. The theatre she created went far beyond the simple slogan 'Votes for Women'. It was a place where women could express themselves and see the reality of their lives reflected from the stage. Sybil Thorndike described her as a 'genius'.[1] Shaw considered that her company, 'by singlemindedness of artistic direction and unflagging activity, did more for the theatrical vanguard than any of the other coterie theatres'[2] – but today Edy and the Pioneer Players have been virtually forgotten.

5. AILSA CRAIG 1869-1908

Edy was born on 9 December 1869, at Gusterd Wood Common, Hertfordshire. Her father, Edward Godwin, was an established architect, archaeologist and a leader of the aesthetic movement; her mother, Ellen Terry, then a little-known actress, was to become a Dame of the British theatre.

According to theatre mythology, Ellen Terry fell passionately in love with Godwin and, tiring of her stage career, eloped with him to the idyllic English countryside. In reality she had no alternative. At the age of sixteen Ellen had married the eminent Victorian painter, George Frederick Watts. Although they were separated, she was still theoretically his wife. At first Ellen's affair with Godwin was a closely guarded secret, but one evening she visited his room in Baker Street and, finding him unwell, stayed until the following morning. Her family considered that she had compromised herself. And it was obvious to Ellen that her liaison was not only embarrassing them, but also alienating her from theatre friends. She knew she must either end the relationship or leave her family and the theatre. On Saturday, 10 October 1868, having finished the evening performance of *The Household Fairy*, she left the New Queen's Theatre and ran away to Hertfordshire with Godwin.

Initially Ellen delighted in the freedom of being alone with her lover, but soon she began to feel isolated. Godwin was always being called away to lecture or attend site meetings. He gave her a bulldog to protect her and then a series of companions: a parrot, a goat, a monkey and finally a child. Many years later Ellen wrote to George Bernard Shaw describing the night that Edith was born.

> I lived in the sweet country — in the middle of a common — and I forgot my pangs whilst reading *The Watching of the Falcon* on a certain bitter sweet night in December when Edy, my first child was born. They were playing in the church 'Oh rest in the Lord'. I

heard them as I passed through the village — alone — feeling
frightfully ill and afraid. I could never forget that music and that
poem. It was all lovely and awful.[1]

If the mother was lonely so was her illegitimate child. Unlike most
Victorian children Edy had no enormous family celebrating her birth,
no brothers or sisters or cousins to play with, no grandparents to
indulge her. She did not speak until she was two years old; Ellen tells
the story in her autobiography of her daughter's first words.

'There's some more.'
She spoke quite distinctly. It was uncanny.
'More what?' I asked in a trembling voice, afraid that having
delivered once, she might lapse into dumbness.
'Birds.'[2]

Edy's silence was not induced just by isolation; both she and her
brother, Edward, who was born in 1872, experienced an exceptional
form of childhood indoctrination. Godwin's involvement with the
aesthetic movement dominated both his own and his children's lives.
After his son was born he built a beautiful house for the family in the
village of Harpenden, not far from Gusterd Wood Common. The floors
of the house were covered in Chinese matting and the nursery wall
lined with Japanese prints and fans. The children were allowed no
'rubbishy picture books'[3] and any tasteless presents were promptly
burnt. A mechanical mouse which had been given to Edy was taken
away despite profuse tears and condemned as being 'realistic and
common'.[4] Eventually the children got the message and when Edy was
presented with a doll in a violent pink dress she exclaimed, much to her
parents' delight, 'Vulgar'.[5]

The family had been living in the country for six years when Ellen
decided to return to the theatre. One day quite unexpectedly she met the
dramatist and novelist, Charles Reade, in a country lane near
Harpenden.

I was driving in a narrow lane, when the wheel of the pony cart
came off. I was standing there, thinking what I should do next,
when a whole crowd of horsemen in 'pink' came leaping over the
hedge into the lane. One of them stopped and asked if he could do
anything. Then he looked hard at me and exclaimed: 'Good God!
It's Nelly!'

The man was Charles Reade.

'Where have you been all these years?' he said.

'I have been having a very happy time,' I answered.

'Well, you've had it long enough. Come back to the stage!'

'No, never!'

'You're a fool! You ought to come back.'

Suddenly I remembered the bailiff in the house a few miles away, and I said laughingly: 'Well, perhaps I would think of it if someone would give me forty pounds a week!'

'Done!' said Charles Reade. 'I'll give you that, and more, if you'll come and play Philippa Chester in *The Wandering Heir*.'[6]

Ellen could not refuse. Her relationship with Godwin was being destroyed by financial worries. He was hopelessly impractical with money and she was continually forced to cajole or charm local tradesmen in order to feed her family. Forty pounds a week was enough to solve all their problems and for Ellen, who had submerged herself completely in her lover's work, Charles Reade's offer was a chance for her to reassert her own creativity. Leaving the children in the country, Ellen and Godwin moved to 23 Taviton Street, a rented house in North London. They took with them Ellen's only close friend from the Harpenden days, Mrs Rumbold, known to Edy and Teddy as Boo. Boo's niece Bo was left in charge of the children.

The Wandering Heir ran for 130 nights at the New Queen's Theatre and then toured the provinces. When Ellen finished the engagement with Charles Reade she was asked by Mrs Bancroft to play Portia in *The Merchant of Venice*. Delighted, she accepted and convinced Mrs Bancroft that Godwin should be employed to work on the costumes and sets. Rehearsals began with Godwin and Ellen working enthusiastically together, but a month before the play was due to open they had a violent argument and separated. The reason for the break is unclear, but it is possible that Godwin felt threatened by Ellen's success as an actress. He never advocated that a woman's place was in the home; in fact he wrote an article for the journal *Women and Work*, suggesting how architects could employ women to revolutionise domestic design. But he may still have found it difficult to play second fiddle to Ellen in the theatre.

A few weeks after Godwin left Taviton Street he tried, unsuccessfully, to get custody of Edy. Horrified, Ellen wrote to their mutual friend, Mr

Wilson, telling him that she no longer wished to communicate with Godwin.

> In all gentleness and kindness of feeling, I must beg you not to act as mediator between Mr Godwin and myself. Our separation was a thing agreed upon by both of us many weeks before it actually took place. The first steps were taken by him and I certainly am much astonished to hear that he professes any strong feeling in the matter. Part of our compact was that we should always maintain a kindly, friendly relation to one another – he has, since Tuesday last, made this an impossibility. He tried by unfair means to get my little girl from me (I had offered to let him have the boy) and I now distinctly refuse to have any communication whatever with him. ...[7]

Edy was old enough to remember the arguments between her parents prior to their separation. Several years later according to her brother, Teddy, she asked him

> if I would like to see a portrait of my father – whom I had not seen since I was three years old and could not remember – and instantly whipped out a terrible drawing someone had made for her of a fiend with long teeth and claws and a tail, and said: 'There – that's him!'[8]

After her father's departure, Edy's life was dominated by women. Her mother's household consisted of Boo and Bo from Harpenden; Audrey Campbell, her understudy; Mrs Harries, the housekeeper; Mrs Bindloss, the governess; the cook and the housemaid. As the years went by still more women joined Ellen's entourage. Many of her most ardent admirers were young women who felt she had found the independence and self-expression that they were groping towards in their struggle for emancipation. They sent her flowers, presents and poetry – begging a brief audience.

As Edy grew up with such a fascinating assortment of women, it is not surprising that she developed a high opinion of her own sex. Whenever she wanted to encourage her brother to do something she would say, 'Come on Teddy, be a woman.'[9] She was nine when she started school. A conventional Victorian school would have quickly taught her that 'being a woman' was not quite what she had imagined, but Edy was lucky; her school was run by a Mrs Cole who held the revolutionary belief that girls should have as good an education as boys.

She was also a pioneer of co-education and all her classes were mixed, so Edy and Teddy attended school together. When Edy outgrew Mrs Cole's school she was handed over to Mrs Cole's sister, Mrs Malleson, who, as well as running a school in Gloucester, was an active campaigner for female suffrage.

In comparison with the women in Edy's childhood most of the men were quite transitory, two-dimensional figures. Her stepfathers, Charles Kelly and James Carew, who entered her life after her parents had separated, were good-looking young actors who exuded a conventional masculinity which Ellen found sexually attractive. Unfortunately, neither of them felt happy in their role as 'Miss Terry's husband', Kelly lasting five years and Carew barely two. Ellen married Kelly in 1876. She managed to get a divorce from Watts shortly after Godwin left her and was eager to re-marry to legitimise her children. Ben Terry, Ellen's father, disliked Kelly, thought he was an alcoholic and likened his daughter's marriage to a duchess marrying a cellarman. But Ellen was respectable again and she and her children were accepted back into the Terry family. Edy was fond of Kelly and found him warm and affectionate, but Teddy loathed him. In 1907 when their mother married her third husband, James Carew, the children, now grown up, found their attitudes reversed. Teddy though James a 'jolly, pleasant fellow', but he described his sister's reaction as 'utterly distraught'. He had little sympathy for Edy's distress and attributed it to a desire to meddle in her mother's affairs and a generalised hostility to men:

> She seems to have thought that others have a say in these matters; she was inexperienced and, I think, ignorant of most things to do with life as it is – and somehow or other, prejudiced in some way against the male sex, though always kind to me.[10]

Carew was four years younger that Teddy; despite accusations that he was an opportunist using Ellen to further his career, he appears to have been genuinely in love with her.

Edy's stepfathers made no lasting impression on her life, but Henry Irving, another of Ellen's lovers, did influence her artistically and emotionally. Ellen became Irving's leading lady at the Lyceum in 1878 and their partnership, which lasted until 1902, became one of the most celebrated in the history of English theatre. When Ellen told her daughter she was having an affair with Irving, Edy listened with her hands in her pockets and after a long silence said, 'I think you've been very badly treated and I'm glad about you and Henry.'[11] Irving had a great affection for Ellen's children and took responsibility for their theatrical education. They were allowed to wander freely about the Lyceum and watch every play with their guardian, Bo, in the Royal Box. He encouraged them to criticise the plays and even his own performance. One day he was rehearsing the part of the vicar in *Olivia* and Edy, who was watching, said, 'Don't go on like that Henry. Why don't you talk as you do to me and Teddy? At home you are the Vicar.'[12] Henry stopped, listened carefully to Edy and altered his characterisation accordingly.

Edy did not find it easy being the daughter of one of England's greatest actresses; she was constantly encouraged to perform and only had to frown and say, 'won't' for Ellen to cry, 'marvellous' and 'hush' to everyone and repeat, 'isn't she marvellous?'[13] At the age of nine she was thrust onto the stage of the Court Theatre for her debut in *Olivia*, by W. G. Wills. Although her career as an actress seemed predetermined Edy was far from acquiescent; as an actress she knew she would live her whole life in her mother's shadow. Eventually, she persuaded Ellen to let her train as a concert pianist. Like most aspiring musicians of her generation she wanted to train in Berlin. When Irving planned a tour of Germany to do research for his major production of *Faust*, mother and daughter went with him. Irving spent hours wandering around antique shops while Ellen took Edy to endless concerts. The trip was a great success. It was agreed that Edy should return to Berlin and study with Alexis Holländer, after training first at the Royal Academy of Music.

It was 1888 and Edy was nineteen when she went back to Germany. Ellen, concerned that she should study hard and not disgrace herself socially, wrote copious letters full of detailed instructions. Years later when Edy re-read these letters she said, 'If I could have done all Mother advised me to do, been all she wanted me to be, I should be a very splendid and wise woman.'[14] Unfortunately, after studying with Holländer for a year Edy developed chronic rheumatism in the joints of her fingers and her hopes of becoming a concert pianist were destroyed.

Depressed and disillusioned, she returned home and Ellen, who could not bear to see her children unhappy, came up with the obvious solution: why didn't Edy become an actress? Ellen had thought of a stage name for her daughter many years before when touring in Scotland with Teddy and Irving. They visited a place called Ailsa

Craig; Ellen said, 'What a good stage name. A pity you can't have it, Ted. I shall give it to Edy.'[15] So in 1890, Ailsa Craig accepted her fate and joined the Lyceum company. Irving cast her in a series of small character parts in which, as she later admitted, she was 'rather good'. Eleonora Duse, the brilliant Italian actress, saw a performance at the Lyceum of *The Lyons Mail* and when Edy, who was playing a very small part, said her line, 'That's the man I served with rum', Duse got quite excited and said, 'Who's that girl? She's the best actress in the company.'[16] Needless to say, as Edy always pointed out when telling this story, her mother was not in that particular production.

Edy never made the transition from being a supporting actress to being a star. She had a good voice, was technically proficient, but became audience-shy when asked to play anything other than minor roles. According to Ellen, she was totally non-competitive within her personal relationships: 'She never tried to compete for anyone, and so probably she'll go to the wall unappreciated.'[17] Perhaps it was a reluctance to compete with her mother that prevented Edy developing as an actress. Ellen, like most actresses of her generation, continued to play young heroines well into her 70s, which not only prevented younger actresses from tackling major roles but also created problems for inexperienced actors, like Ernest Milton, who played opposite her.

> I made my first professional contact with her [Edy] in 1917 when I was engaged to play Bassanio to Ellen Terry's Portia in the Trial Scene from *The Merchant of Venice* at the Pavilion Theatre, Brighton Pier. The Great Actress was then very near the end of her career and there was a wide disparity of age between the two characters. In the course of rehearsals Edith Craig came to me with one of her rarest smiles and said, 'I have a message for you from mother. She says you will wear a beard as Bassanio. You will then pass as her son; but if you don't wear one you will look like her grandson and she feels that won't do.'[18]

Edy played her mother's handmaiden both on and off-stage. After Ellen's admirers had witnessed a few flashes of backstage Terry charm, they were passed on to Edy for disposal. Chris St John, alias Christabel Marshal, who was to play a major part in Edy's life, was just one of many:

> when after a few minutes in her mother's dressing-room, I was

conducted ... to Edy's, which she was sharing with several other
actresses in the company, she gave me a welcome I cannot
truthfully describe as cordial. She was busy mending a mitten (for
her part in *Olivia*, I suppose) and did not put it down before shaking
hands, with the result that I was pricked by the needle.[19]

Edy was continually admonished for her lack of Terry charm. In the
eyes of strangers mother and daughter could not have seemed less alike.
Ellen was short and fair with an enchanting manner that made
everyone adore her; while Edy was tall (5 feet 8 inches), thin and dark,
with the cool detachment of an intelligent critic. In their own ways
both women had such strong personalities that, as George Bernard
Shaw implied to Ellen, the roles of mother and daughter sometimes
seemed reversed. Ellen replied to GBS: 'Edy. I think you think she takes
care of me! Of course she does in her way, because I care what she
thinks and I love her best, but I'm not her child. Lord no!'[20]

Ellen and Edy may have loved each other 'best', but they were still
capable of conflict; during the Lyceum company's 1895 tour of
America, mother and daughter almost came to blows. Edy had wanted
to go to America ever since she heard about the Lyceum's first pioneer
tour in 1883. At that time, according to Ellen: 'there was no living
drama as there is now ... such productions of romantic plays and
Shakespeare as Henry and I brought over from England were
unknown.'[21] Although by 1895 the situation was very different, there
was still an element of excitement and adventure in an American tour.
Amongst other things, the company had to contend with rats,
cockroaches and long, hazardous railway journeys. One night, when
they were crossing a flooded river with the water almost at engine level,
Edy went to check that her mother was all right and was greeted by the
experienced traveller, immaculately dressed, saying, 'Edy darling,
hurry and dress youself properly; we shall probably have to swim.'[22]

The relationship between mother and daughter deteriorated on the
tour when Edy fell passionately in love with a young actor in the
company – Sydney Valentine. Ellen knew that Valentine was married
and decided to put an end to Edy's romance. She told her daughter to
give up Valentine or return to England; Edy gave up Valentine. The
situation was made worse by Ellen forcing the heartbroken Edy to
chaperone her while she indulged in a faintly ludicrous flirtation with
an actor called Frank Cooper.

By the time Edy returned from America in 1886, she was anxious to leave the Lyceum company. The opportunity to do so was provided by one of Ellen's old admirers, George Bernard Shaw. Shaw was famous for his egotism, and perhaps it was Edy's refusal to be impressed by him that cemented their friendship. He never recovered from reading *Arms and the Man* to her, as Ellen explains: 'Edy was present at the reading, and paid the reader so few compliments about his play, that he expressed the opinion that she behaved as if she had been married to him for twenty years.'[23]

To Shaw, Irving was an ogre and the Lyceum the 'Ogre's Castle'[24] filled with old romantic dramas and Shakespearean extravaganzas. For many years he tried to persuade Ellen to break free from her artistic chains. Temporarily despairing of her, he engineered her daughter's escape from the Lyceum. A provincial tour of Shaw's play *Candida* and Ibsen's *A Doll's House* was being organised by Charles Charrington and Janet Achurch under the aegis of the Independent Theatre. Shaw suggested that Edy be employed to play Prossy in his play and Mrs Linde in Ibsen's. He knew exactly how Edy should play Prossy and suggested giving her private rehearsals, he also offered to 'hear her' over Mrs Linde because, as he explained to Ellen: 'Janet is so loathingly sick of rehearsing it with new Lindes that she wants Edy to get through with only one rehearsal.'[25]

Edy had no complaints. She became a dedicated Ibsenite and wrote to Ellen that, should the Independent Theatre decide on *Rosmersholm* for their next production, she would ask to play the housekeeper. Ellen was less enthusiastic; she wrote to Shaw telling him how much she missed Edy and that a clever friend had said: 'If Edy stays long with the Independent Theatre Company she will get dull, heavy, conceited, frowsy, trollopy and dirty! In fact she will look moth-eaten! And no one will see her act, because nobody goes to their theatre.'[26] Edy obviously enjoyed looking 'moth-eaten'; and the political and artistic experience she gained from the Independent Theatre proved invaluable years later when she set up her Pioneer Players.

When the tour ended Edy accepted a part in Mrs Brown Potter's production of *Charlotte Corday* which opened at the Adelphi Theatre in January 1898. While the play was running, Mrs Brown Potter, who was famous for her theatrical tours of China, India, Australia and America, asked Edy if she would like to join her on a South African tour. Edy was delighted, but Ellen was distraught:

The difference between Edy in Manchester and Edy in Africa (Oh, my heart is in my boots as I realize it) is this. If she is in any real difficulty she always sends to me, or comes to me and we pick up her ends together. But when she is in Africa! Oh Lord whom will she go to? ... It's not jealous thought, all this.[27]

Edy went to Africa and Ellen overcame her anxiety by writing copious letters to her daughter.

Well My Ducks,

 I'm a very queer mummy for I'm writing to you all of the time and yet I never put pen to paper. It seemed wonderful to get a note from you so quickly. Bless you for it. For you had by that time passed through the Red Sea and probably been through a great deal of unpleasant hours and I had only gotten up late and gone to bed late and yet had done, as usual nowadays, nothing to mark the time. Cairo. I could scarcely believe it, so quick and such a change. I do hope the seas were kind to you. It must seem to you that you are reading a book to be there — Cairo — and by this time you are sure at work and have sat on Camels and I hope they don't throw people and sit on them. ...

 I am thinking a great deal of how we are all going to make things easier in life for you. Physically it appears to me you seem to be very fairly well, but I know how hard you work for so little recompense and it seems to me too bad you have to rush about so. There never was a truer saying than 'a rolling stone gathers no moss' — to be still in one spot is the sweetest, quickest way to make some of the root of all evil grow and spread and bear fruit, nice little golden fruit — so useful. Of course I know when you're in a train you get some quiet time to read, but it is when you're on your poor old toesies in town I hate to see you. What about importing a camel?[28]

When Edy returned home she was almost thirty, 'in her dark hair, nearer black than brown, there was already one white lock'.[29] Unemployed and with no burning desire to continue acting, Edy contemplated a change of career. She had inherited her father's fascination with theatre design and always created her own costumes, as May Whitty, a young actress who understudied her at the Lyceum, discovered:

Edy played Jessica in *The Merchant of Venice*, and one night was taken ill, and I had to go on in a great hurry in her place. When I was tremblingly making up, and asked for my dress, the dresser produced many scarves and bits and pieces and said Miss Edy always fixed these herself! By the aid of the dresser and many safety pins I managed to adjust these strange, shapeless materials into some semblance of a dress, and decided I must watch Edy at work another time.[30]

Irving, who was obsessed with creating naturalistic settings for his plays, commissioned Edy to redesign the costumes for Sardou's *Robespierre*. She was overjoyed. Since the age of eight Edy had been compiling a reference collection in scrapbooks, boxes and drawers, of pictures of places and people, flowers, dresses and buildings and reproductions of old masters. The *Robespierre* costumes were an unqualified success and Ellen, who was anxious to see her children settled in their careers and self-supporting, provided the necessary finance to establish her daughter as a theatrical costumier. Edy found premises in Henrietta Street and proceeded to build a business which, though financially disastrous, gained a reputation for making the best costumes in London.

In 1899, the same year as the costume business opened, Edy met a woman who was to play as important a part in her life as Ellen. Chris St John was working as a secretary to Lady Randolph Churchill and her son Winston when she first met and fell in love with Edy. She had just come down from Oxford and was trying to write her first novel:

I strove to incorporate much of myself into the hero of the novel, and found him an easier creation than any woman in the story. I did not understand women, I thought, because they love to attract love. They desired to be loved. I felt in myself a burning desire to love, to be the active one who gave, who held the world's record for giving. To be content to receive, to be passive, to be beloved, was not my aim. I saw myself always as the lover.[31]

Chris chose Edy as the object for her love and when Ellen went to America at the end of the year, the two women set up house together in Smith Square. Some years later Chris wrote a thinly disguised account of her relationship with Edy in a novel called *Hungerheart*. In the novel she describes Ellen's jealousy on returning from America and Edy's reaction to it:

You don't know mother. She wants me because I have gone away.
When I lived at home I hardly ever saw her ... partly because she
was never there and partly because she can never bear to be with
any one for long at a time. Please don't think she doesn't love me.
Of course she does – tremendously; at the same time she has all
sorts of ideas and sentiments that she doesn't wish realised. One of
them is my living with her and looking after her. No one can look
after my mother.[32]

Ellen may have been a possessive mother but Chris became an even
more possessive friend. Edy had been living at Smith Square for three
years when she fell in love with a musician called Martin Shaw. Chris
was desolate:

One horrible moment. ... A bomb hurtling through the serene air
of my paradise, exploding with a noise of devils' laughter, tearing
up immemorial trees by the roots, laying waste the greenery of hope
and faith – then filth, stench, corruption – then nothing, no
suffering even – nothing.[33]

When Chris heard that Martin Shaw and Edy were to marry she took
an overdose of cocaine and nearly died. Edy nursed her back to health
but insisted on continuing her relationship with Shaw. Eventually,
Chris discovered that Ellen was also opposed to the marriage and
together they emotionally blackmailed Edy into rejecting her lover.
They justified their actions by saying that Martin Shaw was not good
enough for her; he had a severe birth-mark covering part of his face
and was, they believed, only a second-rate musician. The latter
judgement was contested by Edy's brother, Edward Gordon Craig,
who had collaborated with Shaw while working for the Purcell
Operatic Society. Ellen had been impressed by two of their productions,
Acis and Galatea and *The Masque of Love*, but it was her son's skills, not
Martin Shaw's, that she recognised.

Edy never spoke about the break with Shaw, but years later Chris
wrote, 'I think our life together subsequently was all the happier,
because we did not break open the grave of the thing past which had
threatened to separate us.'[34] Far from being separated, the two women
lived together until Edy's death in 1947. Whether they had an explicit
lesbian relationship or not is open to conjecture, but as Jeffrey Weeks
points out in *Coming Out*, 'Many of the close relations [between women

in the late nineteenth century] might have become "physical" in the modern sense; others did not. To say more than this would be to push modern definitions on to an alien scene.'[35]

In *Hungerheart* Chris describes her emotional relationship with Edy as though it were a marriage.

> Almost from the first we lived beyond our income, but we were too happy to think of the rod we were pickling for our backs. We were as happy as a newly-married pair, perhaps happier; and we certainly disproved the tradition that women were incapable of friendship.
>
> I used to wonder which was the husband and which the wife in the menage![36]

But she implies that Edy was sexually reserved and characterises their physical relationship in terms of warmth and holding hands. In contrast to this demure hesitation Chris describes her relationships, probably fictitious, with a Russian Lady and an Italian Countess. The Russian woman acts as her sexual and intellectual mentor.

> 'No tears,' she said tenderly, putting her arm round my neck. 'Let us keep our hearts on high. You have a tendency to sadness, little one. Well, be sad in your own room. Do not inflict it on others. That is bad manners. I want you to have exquisite manners. The first thing I loved in you was your dear little bow of courtesy. We shall write to each other, shall we not? ... and you shall spend a vacation with me, when you are at Oxford. Now I am going to kiss you. ... Never kiss, cherie, except with your soul ... not man nor woman. A kiss is foolish if it is not sacred.'
>
> Her left arm joined her right around my neck, and hugging me to her she kissed me again and again. Her white teeth seemed to glisten like stars, her face in the dying autumn light was beautiful like a pearl. Each kiss was a seal on what she had taught me. ...[37]

Although *Hungerheart* challenged the Victorian assumption that women were sexually passive, it conformed to the prevalent attitude held by sex psychologists that inversion was either true and congenital or artificial and acquired through temporary influences. By characterising herself in the novel as a congenital lesbian, Chris accepted the implied corollary that she had a male psyche; in *Hungerheart* she calls herself John and in real life she changed her name from Christabel Marshall to the sexually ambiguous Chris St John.

Edy's attitude to their relationship can only be surmised. Most of her personal papers were destroyed by Chris after her death and she was notoriously bad at writing letters, as Cicely Hamilton explains:

> I used to be puzzled, as well as amused, by the stiff little typewritten notes I received which, though signed by Edy, were obviously composed by a secretary. One day I laughed at her about this formal style of correspondence and asked her why she wrote to me as if I were her stockbroker or the Army and Navy stores? Whereupon, to my surprise, she at first looked uncomfortable and then confessed shamefacedly that she didn't write letters if she could help it, as she could never be sure of her spelling.[38]

Ellen's initial reaction to her daughter's relationship is equally open to conjecture. But in 1901 she acknowledged Chris as part of the family, when she bought a farmhouse for the three of them to share as a summer home. Years before, Ellen and Henry Irving had visited Small Hythe, a small Kent village, surrounded by marshland, close to the south coast. On that occasion Ellen had fallen in love with the Tudor farmhouse situated at the far end of the village, but her offer to buy the property had been refused. Ellen asked the old shepherd who rented the house to contact her if the owner decided to sell. In 1901 she received a letter from him saying that the owner had died and the property was up for auction. Immediately she dispatched Edy and Chris to bid at the sale. Edy was enchanted by the house with its thick beams and thatched roof and gazing at the attic filled with fleeces she informed the bemused Chris, 'This will be mother's bedroom.' The property, known as Small Hythe Place, consisted of the farmhouse, a parcel of land, a collection of outhouses, a traditional raised Tudor barn and two cottages, Yew Tree and Priest's House – the latter becoming Chris and Edy's home. Many of Ellen's friends, including Chris, were dubious about the wisdom of the purchase but their fears were misplaced. Ellen spent every summer at her farmhouse until the last years of her life, when she lived there all year round.

Encouraged by her success in providing a home and career for her daughter, Ellen turned her attention to her son. Edward Gordon Craig, like his sister Edy, served his theatrical apprenticeship with Irving at the Lyceum. Despite the fact that he was surrounded by some of the greatest performers on the English stage, he had little sympathy for actors and even less respect for their art. Ben Webster, a young member of the Lyceum company, acted with Edward Gordon Craig in Irving's production of *Cymbeline*; they played two young princes who had to fight their way through an army of battling extras. One night, Ben Webster found that the army were pushing, shoving and hitting him with numerous axes and spears. He turned round and whispered 'What the hell do you think you're doing?' The army wavered and a soldier replied, 'Very sorry, Sir. We thought you was Mr Craig.'[39]

Mr Craig was quite unperturbed by his lack of popularity with the extras. The theatre he envisaged was not dependent on a collective, ensemble spirit, but on individual creative genius. In this respect he was following in his father's footsteps. Godwin, through his involvement in the aesthetic movement, rejected the theatre of the actor-manager, where the leading actor was responsible for the whole play. He established the role of the 'producer', who had artistic control of the entire production and complete power over the performers. When Godwin produced *As You Like It* and Fletcher's *The Faithful Shepherdess* for the Pastoral Players, he created a theatre in which the actors were mere puppets in a series of beautifully coloured and composed, living pictures. In Edward Gordon Craig's work with the Purcell Operatic Society Ellen saw Godwin's genius recreated. When finally she left Irving and the Lyceum in 1902, she decided to use both her money and her skill as an actress to establish Teddy as a theatre producer.

In 1903 Ellen took over the Imperial Theatre in Tothill Street for a Terry-Craig season in which she was to be the star, her daughter the costumier, and her son the producer. Teddy, who was an autocrat, decided the first play would be Ibsen's *The Vikings* and cast his mother in the totally unsuitable role of Hiordis. The rehearsal period was a disaster, with tension between the cast and between the family. Teddy was furious with his sister for making suggestions about the costume designs to Ellen, who would then use her authority in rehearsals to make him accept them. Possibly such manipulation would not have been necessary if Teddy had been prepared to listen to Edy, rather than assume that it was her function as a woman to provide silently for his material and emotional needs, while he indulged in uninterrupted creativity. Years later he had an affair with Isadora Duncan which ended with him shouting at her: 'Why don't you stop this? Why do you want to go on the stage and wave your arms about? Why don't you stay at home and sharpen my pencils?'[40] The women who did stay at home with Teddy's pencils were soon abandoned when they became pregnant. He had ten children, five of whom were illegitimate.

Although Edy, at the time of *The Vikings* production, was not actively involved in the fight for women's emancipation, she was extremely critical of her brother's attitude to women – particularly as he had recently deserted an actress whom Edy knew called Jess Dorynne. Teddy refused to accept any artistic or personal criticism and was in perpetual conflict both with his sister and with her 'obstructionist' friend in the costume department who, according to Teddy:

> saw women as angels come direct from a heaven one cut above the heaven inhabited by God. She saw men as demons come from a hell far worse than that where Satan hung out. She was quite convinced. She would flare up for no reason, about the cut of a cloak of the colour of a cloth, and anathematize me and all the male members of the company, because we were not entirely agreeing with her; she took it as an insult to the whole sex that we should dare to suggest that she could possibly make a mistake.[41]

The conflict between brother and sister merely added to an already disastrous situation; *The Vikings* was a dismal failure and ran for only twenty-four performances. Shaw wrote to Ellen after seeing the production:

> If Master Teddy wants to use plays as stalking horses for his clever effects, let him write them himself. To take an author of Ibsen's importance, and deliberately alter his play to suit the limelight man, is the folly of a child, not the act of a responsible man. ... You cannot run a theatre on moonlight.[42]

Ellen, who had lost a colossal amount of money, persuaded Teddy to replace the Ibsen with a last-minute production of *Much Ado About Nothing* and her Beatrice, which had always been popular with audiences, succeeded in recouping some of the losses.

After two months, Ellen gave up the tenancy of the Imperial Theatre and set out with Edy and Chris on a long and arduous provincial tour to recover the rest of the money invested in the Terry-Craig season. When Edy returned to London, she began yet another career.

6. 'ONE PLAY IS WORTH A HUNDRED SPEECHES': THE PIONEER PLAYERS 1909–14

On 13 October 1905 Sir Henry Irving died in a Bradford theatre. That same evening, in Manchester, the militant suffrage movement was born: an important Liberal meeting in the Free Trade Hall at which Sir Edward Grey and Winston Churchill were to speak was disrupted by two women asking the question, 'What would the Liberal Government do with regard to the emancipation of women?' When it became clear that their question was to remain unanswered, they stood on their chairs and unfurled banners proclaiming 'Votes for Women'. After this unprecedented interruption, the two women, Annie Kenney and Christabel Pankhurst, were evicted from the hall, arrested and imprisoned for three days and seven days respectively.

Sir Henry Irving, who had never concerned himself with women's emancipation, would have been furious to discover that the solemn theatricality of his memorial service at Westminster Abbey was destroyed by chanting women with placards. Arriving at the Abbey, Edy and Chris, who had been touring the country with Ellen, were amazed to find policemen attempting to control a demonstration. When they asked what was happening they were told, 'It's because of the women who want the vote.' According to Chris, it was seeing the suffragettes at Irving's memorial service that persuaded them to join the struggle for the franchise.[1]

Chris became an active campaigner:

> I distributed handbills announcing meetings, chalked 'Votes for Women' on pavements, heckled cabinet ministers when they addressed their public, and knew what it was to be flung into the street by six or seven stewards, who tore my clothes and thumped me on the back with a mad-dog violence that astonished me.[2]

Although they supported the militant suffragettes, neither Chris nor Edy were imprisoned themselves. But they did give refuge – at their flat in Bedford Street — to women who were on the run from the police, or just out of prison.

Propaganda, rather than arson or bricks, became Edy's political weapon. Her experience as a woman, as an actress, musician, costume designer and stage-manager made her the ideal person to create a political theatre for the women's suffrage movement. At first she was hesitant to use her skills to direct plays, but with the encouragement of the AFL play department, Edy began a new career. Her first two productions, *How the Vote was Won* and *The Pageant of Great Women*, were the most successful of the AFL's early repertoire. Unfortunately, her skill as a director was not matched by her diplomacy. Cicely Hamilton, who was a member of the AFL committee, remembers arriving at a meeting to discover that Edy had been involved in 'something like a first-class row':

> The aggrieved committee had decided when I entered, that the matter could not be passed over. A letter must be written to their defiant colleague, pointing out the error of her ways — and, as I was the only literary member present, I was requested to take pen in hand and compose the epistle forthwith. The idea tickled me; I knew my Edy well enough to be fairly certain that, if she had made up her mind to any course of action, the committee's rebuke would have no effect on her — so it could not matter what I wrote on its behalf. ... Next day, in order to observe results, I looked in at Edy's flat and found her, with the letter spread before her, pondering an indignant reply. Had I been at yesterday's committee? she demanded, and did I know about this? I said I did know quite a lot about it, since it was I who had written the letter. 'Well,' said Edy cheerfully, 'as you've helped the committee with their insulting letter, it's only fair you should help me to answer it. You can just sit down and write to them before you go.' And write I did, to Edy's enjoyment and my own. ...
>
> I cannot remember, after all these years, how long this spirited correspondence continued; how many pairs of cut and thrust letters I compiled for the use of the disputants; but when Edy and I thought the joke had gone far enough, I made full confession to the AFL committee.[3]

The committee chose to be amused rather than annoyed by this conspiracy and soon the quarrel was forgotten. But Edy, who at the age

Vice Presidents of the A.F.L.

Lillah McCarthy

Decima Moore

Eva Moore

Lena Ashwell

ow the Vote was Won by Cicely Hamilton. First performed at the Prince's ⸱kating Rink, May 1909.

⸱ana of Dobson's by Cicely Hamilton. First performed at the Kingsway Theatre, ⸱bruary 1908.

The A.F.L. musicians contingent preparing for the demonstration on 17 June 1911. Over 40,000 women marched through London in anticipation of the

...sing of the Conciliation Bill.

Lena Ashwell and C. M. Hallard in the final act of *Diana of Dobson's* by Cicely Hamilton.

Decima Moore entertaining suffragettes boycotting the National Census on the eve of 2 April 1911.

Kitty Marion on her release from prison after being forcibly fed.

Vesta Tilley

Ailsa Craig

Top: Ellen Terry and Edy Craig
Centre: Edy Craig and Cicely Hamilton
Bottom: Edy Craig, Chris St John
and Tony (Clare Atwood) 1943.

of forty was far too individualistic to be dictated to by a committee, decided to form her own theatre company. Capitalising on her contacts in the theatre and the suffrage movement, she created, in 1911, a subscription society to finance a series of Sunday night productions. Contributors to the society were guaranteed a number of seats for each performance. Administratively, Edy's company, the Pioneer Players, was similar to the Independent Theatre or Stage Society, except that all the areas of the company's work were dominated by women. Opportunities to experiment in traditionally male areas of employment abounded; women audited the accounts, designed sets, directed, lit the stage, built the scenery and stage managed.

The publicised objectives of the company were to 'produce plays dealing with all kinds of movements of contemporary interest' and 'to assist societies which have been formed all over the country in support of such movements, by helping them to organise dramatic perform-ances, it having been asserted that "one play is worth a hundred speeches" where propaganda is concerned.'[4] This policy was implemented by a committee that had been hand-picked by Edy to deal with the administration of the company. She was aware of her own organisational limitations, as her legal adviser, Irene Cooper Willis, explains:

> Edy disliked all business formalities; I think that she suspected that there was a catch in them; she always looked immensely relieved when I explained that a letter only meant what it said. 'Oh, is that all?' she would say laughing and looking slightly ashamed. She liked me I think, because I did not fluster her and was able, generally, to set her mind at ease. 'Tell me what I've got in the bank. I can't make out that pass-book.' For years she went without a bank account, keeping her money loose in her purse.[5]

The first performance of the Pioneer Players took place in May 1911. According to the critic from the theatrical journal *Stageland*:

> There was a general atmosphere in the Kingsway Theatre that afternoon of enterprise and courage and cheery comradeship. It impressed me greatly. ... I looked at the packed house, at the rows and rows of women and gloried in them. Such bright, happy women, full of strong life and joyous optimism. Such clever, beautiful women. Pioneers indeed they are, and I wondered what

our grandmammas would have thought of them.

The house was mostly filled with women – one or two men here and there, who did not appear to suffer, as men are supposed to suffer, at the sight of women engaged in a sphere beyond the nursery or the kitchen – and one of these men was Mr George Bernard Shaw, who was mercifully left in peace but was, nevertheless the favoured target of many a kindly womanly glance. Yes, women ruled in this happy house, on stage and off.[6]

Edy had persuaded both Chris St John and Cicely Hamilton to write a short play for the Pioneers' inaugural performance. *The First Actress*[7] by Chris celebrated the struggle of women in the theatre against sex discrimination. The play is set in Restoration England at a time when men, not content with playing Hamlet, Romeo and Macbeth, insisted on their right to play Ophelia, Juliet and Lady Macbeth as well. The impersonation of the 'fair sex' was such an established art that when women began to fight for their right to act they were compared unfavourably with their mimics, who, it was asserted, portrayed the true nature of femininity. The play opens with Margaret Hughes, the first actress of the title, contemplating giving up her fight with the male theatrical establishment and returning to her Restoration kitchen-sink. Suddenly she has a vision in which all the actresses of the future, from the disreputable Nell Gwynne to the respectable Madame Vestris, appear before her and persuade her to struggle on. More of a spectacle than a drama, Chris wrote the play to exploit Edy's skills as a costume designer and to provide cameo roles for famous actresses such as Ellen Terry, May Whitty, Decima Moore and Lena Ashwell, who wanted to support the new company publicly. *The First Actress* 'gladdened the eye and wafted a breath of romance across the stage' and it did attempt, if superficially, to raise the issue of equality in the theatre.

Cicely Hamilton's play, *Jack and Jill and a Friend*,[8] was a light-hearted look at the problems facing a woman writer. Jill, who was played by Athene Seyler, earns her living writing romantic rubbish for a true love weekly. She spends her free time writing novels and visiting her two friends: Jack, another struggling writer and Roger, a painter with a private income. Jill and Jack are in love but too poor to marry. Jack tells Roger that he has entered a literary competition and, should he win, will use the prize money to marry Jill. Unbeknown to him, Jill has also entered the competition and confided a similar intention to their mutual friend. When Jill wins, Jack's ego is shattered and he refuses to marry on her prize money. In the ensuing argument Jill attacks Jack's prejudices:

JILL: Whatever other men do, I didn't imagine that you made it a condition of falling in love that the girl should have no brains at all. And if you think that I'll give up my brains – even for you, and to please you – you are very much mistaken. I've got just as much right as you have to work and win and struggle.

JACK: All right. Go ahead! If working and struggling satisfies you, I won't stand in your way. You're winning right enough – you've beaten me at my own game.

JILL: And you can't forgive it! *(Jack is silent)* That's what it amounts to – you can't forgive it. You wanted me to be your wife; but also, being your wife, you wanted to be able to look down on me – now that you know I'm as good a man as you are – you don't want me any more.[9]

Jack sees the light, overcomes his male chauvinism and accepts Jill as his equal, if not his superior. Typical of many light political comedies of the period, the play resolves the conflicts with illusory ease.

The Pioneers' matinée was widely reviewed; the critics were concerned with the political rather than the artistic content of the programme. As the *Sheffield Daily Telegraph* explained: 'it will be realised that the Society does not confine its pioneering to the purely artistic sphere. Propagandism is very dangerous when mixed with art. It is too early to say yet how valuable the Pioneers will be, but ... one has hopes!'[10]

This optimism was not shared by the critic in the *Evening Standard*:

Ladies, Ladies I must protest! It is not fair. It is not really fair. Not the dramatic critics, but the leader writers, or the critics of abstruse economic essays, or the writers of advice on hygiene and medicine it is that you should invite to these mysterious matinées at which you so cleverly organise your propaganda. ... Personally, if giving women the vote will prevent me having to spend a sunny spring afternoon in a theatre, I hope that women will get the vote very quickly.[11]

Despite their cynicism, the critics had to admit that the majority of the audience enjoyed the matinée. According to *The Stage*, 'each item ...

even if less significant as a drama than stage tract, was received with acclamation by the enthusiasts among the audience.'[12]

This audience consisted of subscribers and their friends; together they were numerous enough to fill a small London theatre, such as the Royalty, Ambassadors, Kingsway or Savoy for a single performance, while their subscriptions, for a twelve-month period, were sufficient to cover the expenses and hire of the theatre for approximately four matinée productions. The Pioneer Players never toured. By restricting each play to a single matinée Edy avoided the problems of multiple casting and limited performance space that she had encountered in the AFL. However, the style and content of the Pioneers' early plays were not dissimilar to the AFL's early repertoire, particularly those dealing with women and work.

The dilemma of the governess, who was expected to behave like a lady while being treated as a servant, was the central conflict of a one-act play by H. de Sélincourt, entitled *Beastie*.[13] A wealthy married couple, aware of their social status, interview a woman for the post of governess. They insult and degrade her while expecting her to flatter and revere them. Although highly sentimentalised, the play did draw attention to the appalling treatment of governesses which, according to Harriet Martineau, had been so bad in the Victorian era that a high percentage of them ended up in mental asylums.

In a double-bill with *Beastie* the Pioneer Players performed a play about women outworkers. *The Thumbscrew*,[14] by Edith Lyttleton, was about a family who lived and worked in a one-room tenement, carding hooks and eyes for ninepence a gross. The critics complained that the play was depressing, lacked action and merely consisted of the family discussing its falling standard of living, the possibility of emigration and the increasing use of women as blackleg labour. They also implied that the family's poverty was exaggerated. In fact, it was disturbingly accurate: 1910 had marked the beginning of a period of massive inflation and by 1912, when the play was performed, many women married to skilled workers had been forced out to work to supplement their family's declining income. Despite the increasing number of women employed in industry, few were unionised; many male trade unionists were reluctant to recruit women as they felt they were doing work that should be done by men and the women, with their new wage packet independence, resisted unionisation if it meant further male domination. The play's uncompromising portrayal of working-class life was intended to reinforce the suffragists' claim that the position of women would only change when they had the vote, and, by raising the issue of blackleg labour, hint at the potential power of women if organised within trades unions.

The majority of the male drama critics complained that the Pioneers' plays about women and work were depressing and boring, but when they were confronted by the plays which dealt explicitly with female sexuality they reacted with undisguised hysteria. The AFL gave preference to plays concerning the legal inequalities faced by women; in contrast the Pioneer Players tended to choose plays which dealt with marriage or prostitution.

In the Workhouse,[15] the company's first marriage drama, was slammed for being a 'brief for bastardy',[16] 'a disgusting drama' and 'a medical pamphlet not a stage play'.[17] One critic was so incensed by the play that he refused to name the dramatist because, 'doubtless by now she is ashamed of having written it'.[18] The woman in question, Margaret Wynne Nevinson, was far from ashamed. She was a Poor Law guardian for Hampstead who had written the play to expose the way British law discriminated against married women. Her attack was aimed at the archaic Coverture Act, which denied a wife any separate legal existence from her husband and placed her under his custody and control. By 1911, when the play was performed, the Infant Custody Act (1886) and Married Women's Property Acts (1870 and 1882) had given a wife some legal independence, but it was not until the 1920s that married women were granted equal custody rights over their children, equality in the divorce courts and the right to a State pension.

Margaret Wynne Nevinson's play is set in the maternity ward of a workhouse. It opens with Lily, a young cockney girl, telling the women who are lying-in that the father of her illegitimate child has agreed to make an honest woman of her. As half the women on the ward are 'honest' and half are 'bad', the news sparks off an argument about the advantages and disadvantages of marriage. The married women are jealous of their polite respectability, but one of the 'bad 'uns', Penelope, tells Lily, 'I was put off marriage at a very early age. I had a drunken beast of a father, as spent 'is time a-drinking by day and a-beating mother by night. One day 'e overdid it and killed 'er.' Just as the argument is beginning to get heated, it is interrupted by the arrival of Mrs Cleaver. She is being held a virtual prisoner in the workhouse because legally she is her husband's property and he is refusing to give her permission to leave. The 'bad' women use her situation to illustrate their argument, and add that married women not only have difficulty leaving the workhouse, they also have difficulty getting into it. Many pregnant women, who supposedly have husbands to support them, have died starving on the workhouse steps. The play ends with Lily talking to her baby:

> LILY: I think we won't get married, my pet! Better keep single, I says, after what we've heard tonight. What I've heard tonight is a lesson to me. I'll not get married, not I. Just look at Mrs Cleaver, an honest married woman. All 'er 'usband 'as done for 'er is to bring 'er and the kids to the 'ouse, and now they say she can't even go out to earn her living. Then look at Pennyloaf, free, rich and prosperous and the kids 'er own. The bad 'uns wins my pet! Vice triumphant, I say!

The Coverture Act knew no class boundaries. *Pains and Penalties*,[19] one of the most lavish Pioneer productions, told the story of Queen Caroline and the cruelty she suffered at the hands of her husband, George IV. The play, written by Laurence Housman, had been banned by the Lord Chamberlain's office, because, 'it made hostile reference upon the stage to the great-grand uncle of our present sovereign'. But the Pioneer Players were a subscription society and were unaffected by the censorship laws. The production stretched the company's limited resources; the cast numbered over fifty and half the scenes took place in the House of Lords or Westminster Abbey. According to an interview in the *Standard*, Edy welcomed the opportunity of directing such an ambitious play:

> 'The subject lends itself to vast spectacle,' said Miss Edith Craig as she turned from rehearsing the 'murmurs' of a crowd of supernumeraries in the Trial Scene. 'The House of Lords and the interior of Westminster Abbey sounds rather ambitious scenic effects for a small society like my Pioneers to tackle, but I am using no scenery at all in either of these acts. The House of Lords will show the stage simply hung with deep red curtains, while red-covered benches will accommodate "my Lords". The Abbey scene is only a retiring-room, shown while the actual Coronation ceremony is proceeding. This also will only have curtains as a background, and this is the scene that was never intended to be used

for a public performance and that the Lord Chamberlain has never seen. Exciting? Yes, of course it is. I'm completely inspired by the whole thing.'[20]

Queen Caroline, played to perfection by Lena Ashwell, was a sublime victim who made her audience weep while offering no solution. The heroines in *The Surprise of His Life*[21] and *Nellie Lambert*[22] are more like 'workhouse Lily' than the queen; they see that marriage oppresses women and look for an alternative. Emily in the first play gives her lover 'the surprise of his life' when she gets pregnant and refuses to marry. Alf, the father of her child, has jilted her for his other sweetheart, Sally. Emily's father forces Alf to do the right thing by his daughter, but Emily points out to her parents that she cannot see how marrying a liar and a blackguard will make an honest woman of her; a sentiment that is shared by Sally, who also rejects Alf. The play ends with Emily's father lighting his pipe and saying 'Well! and 'e'd 'ave married 'er. An' yet Emily said 'e wasn't good enuff for 'er.' To which her mother replies, 'An' you know 'e wasn't!'

As the curtain fell the audiences cheered and called for Jess Dorynne, the playwright. In the play she ignored the problems she had experienced when Edy's brother, the father of her illegitimate child, deserted her. Instead, in the character of Emily, she reflected the militancy of the suffragettes. *Votes for Women* considered that, 'The new spirit among women is rampant in Miss Jess Dorynne's latest play',[23] but the critic from the *Referee* treated the performance with his customary cynicism:

> Miserable man cut a sorry figure ... on Sunday evening, and as I, feeling like a sheep in wolf's clothing shrunk out of King's Hall, Covent Garden ... it did not need the look of scornful triumph in the eyes of all the aesthetic and athletic young suffragists present to convince me that in this home of hard knocks, a blow – a knockout blow – had that evening been struck at every man's very right to existence.[24]

The barmaid in *Nellie Lambert*, who gives her name to the title, shares the anger of Emily Jenkins. Her boss, Mr Potter, is standing for the Borough Council and needs the support of the local church, but the clergyman believes barmaids to be devils incarnate, so Nellie gets the sack. Starvation forces her to marry Potter's son, Tom, who wears a check suit, has a wife already, forges cheques and is the perfect stage villain. Eventually he is dragged off to prison and Nellie, instead of committing suicide like any self-respecting melodrama heroine, joins a suffragette procession determined to find freedom with her sisters. Unfortunately the *Yorkshire Post* felt: 'The play suffers from the faults inseparable from nearly all propaganda plays, lack of interest in the story owing to digressions into the realms of politics and polemics.'[25]

Unemployment and starvation gave Nellie two choices: marriage or prostitution. She opted for marriage with the blackguard Tom. Some of the Pioneer Players' other heroines preferred the brothel to the nuptial bed. The company's prostitution plays reflected the increasing concern in the women's movement over venereal disease and the white slave traffic.

Christabel Pankhurst, in her highly inflammatory book *The Great Scourge*, claimed that 70 per cent of men in Britain were infected with gonorrhoea, 20–25 per cent with syphilis and only 20 per cent were totally free of venereal infection. In the light of these statistics she advised women to avoid marriage and fight for 'Votes for Women and Chastity for Men'. Her figures were considered wildly high by the Royal Commission on Venereal Disease, but even it placed syphilis fourth on the list of killing diseases and attributed 50 per cent of sterility in women to gonorrhoea. Christabel's campaign for sexual purity escalated in 1912 when parliament mutilated a bill intended to eliminate the white slave traffic, and again in 1913 when the Piccadilly Flat scandal broke. The latter was triggered off by the arrest and imprisonment of a brothel madame, named Queenie Gerald. It was known that various politicians had visited her brothel and indulged in sadistic practices. Their names, however, were kept well clear of the case.

The Pioneer Players responded to this demand for sexual purity with two agitational plays about women forced into prostitution. Claire Morgan, the dutiful daughter in H. M. Harwood's *Honour Thy Father*,[26] supports her bankrupt, card-playing father, downtrodden mother and innocent sister out of her immoral earnings. Her family know nothing of her profession until she is exposed by a gambling acquaintance of her father's, Mr Stearn. Mrs Morgan is horrified and tells Claire to beg her father's forgiveness. Infuriated by her parents' bigotry, Claire points out that prostitution is the only profession open to a middle-class girl whose skills consist of playing a piano 'rather nicely' and painting a 'rather pretty watercolour'; and unless her father is prepared to support the family, she must return to her life of sin and degradation. The play, while being useful propaganda on the causes of prostitution, is full of clichés and offensively racist in the character of Stearn, the brutish, Jewish tradesman. Nevertheless, the recognition scene between Claire and Stearn is worth quoting for its unconscious humour.

STEARN: Are you afraid I'm going to bilk you? You needn't be.
CLAIRE: (Breaking away) Oh you don't understand.
STEARN: All right − I don't want to − I know what I do want, though. (Puts his arm round her)
CLAIRE: (Struggling) Don't; let me go!
STEARN: (Holding her easily) All in good time. (She strains back from him, looking at him with her head thrown back and eyes wide open) God! You're a spitfire too − you'd like to bite me, wouldn't you? Well you can if you like. (He puts his face close to hers and then suddenly kisses her violently on the mouth. She struggles to free herself and as he lets her go strikes him in the face and then stands panting facing him. Morgan, who has come in from outside, stands at the door looking at the last part of the struggle)
CLAIRE: You cad![27]

Today this encounter between a hardened prostitute and her ex-customer appears farcical, but in 1912 the audience were shocked by the play's 'very ugly theme'[28] and its 'brutal frankness'.[29] They could accept that prostitution was caused by poverty, but still felt the play must make it clear that a fallen woman was in need of redemption.

In The Street,[30] by Antonia Williams, Margaret Martin is saved from her fate worse than death by the strong, wealthy hero, John Castleton. She is typical of the part-time prostitutes of the period; the poorly paid shopgirls and domestic servants who were forced to accommodate their employers. Margaret's customer is the landlord; she has sacrificed her honour to save her mother and sister from eviction. Castleton, who is a student of life posing as the landlord's rent collector, suspects that Margaret pays the landlord in kind rather than cash and is determined to free her from his evil grasp. The play ends with Castleton proposing to Margaret and reassuring her that she lost her virginity in a good cause, a denouement that Votes for Women described as, 'a bad business well repaired by a man and woman of great qualities − who, lacking heart and courage, might have thrown away their happiness.'

> CASTLETON: You might come to me and say: For those I love, I have parted with honour and hope.
> MARGARET: Mr Castleton!
> CASTLETON: You might even come to me and say: For their sakes I must sell myself again to the most pitiless blackguard who ever lived —
> MARGARET: *(Brokenly)* Don't — I — I — I can't —
> CASTLETON: Wait! Do you know what my answer would be? Greater love has no man! You have done the impossible. You have reconciled death and life. You have made heaven of hell. You have proved that the body is nothing where the spirit is all. You have touched with your own hands the pitiful human, and made it divine.
> *(As her eyes scan his face, at first anxiously and then with confidence, and she realises there the truth and her happiness, she is drawn very slowly but irresistibly forward to his heart)*[31]

The Street was one of several plays produced by the Pioneer Players in which fallen women were saved through the love of man or God.[32] Fortunately, the company also presented a more realistic view of prostitution — Bernard Shaw's *Mrs Warren's Profession* and Richard Wright Kauffman's *The Daughters of Ishmael*.[33] The latter play was an adaptation of a fascinating novel about the extensive white slave traffic in New York. The story centres on the experiences of a young girl who is lured into a brothel, escapes, but cannot live down her past. Jane Comfort, who played one of the whores in Edy's production, remembers how she directed the last scene:

> The girl can't get a job anywhere, because wherever she goes some man recognises her; they know where she's been and she promptly gets the sack. She is literally starving, so she crawls back to the brothel. The girl goes up to the door and rings the bell. The madame opens the door and says, 'No, you're no use to me, you're all in dearie,' and slams the door in her face. The stage was all dark except for an old-fashioned streetlight centre stage. At the dress rehearsal Edy noticed Ben Webster, and said to him, 'Ben, you'll be at the performance won't you, you'll be in evening dress; walk across and stop under the lamp and light a cigarette would you?' That was

how she roped people in to do what she wanted in her plays. At the performance Ben was there beautifully dressed in tails, top hat and everything. He saunters on, stops under the lamp, strikes a match for his cigarette; the girl, who had been sitting on the steps of the brothel, comes up to him and says, 'You going home dearie?'; he blows out the match and passes on. My aunt told me my uncle left in the middle of the play thoroughly sickened, but as she said to me, 'Any man would get upset at the sight of a brothel.'[34]

Many of the Pioneer Players' agitational dramas implied, as did the AFL repertoire, that the vote was the solution to all women's ills. This view was not shared by Edy. Ben Webster's daughter, Margaret, remembers in the 1920s when 'income tax skyrocketed and there were strikes and unemployment and everyone who voted Labour was thought to be a Bolshevik, Edy and her friends in the flat below us went around defiantly in red scarves and Astrakhan caps, thereby clinching the matter'.[35] Edy scattered among the Pioneers' repertoire of plays on the oppression of women in the home, workplace and brothel, several showing the generalised exploitation of labour by capital. The desire to explore the problems involved in organising non-unionised workers, together with the Pioneers' failure to find a woman's play on the subject, led her to take the unprecedented step of producing a one-act play written and performed exclusively by men.

The Great Day,[36] by Cecil Fisher, observes the lives of six poverty-stricken clerks who are scrambling to earn a living in one of the enormous insurance offices in the City of London. For six months the clerks have worked fourteen hours a day with no overtime pay; they are dissatisfied, but the complex office hierarchy divides them and individualises their problems. Their only hope is that their labours will be rewarded on that 'great day' when the company announces the clerks' annual increase. When they discover they have been awarded a paltry ten pounds, the spark of revolution is lit and Armstrong, the socialist, lodges a complaint with the company secretary, Mr Pope. Shocked by their audacity, Mr Pope explains that Mr Montgomery, the managing director, limited the wage rises so that the books could show an increase in the profits and the shareholders receive a 45 per cent dividend. Confused and frightened, with all semblance of unity lost, the clerks have no alternative but to return to work. The last few lines of the play sum up their predicament:

> SIME: Montgomery's only done what any other businessman would do.
>
> ARMSTRONG: Yes that's what he is – a business man. *(He spits out the word 'Business' with unspeakable contempt)* That's what they call business ability.
>
> SIME: *(With finality)* It's take it or leave it – and that's all about it. You can't have anything fairer than that.
>
> ARMSTRONG: *(To himself)* Yes. They've got the whip hand. There's no doubt about that. Ha! *(For a moment he considers the indignity of his position, then realising the futility of defiance, he resumes his work. Silence)*
>
> SLOW CURTAIN[37]

Although the evils of 'business' and the weakness of non-unionised labour were boldly stated in *The Great Day*, the characterisation and dialogue were weak. Edy found similar themes but better drama in the much performed social-realist work of the Dutch dramatist, Herman Heijermans. *The Good Hope*,[38] the play she chose, showed how the Dutch fishing communities were ruthlessly exploited by the shipowners. The play had been translated by Chris St John and performed by Ellen Terry's touring company as part of her attempt to recoup the losses of the Imperial Theatre debacle. Edy used the same translation for her production and persuaded her mother to play Kniertje, the central character, once again. That the Pioneer Players succeeded in broadening the political perspective of their audience with this production is demonstrated by the review in *Votes for Women*:

> *The Good Hope* is a terrible poignant human story, and as such would be almost bound to reveal the conditions of things that the Suffragist is out to revolutionize. It is a sincere picture of the sufferings of humanity under a regime that is being attacked root and branch by the Suffrage movement.[39]

Rarely were the strands of socialist and feminist thought, which ran through Edy's productions, successfully intertwined within a single play. *Rutherford and Son*,[40] by Githa Sowerby, a play she directed for the Little Theatre in 1912, was a notable exception. Set in the industrial north the play tells the story of a family, a factory and the man who rules them. Obsessed with power, Rutherford tyrannises his children and factory hands in his struggle to build the 'works'. His three children, who hate and fear him, identify with the workers who share their oppression. Janet, his eldest child, has been forced to assume her dead mother's role as the mistress of the house. She has grown old and tired serving her father; her one taste of joy is her secret affair with the works foreman, Martin. John, the youngest son, rebels against his father and marries Mary, a poor office girl. His attempt to build a new life in London fails and, together with his wife and small child, he is forced to return to his father's house. Night and day he works on an invention, his one hope of independence, which he intends to sell to his father. Dick, the eldest son, is the only one who, at least partially, has escaped the law of his father; he has become a vicar and embraced the law of God. John, Dick and Martin are totally emasculated by Rutherford; he insults, degrades and manipulates them into betraying each other and the women they love. Martin gives him the secret of John's invention; Dick tells him about Martin and Janet; Martin agrees to renounce Janet to protect his job; and John deserts his wife and child. The women prove more resilient. When Rutherford attacks his daughter for degrading herself with a workman, she strikes back:

> JANET: *(Passionately)* Martin loves me honest. Don't you come near! Don't you touch that! ... You think I'm sorry you found out – you think you've done for me when you use shameful words on me and turn me out o' your house. You've let me out of gaol! Whatever happens to me now, I shan't go on living as I lived here. Whatever Martin's done, he's taken me from you. You've ruined my life, you with your getting on. I've loved in wretchedness, all the joy I ever had made wicked by fear o' you. ... *(Wildly)* Who are you? Who are you? A man – a man that's taken power to himself, power to gather people to him and use them as he wills – a man that'd take the blood of life itself and put it into the Works – into Rutherford's. And what ha' you got by it – what? You've got Dick, that you've bullied till he's a fool – John, that's waiting for the time when he can sell what you've done – and you got me – me to take your boots off at night – to well-nigh wish you dead when I had to touch you. ... Now! ... Now you know![41]

Unrepentant, Rutherford watches his three children leave home, never to return. Only Mary chooses to remain with the old man. She knows his one weakness, the weakness of any patriarch, is that he has no heir to inherit and manage Rutherfords. To protect her child she makes a deal with him: he must support her and the child for ten years and at the end of that time she will give him the boy to educate and train as the new master of the 'works'. Thus Githa Sowerby ends the play — in which all human relationships are determined by the production and profits of Rutherford and Son — with a bargain which exposes the economic roots of family life.

7. BREAKING THE MOULD:
THE PIONEER PLAYERS 1914–25

In the months immediately following the declaration of war in 1914, the majority of the suffrage societies suspended all political activity. Edy and her company were quick to realise that their audience would not be interested in plays about the oppression of women while the newspaper headlines were filled with the atrocities of war. They found themselves in the ridiculous position of having lost an audience while being one of the few theatre companies in the country not reduced to chaos by young men dashing to the front. Two alternatives confronted them: either they follow the lead of the Actresses' Franchise League and devote their skills to troops' entertainment or they build up a new audience with a new repertoire of plays. Having decided on the latter course, they changed their list of objectives to include all good 'plays of ideas'; plays 'which may be outside the province of the commercial theatre, as at present constituted, yet none the less sincere manifestations of the dramatic spirit.'

War, the obsession of the nation, was an obvious initial theme for the Pioneers to tackle. Not the war of heroic deeds and valiant young men, but the war of the women left behind. One of these plays was written by Gwen John, Augustus John's sister. Primarily a painter, she lived the life of a recluse. Her play, *Luck of War*,[1] is a tragic, half-funny story of a woman, Ann, who mistakenly believes that her husband has died in the trenches. Left with three children and only a widow's pension to support them, she decides to remarry. Amos, her second husband, is kind, gentle with the children and an improvement on the first husband, George. But one evening her happiness is destroyed by the unexpected return of the supposedly dead man. Amos conveniently disappears to his temperance meeting, leaving Ann to explain the black-edged memorial on the mantelshelf. He is horrified that she hasn't waited for him and she is furious that he never wrote:

ANN: Then yer might 'a written! I thought happen as you'd been blown up wi' a boom, and nowt left.

GEORGE: 'Ow was I to know yer was getting stuffed up wi' such fairy tales?

ANN: Yer might 'a guessed it if I never 'eard – week in week out. Everybody says if you're missing six months and no news as you're dead. After six months they stop your separation allowance and put you on a pension.

GEORGE: They do, do they? And when do they let you marry again?

ANN: I't' same time. They say it's pretty sure by that time. Then they pay you £39 down and 'a done – at least they do it that road 'ere.

GEORGE: I think it were time I coom back.

ANN: Aye, I've thought so mysen, George. For owt you knew I might 'a been starving.

GEORGE: I left you to t' country, Ann, as a soldier 'as to do. But if you'd been one o' them blatant brassy-haired hussies I shouldn't 'a done it. I knew tha could look after theysen.

ANN: 'Ow did you know t' country was doing right by me?

GEORGE: It expected me to do right by it. Tha mun leave summut to chance.

ANN And tha did leave me to chance![2]

Eventually Ann and George are reconciled and Amos leaves to live with his sister. The play, while never belittling the horrors of the trenches, successfully drew attention to the problems faced by working-class women. It is possible that Gwen John based her play on the experience of Sylvia Pankhurst's East London Federation – one of the few suffrage organisations which had not disintegrated into a morass of jingoism at the outbreak of war. The Federation had grown out of the WSPU East End campaign of 1912. With the help of the Labour member of parliament for Bow and Bromley, George Lansbury, who was a firm supporter of the women's cause, Sylvia Pankhurst had opened a suffrage shop in Bow Street and organised meetings throughout the borough. At first the suffragists encountered violent opposition, particularly in Bethnal Green, where they were pelted with fishes' heads and paper soaked in urine, but gradually they gained the support of the local women. Two years later, in January 1914, Christabel expelled

Sylvia and the Federation from the WSPU. She found her sister's involvement in the campaign to free the imprisoned Irish trade unionist, Jim Larkin, incompatible with the policy of the WSPU, which demanded that all members of the union should refrain from any other political activity until the vote was won. The Federation renamed itself the Women's Suffrage Federation in 1915, and helped East End women survive by setting up childcare facilities and collective kitchens. It also led the fight against the police who harassed women walking alone at night with charges of soliciting, and the bureaucracy which made it difficult for women to collect their allowances as soldiers' dependants.

Relieved of the specific propaganda work of the pre-war period, Edy and her company were loath to restrict their productions to social-realist issue plays such as *Luck of War*. They wanted to move away from the political tracts which relied on the theatrical traditions of the nineteenth century, such as melodrama, society and social drama. Instead, they wanted the freedom to explore the work of foreign dramatists and the enjoyment of experimenting with new theatrical forms.

The Theatre of the Soul,[3] by the Russian playwright Yevreinov, performed in 1915, was their first non-naturalistic production. The play begins with a Professor of Psychophysiology explaining how the researches of Wundt, Freud and Theophile Ribot show that the human soul is composed of several elements: the rational self, the emotional self and the eternal or psychic self. The curtain is raised to reveal the human anatomy: a heart, nerves and lungs. The eternal self, in travelling clothes, sleeps in the foreground while the emotional and rational selves are locked in conflict over the former's love of a cafe singer and the latter's devotion to their wife. They summon up their images of the two women. The emotional self sees the singer as a sensual beauty and the wife as a deformed hag, while the rational self sees the singer as a whore and the wife as a symbol of perfect motherhood. The ugly and beautiful images are forced to fight each other for the supremacy of the man's mind. When the singer wins, the emotional self strangles his rational counterpart. He begs the singer to be his queen but she laughingly rejects him and he shoots himself. As he dies, he is covered by the red streamers which gush from the heart. Meanwhile, the eternal self is led off to Everyone's Town.

Edy excelled in her production of this experimental piece; Chris, in her preface to the published play, describes the visual effects:

> In the production of the play Miss Edith Craig used a queer and fascinating machinery, of the simplest kind, by which little was seen of the three entities of the soul beyond their faces appearing at different levels out of intense darkness. The heart was represented by a glowing red space which appeared to pulsate owing to an effect of light. The concepts of the women were seen in the foreground and were brilliantly lighted. The whole effect was thrilling and beautiful and helped enormously to create a dramatic atmosphere.[4]

The critics described the play as 'a weird and clever piece'[5] that was 'extremely original and striking',[6] but a second performance of the play was banned by the theatre manager because of 'the repulsive incident of a woman's wig being taken off and her bald head displayed.'[7]

Encouraged by the critics, if not by the theatrical establishment, Edy continued her experimental work. But her choice of plays was still influenced by the war — which increasingly affected civilian life. Margaret Webster, who lived in the flat above Edy and Chris in Bedford Street, remembers their first bombing raid:

> On Saturday morning, as my mother and Frances were sitting in the kitchen placidly discussing what form of camel we could have for Sunday lunch, May suddenly caught sight of the planes. They flew in a V-shaped formation gleaming in the sun, beautiful and swift, heading straight for 31 Bedford Street. She called me and I yelled to Edy and Chris below and we all rushed to the nearest window and hung out of it, watching until they were vertically above us. 'How lovely,' we all said. A few seconds later came the crashes and puffs of smoke.[8]

Whereas at first glance Edy's plays appear to have been selected in quite an arbitrary fashion, a closer look reveals that several share a common obsession with death. In *Kanawa*,[9] a Japanese marionette play, a man appeals to an oracle to save him from his wife who has turned into a spirit and cursed him for his unfaithfulness. The oracle offers no help and as the spirit repeats the curse, the man dies. *The Merry Death*,[10] again by Yevreinov, shows how Harlequin welcomes his death with equanimity like Rabelais, whose last words were, 'Let down the curtain; the farce is over.'

The Dear Departing,[11] by Andreiev, the most fascinating of this group of plays, observes the reactions of a crowd of tourists watching a mountain rescue. A stranger is stranded on a rock ledge, high above an alpine cafe. Various attempts to rescue him with ropes and climbing gear have failed. Tourists, of all different nationalities, arrive at the cafe to eat and drink and wait for the stranger to fall to his death. At about midday a special correspondent arrives from the 'European News' to concoct a heartrending piece on the stranger's non-existent wife and child; his arrival is followed by that of a priest, who enlivens the spectacle by granting the stranger absolution for his sins. As evening draws in, the crowd becomes increasingly restless. Suddenly, the stranger yells to the local hotelier demanding his release from the rock and a day's wages. Realising that they have been duped and that the whole drama has been set up to entertain and fleece them, the tourists threaten the hotelier. To assuage their anger, he promises to tie his employee less tightly to the ledge the following day and thus ensure a spectacular death.

The cynicism expressed in this and other Pioneer Players' productions, while no doubt prevalent in a country accustomed to daily lists of dead in its newspapers, was counteracted within the company by the influence of Chris St John. As a devout Catholic, she was attracted to the dramas of the French religious mystic, Paul Claudel. His plays, in which the individual is nothing and only derives meaning from the natural order to which he or she belongs, were performed successfully in America and Germany as well as France. Edy did not share Chris's faith, but she was excited by the poetic symbolism of Claudel's dramas. The Pioneers' most ambitious production of the whole war was *The Tidings Brought to Mary,*[12] a play by Claudel set in medieval France during the war between Joan of Arc and the invading English. According to the *Observer*: 'surely this was drama; this long deliberate, deep-plunging, high-soaring, philosophic, yet passionate, dramatic showing of medieval France ... of all the beautiful things which Miss Craig has done this is the most beautiful that we have seen.'

Edy and Chris began work on this play at a time when their private life was undergoing a considerable change. In 1916, after they had lived together for seventeen years, a third woman joined them at the cottage at Small Hythe. The woman was a painter called Clare Atwood, known to her friends as Tony. Years later Chris St John wrote briefly about her absorption into the household:

the bond between Edy and me was strengthened, not weakened, by Tony's association with us. It is, however, clear that Edy, who was aware that I was not so immune from jealousy as she — her immunity was indeed absolute — had some qualms at first about the success of the *ménage à trois*, for Tony told me years later that when it was being arranged, Edy said: 'I must warn you that if Chris does not like your being here, and feels you are interfering with our friendship, out you go.'[13]

Tony was absorbed, not only into the Small Hythe menage, but also into the Pioneer Players. Whereas Chris was responsible for translating and adapting plays for the company, Tony was expected to paint flats and build scenery. In 1919 Edy, Chris and Tony began work on another of Claudel's dramas, *The Hostage*.[14] Tony was responsible for a crucifix:

> Edy decided that the first act should be dominated by an enormous Crucifix, which was to be in the round, not painted in cloth. The stage was a very large one, the flats were sixteen feet high; the Crucifix was to be as high as the flats and the figure twelve feet. My heart sank at the thought of this task — even though one knew that Edy would never ask the impossible. ... I expect Edy knew the fix I was in, though she said nothing until the week before the date of the production. Then she suddenly announced that she had had a cross made in a scene painter's workshop at Turnham Green, that it would be ready on Tuesday, and that I would find there all the materials necessary for constructing the figure. Down I went, across the snow which lay on the Green, into an out-house containing the wooden cross, a sack of paper and cardboard, some wood, a large pot of glue and a great ball of string. Two days to do the work! The lorry was fetching it on Thursday! A feeling of desperation and blank despair had settled on me, when, quite suddenly it came to me that Edy had no doubt the work could be done, and would be done. And it was.[15]

The Hostage, which is set in Napoleonic France, tells the story of Synge, a woman who represents the dying feudal order, and her struggle to preserve her identity in an alien world. In order to save the lives of her cousin and the pope, who are in hiding on her estate, Synge agrees to marry the Baron Turelure, a man of the new order and a servant of

Napoleon. In accordance with her marriage vows she obeys her husband in all things and bears him a child towards whom she can feel nothing but hatred. Her sacrifices for the men in her life (her cousin, the priests and her husband) have left her not a saint, but a broken woman. Tired of life, she deliberately intercepts a bullet intended for Turelure. Finally close to death, she rebels against the will of God and ignores the priest's entreaties that she forgive her enemies. He refuses to give her absolution for her sins and her soul is condemned to everlasting damnation.

Synge was played by Sybil Thorndike, who first met Edy at the Old Vic in 1914:

> It was at the Old Vic from 1914 that I began to know her. She would come and play for our special Shakespeare birthday shows with her mother, who gave us excerpts from the Shakespeare plays in which she had acted with Sir Henry Irving. I can see Edy now sitting in the wings, and always having to re-introduce us to Ellen Terry who never really remembered any of us. Edy said she never recalled my name but always said, 'You know − that big girl', which slightly hurt my pride, because, as I wasn't tall, I knew it must have referred to my rather square bounciness, as was proved afterwards by Edy saying to me so frequently 'keep still − don't flounce and bounce'.[16]

Sybil Thorndike described the part of Synge as one of her 'biggest spiritual experiences in the theatre':

> I remember arriving for the first rehearsal at Edy's flat in Bedford Street, full of beans, loving the words of the play even when I didn't know what on earth they meant, but dashing at them in the forthright way one dashed at Shakespeare, hoping that verve and nerve would carry one through, then being laid completely low by Edy, who could 'scathe' as few people know how. But with her scathing and mocking discouragements came a bigger thing − a sense of beauty hidden, waiting to be unfolded. One particular time I remember when she was showing me what she meant about a certain line. (Edy could always show you − she didn't just talk − just as Granville Barker used to be able to show an actor, not exactly how to do it, but with a significant suggestion.) She used her hand, in a pause, to convey the carrying on through, and her hand gave

me suddenly a jump, realising beauty. To me, it was like seeing the da Vinci hands for the first time, or a chord of Bach – putting me in a place where I was able to grasp and convey the meaning myself.[17]

Opportunities for Sybil, or any other actress, to play characters with the passion and dynamism of Claudel's heroines were rare; but the Pioneer Players' repertoire, particularly after the war, provided actresses with unusual and demanding roles. Strong female characters were to be found in the work of foreign dramatists such as Herman Heijermans (who was known in Holland as the mouthpiece of the oppressed), Chekhov and the Frenchman Saint-George de Bouhelier.

Although the company created excellent work for actresses, it increasingly neglected women playwrights. Over half of all the plays produced in the pre-war repertoire were written by women, but by 1921 the proportion had fallen to less than one-third. Fortunately, one woman writer the Pioneers did not overlook was the American novelist and dramatist, Susan Glaspell. A number of her one-act plays and her first three-act piece, *Bernice*, were performed prior to 1915 by the American theatre company, the Provincetown Players. Her most famous play, *Alison's House*, won the Pulitzer Prize in 1930.

Trifles,[18] the first Glaspell play produced by the Pioneers, is a murder mystery with a difference. Minnie Wright has been arrested for the murder of her husband, John; but the county attorney knows the jury will acquit her if he cannot establish an obvious motive for the killing. Together with Mr Hale, the chief witness, Mr Peters, the Sheriff, and their wives, he visits the Wrights' home. The men go upstairs to the bedroom where the strangled man was found, leaving the women alone in the kitchen. As they tidy the room Mrs Hale reminds Mrs Peters how young, pretty and full of life Minnie was as a girl. She feels guilty about never visiting her childhood companion but explains that John Wright was a hard and difficult man who disliked visitors. They notice an empty birdcage in the cupboard and then, while sorting Minnie's patchwork, they find a strangled bird in a box.

MRS HALE: I wonder how it would have seemed never to have any children round. *(pause)* No, Wright wouldn't like the bird – a thing that sang. She used to sing. He killed that too.

MRS PETERS: *(Moving uneasily)* We don't know who killed the bird.

MRS HALE: I knew John Wright.

MRS PETERS: It was an awful thing was done in this house that night, Mrs Hale. Killing a man while he slept, slipping a rope around his neck that choked the life out of him.

MRS HALE: His neck. Choked the life out of him.

(Her hand goes out and rests on the birdcage)

MRS PETERS: We don't know who killed him. We don't know.

MRS HALE: If there'd been years and years of nothing, then a bird to sing to you, it would be awful still, after the bird was still.

MRS PETERS: I know what stillness is. When we homesteaded in Dakota, and my first baby died – after he was two years old, and me with no other then. ...

MRS HALE: I might have known she needed help! I know how things can be for a woman. I tell you, it's queer, Mrs Peters. We live close together and we live far apart. We all go through the same things – it's all just a different kind of same thing.[19]

Hearing the men's footsteps on the stairs, Mrs Peters tries to hide the box with the dead bird in her handbag. It is too big. Mrs Hale snatches the box and puts it in her coat pocket. The men enter the kitchen; they have found no clue as to the motive for the murder and are resigned to the fact that Minnie will be acquitted. The women, united in their sympathy for the accused woman, say nothing and their silence conveys the message of the play.

In 1921, financial difficulties curtailed the work of the Pioneer Players. Theatre rents and production costs quadrupled during the war and a Sunday night theatre society relying on subscriptions was not economically viable. Increasingly, the actor-managers were being ousted from the West End theatres by investors who backed popular farces and musical comedies, hoping for long runs. After a performance in 1921, Edy made a speech in which she claimed that the Pioneer Players had produced fifty-two plays for £2,000 – an amount considerably less than that spent on one contemporary musical comedy.[20] Unfortunately, she added, with less than £100 in the bank, the company's activities would have to be suspended indefinitely.

As well as dealing with the company's financial difficulties in the early 1920s, Edy had to cope with her mother's imminent bankruptcy. In her heyday Ellen had been paid enormous salaries, but had developed a reckless generosity which resulted in scores of dependants – including such tenuous relations as the sisters of her second husband's first wife.

By 1921 her financial affairs were in chaos. Her dependants expected £700 from her each year, but her income was only £380 and she had an overdraft of £1,600. Her London home, 215 Kings Road, Chelsea, had to be sold, together with various possessions, and a small flat found for her in St Martin's Lane close to the theatres and her favourite restaurant, Le Gourmet in Lisle Street. Fortunately, Small Hythe was considered of little value by the accountants and was left unscathed.

Ellen managed to supplement her income in the seven years before her death with several film appearances, but her health precluded any theatre work. Her last stage role was as the nurse in Doris Keane's 1919 production of *Romeo and Juliet*, and although she was praised for her performance it was rumoured that Edy was hiding behind every flowerpot feeding her the lines. She did make one final stage appearance in the summer of 1921 at the Gaiety Theatre, Manchester, when it was being transformed into a cinema. This event was rather inappropriately celebrated with excerpts from Ellen Terry's most famous roles. A more formal recognition of her influence in the theatre came in 1925 when she was created a Dame of the British Empire. On being asked by reporters what she felt about the gold cross she replied: 'I am delighted. It is an honour to my profession, an honour to women and very pleasant for me.'[21]

In the same year as Ellen became a Dame, the Pioneer Players gave their very last performance. After a gap of four years, Edy found in Susan Glaspell's *The Verge*[22] a suitable play for the company's swansong. After receiving the following letter from Sybil Thorndike, she had decided to buy the English rights of the play with the Pioneers' precious £100.

> Edy darling – *The Verge*. Are you really going to do it – we're mad about it and I'm longing to play it – The Stage Society is sure to bag it if you don't – and it would be sickening – I could do it early in the year ... it would be such fun. Do let me know, angel. ... I've never wanted to play anything so much. *Do do it*.
>   Yrs Sybil
>   That woman says everything I want to say!![23]

Edy had no difficulty in getting advance publicity for her production; the critics were anxious to pass judgement on a woman playwright who was billed in America as a new Ibsen. The *Yorkshire Post* interviewed

Edy during the rehearsals and championed Susan Glaspell as a brilliant new playwright: 'in the opinion of many Americans Susan Glaspell is one of the most important of contemporary American dramatists and in the opinion of almost all she vies for first place with Eugene O'Neill.' But the reporter could not restrain from asking, 'will she, with no axe to grind for feminism and with all the detachment of the artist, show us in what direction the theatre tomorrow will be influenced by the new feminine mind?[24] With such dubious expectations it is hardly surprising that many of the critics were confused by the fusing of feminist politics and poetic symbolism in *The Verge*.

Claire, the central character, is a female Faustus whose desire for knowledge leads her to live on the verge of existence: the border between sanity and insanity. She challenges God by breaking down old life-forms in order to create new plant life. She is not a comfortable, nurturing, mother-earth figure, but a passionate explorer who longs to reach 'otherness' and escape the mundane routine of normal existence. The play opens in Claire's laboratory, the greenhouse. It is mid-winter and snow covers the ground. Owing to a fault in the central heating system, Claire has been forced to redirect the heat from the house to the greenhouse to protect her plants, leaving her second husband, Harry, her close friend, Tom and her lover, Dick, to freeze in the house. In a comical scene they beg permission to eat breakfast with the plants. As their names suggest Harry and Dick, despite their respective careers as an aviator and artist, are the personification of conformity; only Tom has any understanding of Claire's vision. Breakfast is interrupted by the arrival of Claire's daughter by her first marriage, Elizabeth. She is the product of an upper-class finishing school and is obsessed by 'what one does and does not do'.

> (*Claire, who has not fully ascended, looks at Elizabeth, hesitates, then starts back down the stairs of the cellar*)
> HARRY: (*Outraged*) Claire! (*Slowly she re-ascends – sits on the top step*) (*After a long pause in which he has waited for Claire to open a conversation with her daughter*) Well, and what have you been doing at school all this time?
> ELIZABETH: Oh – studying.
> CLAIRE: Studying what?
> ELIZABETH: Why – the things one studies, mother.
> CLAIRE: Oh! The things one studies. (*Looks down the cellar again*)

DICK: *(After another wait)* And what have you been doing besides
studying?

ELIZABETH: Oh – the things one does. Tennis and skating, and
dancing and –

CLAIRE: The things one does.

ELIZABETH: Yes. All the things. The – things one does. Though I
haven't been in school these last few months, you know. Miss
Lane took us to Europe.

TOM: And how did you like Europe?

ELIZABETH: *(Capably)* Oh, I thought it was awfully amusing. All
the girls were quite mad about Europe. Of course, I'm glad I'm
an American.

CLAIRE: Why?

ELIZABETH: *(Laughing)* Why – mother! Of course one is glad one
is an American. All the girls –

CLAIRE: *(Turning away)* O-h! *(A moan under her breath)*
....

CLAIRE: *(Pointing to Elizabeth – and the words come from mighty roots)*
To think that object ever moved my belly and sucked my breasts.
(Elizabeth hides her face as if struck)[25]

The second act is set in Claire's retreat, the irregular tower. The family,
fearing she is insane, have invited a psychiatrist to the house. Harry,
together with Claire's sister, Adelaide – in language which expresses
their total lack of imagination and vision – attempt to bully her into
meeting him. Eventually Claire is left alone with Tom; they are
irresistibly drawn together and merge into a spoken love duet.
Suddenly, banal romantic music blares from the record player
downstairs and Tom breaks away, frightened that their vision of love is
an illusion and that reality will be cosy conformity. Claire, terrified by
her apparent insanity, calls her lover, Dick, and begs him to take her to
a faraway place where she can disappear into 'nothingness'. He is
horrified by her hysteria and embarrassed that their secret affair has
been revealed to Harry.

Next morning, Harry threatens Dick with his revolver and chases
him round the garden. Eventually they become bored with this game of
sexual jealousy and return to the greenhouse to find Claire. She is totally
absorbed in her latest creation, 'the Breath of Life', which has bloomed
during the night. Dick and Harry are delighted that her 'flower' is a

success. Only Tom understands the importance of this new life-form which has crossed into 'otherness'. Once again he declares his love for Claire, but now it is she who sees love as a threat to creativity. As she slips into insanity she strangles him, sacrificing his beauty to her 'Breath of Life'. This final madness is not a female weakness, but a progression in Claire's exploration of life. Although a victim of claustrophobic family life, like Ibsen's Nora and Hedda, she has moved beyond its confines to discover her own creativity and vision. The play's overt challenge to conventional assumptions about the natural role of women as mothers and wives made it the perfect finale to the Pioneers' repertoire.

Reactions to the play were extreme. *The Lady* found the play:

> left a huge audience gasping with surprise and enthusiasm. A comment that was overheard as the crowd left the theatre was illuminating. 'I don't know what it was all about but it was the most thrilling thing I have ever seen.' And that is exactly how *The Verge* affected a large number of people.[26]

In contrast, the critic from the *Evening Standard* entitled his review *On the Verge*, and included the following notes for 'mad horticulturalists':

1. The strange new flower, unknown, called the Breath of Life, is a begonia with the leaves of an aspidistra, at least so it appeared to me. ...
2. The success of a conservatory depends on it having in it practically no plants. It should however have a trap door through which its proprietress can emerge at intervals carrying little boxes of lice and the like, which carry on a mysterious process of cultivation.
3. Translate into French: Where is the female gardener? She is getting the pepper for the boiled egg of the retired aviator.
4. You should always carry a revolver in your hand and *Hymns Ancient and Modern* in your head if you wish to succeed in horticulture.

Need I say that Miss Sybil Thorndike obviously enjoyed herself and her splendid memory served her well. Like all tragic players, she's entitled to a little breaking out once in a while. I've no doubt this provided her with exactly the same relaxation as the cheerful play at the Little Theatre, when mad old ladies put her eyes out with knitting needles.[27]

Among the many letters Edy received praising the production were a number from the 'old contemptibles' – the women who had worked with the Pioneer Players in the early suffrage days:

> My dear Miss Craig,
>   It is superfluous to say it, but you are the only producer who can bring out every ounce of meaning in a play so that it can plead its own case. It is a marvellous performance and you draw everything out of both play and players. What a treat and how inadequate it sounds to say so.
>   Yours sincerely,
>   Gwen John
>   P.S. You are the only producer who could produce a play like this, as one thinks of it.[28]

Despite the success of *The Verge* and the great respect Edy inspired as a director, there was no way that the Pioneer Players could be permanently revived. The company finally died in 1925. Little regard has been paid to its work in the theatre history books, though the Pioneers' main rival, the Stage Society, has received considerable attention. Created in 1899 the Stage Society survived until 1939. Initially it specialised in Shaw's plays, but after the First World War it produced the work of foreign dramatists such as Hauptmann, Gorky, Gogol, Wedekind, Pirandello, Cocteau and Odets. Although the Pioneers were overshadowed by the Stage Society, the importance of the company's work can be estimated by the comparisons made by Saint-George de Bouhelier between Edy, her brother, Lugné Poë, Meyerhold and Reinhardt. The French dramatist saw that they were all, in their own way, fighting against worn-out, nineteenth-century naturalism. They all opposed the star system, which encouraged actor-managers to build a production around a single performance, and were instrumental in developing an ensemble method of working. Craig developed a new theory of stage design which instead of providing pretty backdrops for actors focused on abstract setting which encompassed the spirit of a play. He influenced the Austrian actor and director, Max Reinhardt, who was renowned for his technique of using crowds to create rhythmic mass movements. A similarly abstract, stylised theatre was developed by the Russian actor and director, Meyerhold and the French director, Lugné Poë. By equating Edy with these men, Saint-George de Bouhelier was drawing attention to her own attempts to create a more symbolic theatre.

This view of Edy as a theatrical innovator is confirmed by one of her actors, Ernest Milton:

> Effects obtained by her Pioneer Players ... indulgently smiled at, at the time, as high brow and freakish, have since been used with impressive and remunerative results in the non-experimental theatre. I recall a recent production which from rise to fall of curtain reminded me of Edy Craig's productions years ago, and the young, eclectic producer, who so recently and so blithely copied her methods, was considered modern, daring, unconventional and in the same breath sane.[29]

Edy devoted ten years of her life to the Pioneer Players; she directed nearly all the productions and designed most of the sets and costumes. But her work was not confined to the company and in 1925, at the age of fifty-six, she put the Pioneers behind her and moved on. 'Edy had that mysterious quality none of us can put a name to,' replied Sybil Thorndike when asked about her work with the Pioneers, 'but when we meet it in a producer we call it genius. I adored working for her. Marvellous woman. Always breaking the mould and moving on to something fresh.'

8. THE SMALL HYTHE *MÉNAGE À TROIS* 1925–47

Edy, the Small Hythe matriarch, presided over the household at mealtimes from her large oak chair at the head of the refectory table. According to Vita Sackville West,[1] Chris and Tony indulged her, for the twenty years that they lived together, more through love than fear as they had equally strong personalities. They quarrelled, teased, joked, argued and interrupted each other incessantly until such time as Tony assumed her role as peacemaker and restored harmony. Chris believed that the *ménage à trois* was successful because all three women had another life apart from each other, in their work. A visitor to Priest's House was likely to find Tony, looking a bit like a tropical tea planter in her white jacket, trousers and much too large panama hat, painting in her studio; Chris sitting at her desk working on her latest article, play or translation; while Edy, in a red or blue Kentish smock of hand-loomed linen and open sandals, paced about making plans for her next production.

When they did venture out from the seclusion of Small Hythe to visit a theatre, cinema or art gallery, the journey was as important as the destination. Edy adored the sensation of speed; as a child this passion had been satisfied by four-wheeled phaetons, as an adult it was satiated by motorcars. Although Edy had her own car, named Belinda, she never drove herself; instead she sat next to the chauffeur (who doubled as the gardener) while Tony and Chris were squashed in the back. Unfortunately, a combination of rising petrol costs and engine fatigue relegated Belinda to the scrap-heap. When at home and not working, the three women spent many hours together turning the flat potato patch outside the cottage into a beautiful English garden with apple-trees, lilies, red-hot pokers, willows and a wall of Kentish rag-stone. This love of nature they extended to animals, particularly birds, dogs and cats. In the garden there was a little stone pietà which said: 'Dear

Dog' – 'We couldn't put Good Dog', they explained, 'because he wasn't, but he was so dear, we put that.'[2]

Although Edy, Tony and Chris were self-sufficient they were also extremely gregarious. Late in the 1920s they befriended two writers who lived in Kent, Radclyffe Hall and Vita Sackville West. Both were wealthy women and advocates of sexual freedom, but they had little connection with each other except through the Small Hythe ménage. Radclyffe Hall was the more militant of the two; she believed it was essential for lesbians to assert their sexual identity in the face of a hostile world. For many years she lived quite openly with her lover, Una Troubridge, in Rye, where they shocked the local inhabitants by their relationship, male attire and habit of smoking small, green cigars. But personal liberation alone was not sufficient for Radclyffe Hall; she wanted to win acceptance for homosexuals from heterosexual society. To this end she wrote a novel in 1928 entitled *The Well of Loneliness*, which tells the story of the loves and sorrows of Stephen Gordon, a lesbian. The advanced publicity was so scandalous that Jonathan Cape, the publishers, got cold feet and sent the plates to Paris for printing. When copies of the book eventually found their way back to England, they were seized under the Obscene Publications Act. The literary world was outraged by the suppression of the novel and a letter of protest was sent to *The Times* signed by, amongst others, Leonard and Virginia Woolf, G. B. Shaw and Vita Sackville West.

Vita supported Radclyffe Hall, but her own literary work was more discreet. Consequently, in *Triptych*, a short tribute to the Small Hythe ménage written after Edy's death, she is vague about the nature of their relationship. In Vita's personal life there was no such hesitancy. Virginia Woolf, with whom she had an affair in the late 1920s, wrote of her:

> These Sapphists love women: friendship is never untinged with amorosity. ... I like her and being with her and the splendour – she shines in the grocer's shop in Sevenoaks with a candle lit radiance, stalking on legs like beech trees, pink glowing, grape clustered, pearl hung. That is the secret of glamour I suppose.[3]

Virginia Woolf's affair with Vita was reflected in her novel *Orlando*. Published in 1928, it was both critically and financially successful, partly, as Vanessa Bell pointed out, because it inadvertently capitalised on the publicity surrounding *The Well of Loneliness*.

Lesbianism was not merely regarded as an *avant-garde* literary theme in the 1920s. In 1918 a Member of parliament, Noel Pemberton Billing, claimed to have uncovered a 'Black Book' prepared by the German Secret Service containing the names of 47,000 English male and female 'sexual perverts'. In his newspaper *The Vigilante* he printed an obnoxious article entitled *The Cult of the Clitoris* which implied that a well-known dancer, Maud Allen, who at that time was performing the dance of the seven veils in Wilde's *Salome*, together with the majority of her audience, was named in the 'Black Book'. Despite the spurious nature of Pemberton Billing's claims, the House of Commons reacted to the scandal by proposing that a new clause be added to the Criminal Law Amendment Act to prevent 'acts of gross indecency by females'. Although the majority of the Commons voted in favour of the clause the House of Lords voted solidly against it because, as Lord Desart pointed out, 'You are going to tell the whole world that there is such an offence, to bring it to the notice of women who have never heard of it, never thought of it, never dreamed of it. I think that is a very great mischief.'[4] Fortunately, the Lords prevailed and the clause never made the statute book, but this fear of a 'lesbian epidemic' encouraged hostility to all women who chose to live independently of men.

The Small Hythe *ménage à trois*, with its unconventional life-style and acquaintances, must have been an obvious target for the public morality crusaders. With hindsight it is possible to interpret the criticisms levelled at Edy over the deliberate isolation of her mother during her final illness and her own subsequent failure to secure work in the commercial theatre as part of this reaction. In the 1920s, as the Pioneer Players declined, Edy attempted to earn her living as a freelance director. The refusal of the West End managers to employ her was greeted with disbelief by her many friends who had great respect for her theatrical skills. The attitude of the London managements reflected not only their sexual prejudices but also their dedication to a safe, sterile theatre which had ignored the most exciting theatrical innovators of the epoch—directors like Granville Barker, William Poel and Edward Gordon Craig. Even Lilian Baylis of the Old Vic, when asked if she would employ Edy, replied, 'We don't want another woman here. And anyhow we don't want Edy. She would upset the staff.'[5] There was perhaps some truth in this, as Harcourt Williams pointed out:

Perhaps it was fastidiousness, a demand for perfection and complete control – qualities that could hardly be satisfied in the commercial theatre. No one could say that she was lazy – but she was a born director and so possibly the habit grew of moving pawns. Her work was strenuous enough but sometimes too vicarious. Even in her gardening it was her friends who jumped to do the heavy jobs, and woe betide them if they jumped in the wrong direction.[6]

Virtually exiled from the London theatres Edy spent several years working in Leeds, Letchworth, York and Hampstead, in the fast developing Little Theatre movement, so called because it comprised amateur groups who owned or leased theatres. When she did venture back into the West End it was, by strange coincidence, to produce the play that had made her father's theatrical reputation with the Pastoral Players, an amateur group which specialised in outdoor performances in beautiful settings. The daughter, like her father so many years before, found in *The Faithful Shepherdesse* an ideal vehicle for her theatrical vision. The play was written by Fletcher in 1608-9 as an English version of the Italian pastoral poetry or shepherd plays. Pepys saw it in 1663 and described it as 'a most simple thing, and yet much thronged after and often shown, but it is only for the scenes sake, which is very fine indeed and worth seeing.' Sir Thomas Beecham offered to select, arrange and conduct the music and Norman Wilkins offered to design the set, thus leaving Edy with the supreme task of unifying and harmonising words, pictures, movement and music. Despite the success of this and other provincial productions, the theatrical establishment still refused to accept her, so in 1928 Edy gave up the unequal struggle, accepted that she would never win the recognition she deserved and retreated to Small Hythe. She made this decision to leave the commercial theatre at a time when she was under great emotional strain, due to the rapid decline in her mother's health.

Old age was not kind to the great actress: she was blind, crippled with arthritis and always short of money. In the last years of her life Ellen became mentally confused, and this manifestation of senility, coupled with increasing irritability, made her a difficult employer. In five years she got through twenty-seven personal maids and acquired such a bad reputation that she was blacklisted by the major domestic employment agencies. Luckily, number twenty-eight, or Barney as she was known by the family, stayed, and proved to be an obstinate and loyal friend to Ellen. As well as dealing with all her physical needs,

Barney had to get rid of Ellen's unwelcome admirers because the doctor had told Edy, 'it is very important that she should lead a very quiet life. Indeed it is wiser for her not to see more than one or two persons at a time'.[7] The antagonism provoked by Ellen's enforced isolation was directed mostly at Edy.

During the summer of 1928 a constant watch was kept over Ellen and on the morning of 17 July Tony took the habitual walk through the orchard, which separated Priest's House from the farmhouse, to find out if she had had a quiet night. She found her in good spirits but within two hours Ellen had had a stroke which left her paralysed and blind. Edy, who was working in London, was rung immediately. By chance her brother, who had been living abroad for many years, was also in London. Edy contacted him, but by the time they arrived in the late afternoon their mother was unconscious. For the next four days Ellen lay paralysed, regaining consciousness for brief spells and then lapsing back into a coma. When Edy and her brother were not sitting by her bed they walked together in the orchard. Teddy's son Edward was also there:

> The weather was oppressive. The prowling photographers and the newspaper men disgusted us. But there were old friends too, who walked with us in the orchard talking in undertones. It was wonderful to see father and his sister suddenly brought together again – children once more – but sad they should be reunited by impending tragedy.[8]

Some years later Teddy wrote down his impression of his mother's death:

> she died in the morning sun, which shone warm and yellow on her. She sat up suddenly – opened her eyes – fell back and threw off fifty years as she fell. She became twenty-five to look at – and in truth, she became once more Nelly Terry back again at Harpenden with little Edy and little Teddy and the one she loved better than all the world.[9]

Edy overcame her grief at her mother's death by resolving to keep the memory of Ellen Terry the artist alive for future generations. This conflicted with Teddy's desire, reflected in his account of Ellen's death, to preserve his sentimentalised image of Nelly, the loving mother and wife. Edy's struggle to immortalise her mother's name began almost immediately after the funeral. Permission had been given for the service to be held in St Paul's, but it took over a year before Edy obtained a faculty for placing Ellen's ashes in the church. During the year-long negotiations with the ecclesiastical bureaucracy, Edy created another memorial to Ellen at Small Hythe. The farmhouse was converted into a museum and the Tudor barn into a theatre. The large sums of money needed for the conversion were begged, stolen or borrowed from old friends and admirers of Ellen, including an American millionaire. To boost the funds a benefit was held at the Palace Theatre, the cast of which consisted of all the actors and actresses who had ever appeared on stage with Ellen Terry. Allan Wade remembers it:

> an amusing occasion: people who had not seen each other for years; elderly gentlemen who had retired and grown beards presented a problem in recognition; how many mustered I don't know, but considerably more than the Palace could accommodate, and the dressing rooms of nearby theatres had to be pressed into service.[10]

Once the money had been raised and the Barn Theatre finished, Edy began work on the first of many Shakespeare productions commemorating the anniversary of Ellen's death. Although the plays were rehearsed in London, the actors had to travel the sixty-five miles to Small Hythe for the one Sunday night performance in July. The star-studded casts, which included John Gielgud, Lewis Casson and Sybil Thorndike — together with the distinguished audiences — were a tribute to both Ellen's memory and Edy's persuasiveness.

The success of these Shakespeare evenings encouraged Edy to expand the activities of the Barn Theatre; a subscription society, similar in structure to the Pioneer Players, was established in 1931 to facilitate the production of four or five rare and unknown plays each summer.

The museum and the Shakespeare productions revered Ellen the actress, but Edy was determined that Ellen the writer should also be recognised. To this end she arranged that Ellen's correspondence with George Bernard Shaw, which had begun while she was at the Lyceum Theatre with Irving and continued for most of her career, should be published, and that her lectures on Shakespeare's women be revived. Florence Locke, a young actress chosen to perform the lectures, was summoned to Small Hythe to be directed by Edy. She arrived to find the house in turmoil and the only available rehearsal space a garden shed filled with 'flower pots, odd straps and bits of metal suspended from nails'.

Edy was seated upon the only chair – an old somewhat crippled wicker one, I think. Eleanor was perched upon a lawnmower, preparing to take notes – I began ... 'It gives a very echo to the seat, where love is throned' – when a tremendous thump came on the shed wall just beside Edy's chair and a man's voice roared (he evidently felt that it would be hard to make her hear): 'Edy, where's the large axe?'

'I don't know,' she shouted back, 'Use the little one.'

'It's broken', came the answer.

'Well, go to Tenterden and get another. Don't bother me.' The tone suggested that he might go further than Tenterden and not be missed.

Then to me: 'You are not making enough of the word "seat" in those lines. Mother used to let it ring out, as though the tune had pierced to her very heart – try it again!'

'It gives a very echo', said I, when a shrill 'Yoo-hoo' came through a knot hole in the shed.

'Edy, dear, can we have ices?'

'What do you want ices for – you've just had lunch?'

'We are going to Tenterden. ...'

'For goodness' sake, go then, and don't bother me.'

'Can we have ices then?'

'Yes, but go away!' Then to me, quite sternly: 'I don't yet hear quite the right tone for Viola, but go on, you are all right – you'll get it.'[11]

Emerging from the garden shed after the rehearsal, Florence followed Edy back into the chaos of the house. Contrary to her expectations the household's hyperactivity had nothing whatsoever to do with the Ellen Terry museum or the Barn Theatre, but was caused by the preparations for a village pageant.

One of Edy's first and most successful productions for the suffrage cause had been *A Pageant of Great Women* and it was to the pageant, as a theatrical form, that she returned in the last years of her life. Commissions to organise pageants on English history, literature or theatre came from villages and towns all over the country. Before each production a few old suffrage and theatre friends were gathered together and assigned tasks. There were no objections for, as Vita pointed out 'No one could ever say no to Edy,'[12] but everyone, including Chris and Tony who had been Edy's serfs on countless productions, found working for the pageants exhausting. On more than one occasion Tony was caught muttering – 'This time Edy's bitten off more than we can chew.'[13]

The friends helped with design, costumes and organisation, but the casts were made up of local people. Edy expected these amateurs to show the same dedication and discipline as hardened professionals. While working on the Mount Grace Priory Pageant she encountered a stubborn Yorkshireman who refused to take her direction. After she had shouted at him in front of the whole company a friend whispered in her ear, 'I should be careful what I said to Sir Thomas. He is one of the biggest ironmasters in Yorkshire.' To which she replied loudly, 'I don't care if he is the biggest ironmonger in Europe: he has got to do what I tell him.'[14]

In 1938 at last Edy was officially recognised by the theatrical establishment. Sybil Thorndike presided over a dinner at the Savoy Hotel in her honour and Queen Mary sent a message of congratulations and best wishes. Edy was presented with a scroll containing the names of all present and a cheque in appreciation of her services to English theatre.

Her swansong was the Chilham Pageant. She was seventy-six, and suffering from arthritis, rheumatism and a heart condition, when she undertook this massive pageant based on the classics of English literature. Despite long hours of preparation the dress rehearsal was a fiasco. Chris St John remembers watching Edy

> pacing to and fro over the damp grass in the twilight after the rehearsal had dragged its slow length along, not even to the end, for it had not reached the final scenes. She looked calm and dignified in the friar's habit she always wore at dress-rehearsals and performances of pageants so that she would go on the scene to put right anything that had gone wrong. Her hands were clasped behind her back. ... Boney was one of Edy's nicknames. She lived up to it in this hour.[15]

Edy gathered her friends around her and issued detailed directions. Her years of experience did not fail her and next day the first performance combined the visual beauty and emotional intensity of her best work.

Recreating an image of a pageant producer without photographs, actors' reminiscences and press reviews is a daunting task. Luckily, a vivid portrait of Edy in this role can be found in Virginia Woolf's novel *Between the Acts*.[16] Vita introduced her lover to Edy and Chris as early as 1933. In September of that year Virginia wrote to Vita:

> I'm longing to see the Ellen Terry house. Will you thank, rather late in the day, Miss Craig or St John, for offering lunch? I'm going to join the society, I mean nothing more than subscribe to The Barn, as soon as I can summon resolution to write a letter or cheque.[17]

Miss La Trobe who 'gets up' a pageant in the novel wears a 'smock-frock', 'makes everyone do something', is nicknamed 'Bossy' and muses in the pub over 'the actress who had shared her bed'.

> Miss La Trobe was pacing to and fro between the leaning birch trees. One hand was deep stuck in her jacket pocket; the other held a foolscap sheet. She was reading what was written there. She had the look of a commander pacing his deck. The leaning graceful trees with black bracelets circling the silver bark were distant about a ship's length.
>
> Wet would it be, or fine? Out came the sun; and, shading her eyes in the attitude proper to an Admiral on his quarter-deck, she decided to risk the engagement out of doors. Doubts were over. All stage properties, she commanded, must be moved from the Barn to the bushes. It was done. And the actors, while she paced, taking all responsibility and plumping for fine, not wet, dressed among the brambles. Hence the laughter.[18]

It was not merely the external description which concurs with Edy. Through Miss La Trobe, Virginia Woolf strives towards an expression of the woman artist who uses the commonplace to create her illusion. She uses 'scouring-pads' and 'bed-spreads' to recreate the court of Queen Elizabeth, just as Edy, according to Ernest Milton, 'could transmute sacking, dyed and stencilled, into royal robes that completely nullified such paltry alternatives as cloth of gold and ermine.'[19] People as well an inanimate objects are the raw material of Miss La Trobe's art. She inspires Albert, the village idiot, Eliza Clark, who runs the village shop, and Mrs Swithin, to rediscover what is hidden within them:

Mrs Swithin, laying hold desperately of a fraction of her meaning, said: 'What a small part I've had to play! But you've made me feel I could have played ... Cleopatra!' She nodded between trembling bushes and ambled off. The villagers winked. 'Batty' was the word for old Flimsy, breaking through the bushes. 'I might have been – Cleopatra,' Miss La Trobe repeated. 'You've stirred in me my unacted part,' she meant.[20]

Pageants are communal art; Edy and Miss La Trobe dispensed with the trappings of professional theatre in order to create collective experiences. The village actors in *Between the Acts* relive English history while live history evolves around them. When they reach the act entitled 'Ourselves', actors and audience merge to experience 'ten mins. of present time. Swallows, cows, etc.' A shower of rain, nature's contribution to the pageant, breaks reality only to reinforce its spell; finally, the actors, portraying ourselves, reflect the image of the audience in broken slivers of glass. This haunting image of art as a fractured mirror, disturbing and challenging its audience, aptly describes the theatre of Edith Craig.

George Bernard Shaw, one of the mentors of Edy's youth, wrote after her death, 'Gordon Craig has made himself the most famous producer in Europe by dint of never producing anything, while Edith Craig remains the most obscure by dint of producing everything.' Edy's influence within the theatre was underestimated during her life time and has been ignored since her death. She was demanding, aggressive and impatient, but these qualities were essential to the survival of any woman director in the early years of the twentieth century. Although she alienated some actors by the brusqueness of her manner, she inspired many more by the brilliance of her theatrical vision.

In the latter years of her life she delighted in meeting the children of her theatre friends, and perhaps it is from their reminiscences that the clearest picture of Edy emerges. Margaret Webster, the daughter of Ben Webster and May Whitty, remembers a vivid picture of Edy through her childhood:

sitting huddled over a gas fire in an old turquoise-blue dressing gown, her white hair gleaming, her brilliant brown eyes looking right into mine. ... She would discuss anything and everything, often way above my head, but striking sparks from me all the same.[21]

while Violet Pym, who still lives a few miles from Small Hythe, remembers Edy's relationship with her daughter and sons:

> The two-year-old ... solemnly calls her 'Miss Edy' and to Edy she is equally solemnly 'Miss Jane'; she is the proud possessor of a ticket on which Edy has written 'Permanent Pass to the Barn Theatre. Admit Miss Jane, "On the Nod" '. She is the one who claims the right to sit with Edy in the bathchair which the older brothers wheel so proudly and carefully down the garden path.[22]

Edy died on 27 March 1947; her timing in death was as perfect as in life. In her last year she directed the Chilham Pageant, attended the St Paul's service commemorating the centenary of her mother's birth and arranged with the National Trust that the Ellen Terry museum be preserved for future generations. The Small Hythe *ménage à trois* were discussing the coming Barn Theatre season when Edy cried out, 'It's all black ... who's put out the light,'[23] and died. Teddy, when he heard of his sister's death, wrote:

> A quiet or quick or slow going is, all the same, a going – into the darkness which she rightly said was black; soot – night-time all such darkness is not black, but where there is nothing that gulf-like shade of black, can only be.[24]

On 28 March, her obituary appeared in *The Times*. It included the following sentence:

> Her devotion to her mother shone out more brightly than the remarkable theatrical talent which never, perhaps, received its due attention.

9. EPILOGUE

In 1972, twenty-five years after Edy's death, a new women's theatre company was created. It was the first of many to emerge during the 1970s and today more than a dozen are touring the country. In each company the same questions are being asked: What is feminist theatre? Should it be primarily propagandist and documentary in style or should it create a new verbal and visual language? How far are our assumptions about theatrical structure, relationship to the audience and even length of performance conditioned by our experience of male-dominated theatre? Is it essential to work in all-women groups or can one create feminist theatre in a company which includes men? How can a performer express her sexuality on stage when the audience is conditioned to see her as a sex object? What is feminist humour? In all these discussions there is an implicit assumption that it is the first time women theatre workers have grappled with these issues. Yet almost a century ago Elizabeth Robins wrote:

> we had further seen how freedom in the practice of our art, how the bare opportunity to practise it at all, depended, for the actress, on considerations humiliatingly different from those that confronted the actor. The stage career of an actress was inextricably involved in the fact that she was a woman and that those who were masters of the theatre were men. These conditions did not belong to art; they stultified art. We dreamed of escape, through hard work, and through deliberate abandonment of the idea of making money. ...

The lives of Elizabeth Robins and Edy Craig, the work of the Actresses' Franchise League and the Pioneer Players are just part of a lost tradition that must inform and influence the women's theatre of today. When I began reading about the Victorian and Edwardian actresses I was presented with a picture of them as handmaidens to the great actor-managers, male dramatists and directors of the day; I had no idea that they had created their own theatre. Now I cannot help thinking that whenever and wherever women have fought for equality a women's theatre is there, hidden behind a curtain, waiting to be re-discovered.

Part Four

PLAYS

The three propaganda plays in this collection give an impression of the variety of subjects and styles within the AFL repertoire. The first, *Jim's Leg*, by L. S. Phibbs, was published in *Votes for Women* on 29 January 1911, but it is typical of the monologues performed by actresses at suffrage meetings from the spring of 1909. L. S. Phibbs and the writer of the second play in the collection, Joan Dugdale, were not professional playwrights. The latter was a secretary of the AFL but had to give up the post when she joined a company that was touring the provinces. Her one play, *10 Clowning Street*, was performed in 1913 and published in *Votes for Women* with photographs of the production on 23 December 1913. This play is similar in style to *How the Vote Was Won* and builds its climax with the arrival of a series of militant suffragettes.

The last and most sophisticated play is by Evelyn Glover, who wrote a number of one-act plays and had a full-length play, *Time to Wake Up*, performed in 1919 at the New Theatre. Her play, *Miss Appleyard's Awakening*, was published by the AFL in 1913 and first performed by the League at the Rehearsal Theatre in 1911. It is typical of the duologues which dominated the AFL repertoire right up until the war. Evelyn Glover also wrote *A Chat with Mrs Chicky*, one of the most popular plays performed by the League.

JIM'S LEG

A Monologue

by L. S. Phibbs

The best thing as ever happened to me was when my Jim lost 'is leg. Afore then 'e was always a-grumbling, and saying as women wasn't of no account, and my eyes – as mother used to say was a lovely brown – was most times a nugly black, for Jim was that free with 'is fists when 'e'd 'ad a drop too much. And, bless you, to 'ear 'im 'old forth on pollyticks and votes for women! Why according to 'im, women 'ardly deserved to be let live, and men only let 'em because of cooking dinners, and mending clothes and the like.

'What 'ave *you* to do?' he'd say. 'You can jest sit at 'ome and amoose yerself, lookin' after the kiddies and cleanin' up. Why, that's only play, that is. Where's *your* responsibilities? And 'oo's *you* to 'ave a vote? Thinkin' yourselves on a level with us men!'

Well, one day as 'e was a-coming out of the Red Lion, and none too steady on 'is feet, 'e was run into by a motor bus. 'E would stop in the middle of the street to argue with it, and it 'adn't any time to listen, and it went over 'is leg, and 'e was took to the 'orspital and 'is leg was took off. And there was me, with six children at 'ome, and only my eldest, Ethel Emerly – 'oo was fourteen – in service.

Well, I got took on in Jim's place: 'ee was bottle washer at a brewery, and o' course they said they couldn't give me as much as 'e ad, 'cos I was only a woman.

'Not if I does as much work as 'e do?' say I and they only laughs and says, 'Women can't do men's work.'

'Can't they', says I. 'You'll see.' But give me more than twelve shillin' a week they would not, not if I washed them bottles ever so, and a lick and a wipe was never my way.

Well I got Gladys Matilder, as was thirteen, a little place, and Vilet Muriel 'ad to look after the little 'uns, and we got on some'ow till Jim 'e come out o' the 'ospital, just able to 'op about on a crutch. And when 'e come 'ome I says to 'im, 'Now you've got to take care of the 'ouse and do my work while I does yours. You says there aint nothing for the mother of a family to do, so let's 'ope you'll find it easy.'

'That's all right,' says 'e, careless, but when I come 'ome at night 'e 'ad a different tale to tell. The 'ouse looked as if all the monkeys out of the Zoo 'ad bin turned loose in it. E'd forgotten to cook any supper, the fire was out, all the children was a-crying, and 'e was sitting in the middle of the room with his 'ed in s'ands, the very picter of misery.

' 'Ope you've enjoyed yer little 'oliday,' says I, perky like, and pretending to see nothing.

' 'Olliday?' 'e groans, 'I'd rather do a month's 'ard. The kids ain't stopped 'ollering, ollering all day, and the biby's the wussest of um all.'

'No wonder, with a pin sticking into the precious lamb,' says I. 'Call that dressing 'im? Every blessed thing's on wrong. Well, you've cleaned up, I s'pose?'

'Clean,' says 'e, miserable like. 'I've bin cleanin' the 'ole time and it don't seem to get nothing but dirtier every minit.'

'You'll do better soon,' says I, 'when you've 'ad practice. You'll see 'ow nice it is to set at 'ome and do nothing, as you says. Now let's 'ave supper. Somethin' 'ot and tysty, I 'ope?'

'There aint none,' says 'e, 'I aint 'ad time to think of it.'

'Ain't 'ad time?' says I. 'You 'ad all day jus' as much time as I 'ave.' I couldn't 'elp feeling' pityin' in my 'art, 'e did look that wretched sittin' in a sloppy floor as 'e'd bin trying to wash, but I says, 'Things is changed. I'm going to clean myself and take the children out. You can set to work and put the biby to bed and 'ave things tidy when we comes 'ome.'

'Go out and leave me?' 'e cries.

'Why not?' says I. 'You ain't done nothing all day but amoose yourself. I'm going out after my 'ard day's work same as you used to. There's a Sufferagette meeting as I means to attend, to learn 'ow to stand up for my rights.'

'You don't want no learnin',' says 'e. 'You might stop and keep me company when I've bin shut up 'ere with the kids all day.'

'Company?' says I. ' 'Ow often 'ave you told me the children was all the company I needed? No, a little peaceful time to think is what you're needin',' says I, and off I goes. Pore Jim! After three days 'e'ed got things in such a muddle that I scarcely knew 'ow to put up with it, 'aving found a saucepan lid under the biby's pillow and my best stockins used as a kettle-'older. Then comes washin' day, and I 'eard

Jim a mutterin' about 'is clean collar, which indeed 'e wanted badly.

' 'Oo's goin' to do the washin'?' he asks as 'e sees me going out as usual.

'Why, you are, of course,' says I. ' 'Oo else?'

'Me?' says 'e. 'Me do the washin', with only one leg?'

'Bless the man,' says I. 'You don't wash with your legs you wash with your 'ands. And then there's the manglin', and next day the starchin' and ironin', and I 'ope you'll like the job. I'm sendin' Vilet Muriel round to 'elp 'er aunt a bit 'as 'ad the collect cruel, so you must look after the little 'uns extry speshul. Good bye.'

'Well, 'ave you finished the wash?' says I that evening.

'The wash 'as finished me,' says 'e a-gaspin', and indeed 'e looked like it. ' 'Ow you ever gets done', says 'e, 'I don't know. Them things 'ave bin bilin' and bilin', and don't get no cleaner.'

You should have seen the way 'e'ed washed 'em! All biled up, on my saucepans, and no rinsin' nor nothin' and as to 'is manglin' – well, mangled they was indeed. The pore children 'adnt a pinny 'ole among 'em, and my lace curtains jus' fell to pieces when you touched 'em like a spider's web. But the ruinin' of them clothes and things was the makin' of Jim. 'E began to see for the fust time in 'is life what a woman's work meant, and by the time 'e could go back to 'is bottle washin', 'e was a changed man. 'Andy 'e could never be, and sometimes I wished 'e'd lost an arm instead of a leg – 'e'd 'ave missed it less. But one night 'e 'opped along of me to a Sufferagette meeting and comin' out 'e says, says 'e, 'Esther,' says 'e, 'I'm a goin' to be a Sufferagette myself. As soon as I gets my noo leg I'll join. One 'as to be an 'ole man to be up to them women. And you did ought to 'ave a vote, Esther,' says 'e. 'Bottle washin' is play to byby mindin' and 'ome work what aint never over. And if I ever gives you a black eye again, well –'

'I'll give you one back with your own noo leg,' says I smilin' friendly-like. But lor', there ain't bin no need to. And we're all Sufferagettes and the children too, bless their 'arts down to the noo byby as is an 'owling 'er precious 'ed off, as tho' to say, 'I won't be 'appy till I gets it.'

10 CLOWNING STREET

by Joan Dugdale

CHARACTERS:

The Right Hon. Anthony Foljambe, MP	The prime minister
Arthur Featherstone	His private secretary
The Hon. Geoffrey de Haughten	His assistant secretary
Isabella	
Judith	His daughters
Enid	
Mr Marchmount	Editor of the *Daily Discriminator*, a leading London paper

SCENE: The prime minister's study in Clowning Street

TIME: About 11 a.m.

(The room is furnished in the usual fashion of men's studies; everything — the leather chairs, writing-table, placed like an altar in the centre of the room, waste-paper basket and massive clock on the mantelpiece — being on a large scale. The writing-table is covered with neatly arranged reference books and official-looking papers. At the back of the room is a door, leading to an ante-room, through which visitors are ushered; another door to the right leads into the passage.

Geoffrey de Haughten, *seated at the writing-table, engaged in sorting letters and placing them in separate heaps before him. He is a young man of weedy, aristocratic appearance, to whom every movement seems an effort; takes up the letters in the tips of his long fingers, eyes them vacantly, and is so slow and unbusinesslike, that if one did not know that his father had won fame as the*

'Tory Renegade Peer', one would wonder what qualifications had secured him his post. He ponders some moments over each letter, murmuring, 'Private, public. Public, private', to himself all the while.

    Enter Arthur Featherstone, *a fair-haired, nice-looking, carefully dressed young man, who would not strike one at first sight as possessing capabilities beyond the average. He carries a leather dispatch-box and places it on the table with an important air, then looks at the clock and exclaims joyfully)*

DE HAUGHTEN: *(Looking up)* Hullo!

FEATHERSTONE: *(Approaching the table)* Hullo! What are you sitting there for? Get out of that. You're not the Prime Minister. That's my place till he comes.

(De Haughten *slips out of the chair and sits down opposite,* Featherstone *taking his place)*

FEATHERSTONE: *(Grumbling, taking up one of the piles of letters)* Good Lord! How many more! I shan't be able to get my game of golf in this afternoon, with all these fools to answer!

DE HAUGHTEN: *(Priggishly)* Surely the good of the State comes before games!

FEATHERSTONE: Good of the State be — *(can't find the right word)*. You won't spout that sort of stuff when you've been here as long as I have, my boy! *(Flings the letters over to him)* Go on opening them and read out any that are important.

DE HAUGHTEN: *(Innocently)* The ones that want something, I suppose?

FEATHERSTONE: You won't find one that doesn't want something! That's the rotten part of a Democratic Government! Gives the people absurd ideas of their own importance, still they think they can dictate to us through the post, and that this is a sort of Ask-and-You-Shall-Receive Bureau. It's getting worse every day!

DE HAUGHTEN: *(Shocked)* Oh, I say! If people heard you say that, they'd think you a Tory!

FEATHERSTONE: No fear! I know which way my bread's buttered! Get on with those as quick as you can, while I draft this Bill out. *(Buries his head first in the dispatch-box, and then in the mass of papers he extracts. Both proceed in silence a few moments)*

DE HAUGHTEN: *(Looking up, suddenly)* Oh, I say, Featherstone. The PM sent down word he'd be rather late this morning, because he's having a bath for his rheumatism with some new salt from Germany!

FEATHERSTONE: Damn his rheumatism! That means I shall have to do everything. It's beastly unfair taking salt baths, instead of doing the job he's paid for!

DE HAUGHTEN: *(After a few moments' silence)* Featherstone! *(No answer) (Again, rather timidly)* Featherstone! *(No answer from Featherstone, who, from his expression, is in the throes of a difficulty himself)* I say, Featherstone!

FEATHERSTONE: *(Without looking up)* What?

DE HAUGHTEN: I say, is this important? It's from the United Brotherhood of Northern Mining Independents.

FEATHERSTONE: *(Impatiently)* Well, what do they want?

DE HAUGHTEN: *(Reading)* Increase of wages –

FEATHERSTONE: Of course!

DE HAUGHTEN: Shorter hours –

FEATHERSTONE: *(Snorts)*

DE HAUGHTEN: And a coal benefit once a fortnight –

FEATHERSTONE: What next?

DE HAUGHTEN: *(Still looking at the letter)* The owner, a 'something' Tory, has refused point blank to concede their demands –

FEATHERSTONE: Quite right. I admire his spirit!

DE HAUGHTEN: *(Reading)* 'Will the prime minister receive a deputation on the subject? Next week, or at your earliest convenience?'

FEATHERSTONE: I like their cheek! Why, he's got more deputations than he'll have breath for, next week! Chuck it away. No, wait a sec. Better look up how many votes they've got, between 'em.

DE HAUGHTEN: *(Consults a reference book on the table and reads out)* United Brotherhood of Northern Mining Independents – a large and powerful body, founded on a religious basis. Said to control 7,000 votes.

FEATHERSTONE: *(Groans)* We shall have to have them. *(Turns over the pages of a diary, biting his nails, with a worried brow)* Wonder if I can sandwich them in between the Druid Bards and the Street Noises people? ... Not a moment, unless he sees them in his bath! Like Robespierre, the chap who was murdered by a Suffragette! *(Laughs at his own wit)*

DE HAUGHTEN: *(In doubt)* Was it Robespierre? I thought he escaped to America and founded the United States?

FEATHERSTONE: Not he! She did for him, right enough. By the way, we haven't heard much of the Suffs lately! They'll be quite snuffed out when the PM's Bill comes in ... I wonder what Clementina will take on next?

(Telephone bell rings)

FEATHERSTONE: Go on, answer it.

DE HAUGHTEN: *(Answering)* Yes? Yes? What? What? What name? I can't hear ... Mr Marchmount. Oh, all right. *(Cuts off connection)* Mr Marchmount says he's coming round at once to see the PM about some Bill or other.

FEATHERSTONE: The Women's National Service Bill, I suppose? What on earth did you cut him off for? You ought to have let me speak to him.

DE HAUGHTEN: *(Huffed)* He didn't ask for you.

FEATHERSTONE: What else did he say?

DE HAUGHTEN: *(Stiffly)* He said he would rather not bring it out in the Press until he had talked to the PM about it. *(Goes on opening letters, and sticks at one of them) (After a pause)* I say, Featherstone, this is rather funny! Listen to this: *(reads)* 'Dear Father, I am writing to tell you that I think it will be very difficult for me to remain here much longer. When you spoke of my filling a place in the world and doing my duty to my country, I had no idea it would be so unpleasant. I feel my patriotism has degenerated since I have been here; I —'

FEATHERSTONE: *(Suddenly waking up and seizing the letter. Turning to the signature)* I say, hold hard! It's from Isabella! You've no business to open letters marked 'Private'.

DE HAUGHTEN: *(Aggrieved, taking up the envelope)* It's not marked 'Private'.

FEATHERSTONE: *(Scanning the rest of it)* I say, this is awful! There'll be a nice row if this comes out! The PM will be furious.

(Knock at the door. A voice outside, 'Telegram, sir'. De Haughten goes to the door and brings the telegram to Featherstone, who opens it)

FEATHERSTONE: *(Reading)* 'Have left Stevenson and Brown, and am on my way home — Enid.' *(To himself)* Great Scott! This will upset everything!

(De Haughten eyes him in amazement. Telephone bell rings)

DE HAUGHTEN: *(Answering)* Yes?

FEATHERSTONE: Who is it?

DE HAUGHTEN: *(Into the telephone)* Who is it? *(To Featherstone)* There seems to be someone very angry the other side!

*(*Featherstone *tries to take the receiver, but* de Haughten *clings to it as though hypnotised)*

DE HAUGHTEN: *(Into the 'phone)* I'm de Haughten, the prime minister's assistant secretary. What? Oh! ... *(Listens, his eyes widening with surprise and horror. Puts the receiver down with a gasp)* I say, someone using most awful language! Things I can't repeat! Something about the Bill and letting it go to the devil. Couldn't make out who it was. Perhaps she thought I was you! She said she was Judith!

FEATHERSTONE: *(In consternation)* Judith! Then it's all up!

(Enter Mr Foljambe, *the prime minister, a heavily built, square-faced man, with a large nose of the type that denotes a certain amount of acquired intelligence, small eyes, without any sympathy in them, and a large, weak mouth. Walks in with the air of a man thoroughly satisfied with himself)*

PM: Good morning, both of you. *(To* de Haughten*)* How are you getting on?

DE HAUGHTEN: *(Innocently, with the self-confidence of incompetency)* Oh quite well, thank you, Sir.

PM: *(To* Featherstone*)* Anything to see to, Featherstone?

FEATHERSTONE: *(Guiltily, hiding the letter and telegram hastily under some papers)* Oh – I – er – ah – I've been looking up the date for you to see some coal people. They –

PM: *(Going to mirror and adjusting his tie, while he eyes himself complacently)* Nothing important I suppose? Read it out. By the way, before you do anything else, I want a very polite letter written to Messrs. Saltz-Krantz, the German salt people. They've been very civil, sending me a large case of anti-rheumatic salt, and I want to thank them for it. Wonderful stuff! I feel I could tackle anything, even a Suffragette, after that bath this morning. I'll sign the letter myself.

FEATHERSTONE: Very well, Sir. *(Writes busily for a moment, while the PM looks through a newspaper. Telephone bell in corner rings)*

FEATHERSTONE: *(Answering it, addressing the PM)* Mr Marchmount is here, Sir.

PM: *(Roused out of his paper)* About that Woman's Bill business, I suppose. Ask him to come up. *(Resumes his reading, and* Featherstone *his laborious attempts at a German letter, with the aid of a dictionary)*

(Enter Mr Marchmount, *an individual of the Yankee type, with an alert mind and a keen eye for business. His attitude towards the PM is that of a*

social inferior, who is able to confer benefits the former cannot do without. His tone is therefore assured, and at times familiar)

PM: *(Rising to greet him with great cordiality)* Glad to see you Marchmount. Sit down. (Marchmount *sits to right of* PM. Featherstone *gives whispered instructions to* de Haughten *and they both go out)* You're looking well.

MARCHMOUNT: So are you.

PM: Yes. It's some salt from Germany I've been trying. You might make a good thing out of it, perhaps, if you puffed it in your papers a bit.

MARCHMOUNT: On the Standard Bread system, I suppose!

PM: *(Laughs, then suddenly assumes a serious manner)* You wanted to see me about the Woman's Bill, didn't you? My Bill?

MARCHMOUNT: Yes. Dove-Williams told me something about it last night, and I'd like to get it out before anyone else. He said it was a wonderful idea.

PM: It is. It knocks all the others we have brought out into a cocked hat.

MARCHMOUNT: Really? Who is responsible?

PM: Dove-Williams and I thought it out between us. You see, we have had about enough of these Suffrage women and their antics. We shan't hear them again when my Bill is law.

MARCHMOUNT: I suppose you haven't let them get wind of it, have you?

PM: No, not a word. The only women who know about it are my daughters, and they are all Anti-Suffrage to the backbone. *(Triumphantly)* I tell you, Marchmount, it's going to take those Suffrage women completely by surprise. It will be passed into law at once, and then they will pass into its clutches.

MARCHMOUNT: They may kick at it, then.

PM: They won't be able to. My Bill is specially framed to take the kicking out of them.

MARCHMOUNT: I'd like to know how you're going to perform that miracle!

PM: *(After a pause, which he means to be very significant)* To make a long matter short, Dove-Williams and I have discovered that the women at the bottom of this agitation are the unmarried ones; those at a 'loose end', as Binston so aptly remarks. Unfortunately, we can't provide them all with husbands; there aren't enough to go round. ...

What can you give them? ... Work. ... That's the answer. Something to do. Let them feel they are some use in the world, these unmarried females clamouring for Votes, in other words, for attention, and they'll soon stop shouting.

MARCHMOUNT: I doubt if Clementina and the Red Hot Ones will. It'll take a good deal to muzzle them, I should say.

PM: *(Rather irritated)* I tell you it's been worked out scientifically to meet every case. We put Sir James Crouchington, of the Eugenics Society, on to it, and he says there's no doubt these women are possessed. We can't allow the nation to deteriorate through this sort of thing. It's got to be stopped, and my Bill is going to stop it.

MARCHMOUNT: Rather a pity all this wasn't discovered before.

PM: No. One has to wait and see how these agitations take shape before coming to grips with them. Science and deep thinking have solved this problem in one word, and now the cure is going to be applied as soon as possible.

MARCHMOUNT: Sort of kill and cure together!

PM: Exactly. *(Opens a drawer and takes out a sheaf of papers fastened together)* Now I'll give you the details if you will listen. To put it in a nutshell: it obliges every unmarried, or otherwise unattached, unemployed woman in the country, over the age of twenty-one, to go out and enter some employment.

MARCHMOUNT: *(Astonished)* You don't mean to say it's to apply to women of all classes?

PM: Certainly. How should I get the support of the Labour men, otherwise? You know how important it is to keep in with them now. Mackenzie swallowed the Bill whole directly he heard peers' daughters would not be exempt.

MARCHMOUNT: I don't quite see how you are going to work it, though? Half the girls in the country know about nothing but love-making and curling their hair!

PM: Those are the marrying sort, so we shan't have to do with many of them. Lady Grantham thinks this Bill will not only kill Woman Suffrage, but solve the Domestic Servant Problem!

MARCHMOUNT: Oh! Lady Grantham's got her finger in the pie, too, has she?

PM: *(With dignity)* Lady Grantham has given it the feminine touch it needed by advising me on several small matters. She's delighted, because she says it will encourage early marriages.

MARCHMOUNT: *(Warningly)* Don't let that out, then. You'll put every Suffragette's back up if you do. She's President of the Anti's, isn't she?

PM: Yes; but she won't be President much longer.

MARCHMOUNT: What? D'you mean to say she's turned the other way about?

PM: Of course not. She's going to dissolve the League next week, to show there's nothing left to fight against. Her resignation and the Anti Suffrage dissolution will follow the introduction of my Bill.

MARCHMOUNT: I see. The final stamp on the Suffragettes' grave.

PM: I hope so. *(Turns over pages of the document in his hand)* Naturally, it will pass without opposition, being a Government measure. The Opposition are voting with us. We're all one at bottom on Woman Suffrage, you know; don't want it at any price.

MARCHMOUNT: Better not let *that* out, I suppose.

PM: Safest not, though it's an open secret. I want you to work all this very cleverly. On the lines of Standard Bread and the Boy Scouts. I want the women in the country to take to it, and there's one great thing to start upon — the fact that the three daughters of the Prime Minister have already gone out to work.

MARCHMOUNT: *(Astonished)* What?

PM: Yes, last week, under assumed names. They wanted to rush off directly, they were so keen.

MARCHMOUNT: *(Overcome)* Well, I don't know which is the most wonderful; your daughters or the advertisement!

PM: What remains now is to work up the young women of Great Britain to follow their example.

MARCHMOUNT: *(Musing)* I see. You want me to make it the fashion?

PM: *(With averted head, in a broken voice)* Naturally, parting with my three darlings has been most painful to me — wrenched me to the uttermost depths of my being; but I want to show the country that I am prepared to sacrifice even my nearest and dearest for its benefit.

MARCHMOUNT: *(Taking out a gold pencil and writing on the back of an envelope)* I'll put that in verbatim. Anything in the family sentiment line takes like hot cakes with the British public. What do you think of headlines like these: 'Prime Minister's Daughters Set Example of National Devotion and Duty', or 'Prime Minister Parts with his Daughters — Tearful yet Resolute'? I wish I had some photographs to illustrate it with.

PM: *(Suddenly inspired)* Why not go and interview them?

MARCHMOUNT: *(Delighted)* That's a good idea. I'll send off a special reporter to each of them at once. Where are they?

PM: Well, Isabella, the eldest, confessed she had always longed to be a parlourmaid, and has gone off in that capacity to one of the Labour Members; Judith developed a sudden passion for laundry work, and is in the Snowdrop Laundry at Stonehenge; while Enid is measuring ribbons behind the counter in Birmingham.

MARCHMOUNT: *(Still overcome)* Well, you ought to carry the country and the Bill on that! Poor Clementina, her day is done!

PM: Oh, she'll marry. I know several nice young members who admire her complexion.

MARCHMOUNT: She may. One always finds those sort of women tame down wonderfully in matrimonial harness.

PM: *(Regretfully)* I wish she were tame now. There are some points in my Bill I'd like to discuss with her.

MARCHMOUNT: *(Rises)* I must be off. You can trust me to make as big a thing out of it as possible.

PM: Send me the papers as soon as you can, won't you?

MARCHMOUNT: You shall have the first copy that's rolled off by special messenger.

(Voices raised in the ante-room. Featherstone expostulating. A girl's voice very loud and clear: 'I don't care if all the editors in London are with him. I'm going in!')

PM: What's that? It sounds like –

(Enter a girl dressed in an ill-fitting black serge coat and skirt and a cheap black sailor hat perched on her coppery hair. Her face is flushed and her brown eyes are shining with anger. In spite of the humbleness of her attire, her manner is full of authority, determination and fearlessness)

PM: *(Eyeing her in amazement)* Judith! What the –? Why? Where have you come from? (Featherstone, *who has followed her into the room, and* Marchmount *eye her with interest and curiosity)*

JUDITH: *(Coolly, sitting down and taking off her hat)* From the Snowdrop Laundry, Stonehenge. Didn't you get my message?

PM: *(Still groping)* Oh, I see, they've given you a holiday?

JUDITH: No. I've taken one, a permanent one.

PM: *(The truth dawning on him)* What do you mean?

JUDITH: I mean that I'm not going back.

PM: *(Furious)* What? Do you mean to say you have thrown it up already? After all your promises and fine language? Faugh! I'm disgusted with you. Just like a woman!

JUDITH: *(Unmoved)* I'm very sorry, but I can't help it. *(Shuddering)* Ugh! I couldn't stay there.

PM: *(Furiously)* But you must, you shall. You agreed to go, and you must stick to it. *(Turning to* Marchmount*)* Why, you are coming out in the *Daily Distractor* and a host of other papers to-morrow, photographs, interviews, and I don't know what beside.

JUDITH: Mr Marchmount can interview me here. I shall be delighted to give him my experiences.

(Marchmount bows and takes out his gold pencil)

JUDITH: *(Addressing* Marchmount*)* I suppose the PM has been telling you about his Bill, hasn't he?

MARCHMOUNT: *(Trying to smooth matters)* Yes, and I'm tremendously interested. It's going to smash up Woman Suffrage for good. You approve of that, surely, don't you?

PM: *(Swallowing his wrath)* Of course she does. Why, she's a Vice-President of the Anti-Suffragists, and has secured thousands of names for their petition. Haven't you Judy?

JUDITH: *(Doggedly)* I shan't get any more.

PM: *(Triumphantly)* You won't need to, the Anti's are dissolving next week, becuase there's no further need of them. The Suffragettes will be as extinct as the Dodo when my Bill comes in.

JUDITH: Not quite. Directly your Bill becomes law, I'm going to join the Militants, Red-Hot-Ones. They'll have one fresh recruit, at any rate!

PM: My dear Judith, if you say things like that we shall think you are going off your head. Something has upset you. I think you had better go to your room and compose yourself.

JUDITH: *(Without stirring)* I may have been mad a week ago, but I'm not now. It's your Bill that's mad. *(Continuing, gradually firing up as she speaks)* What do you know about women's work and its conditions? If you did, you had no business to send me off as you did in cold blood to that laundry. You know nothing about it, so you have no business to legislate for it. Why, I know a thousand times more than you now ... I'm thankful I've had my week's misery. It's opened my eyes; taught me what women have to go through when they're not sheltered behind padded front doors like ours. *(Takes off her jacket, and walks across the room to place it on a chair opposite)* I know laundries from top to toe now. I'll take Lady Grantham's place when there's any laundry legislation to be done in future. I'm an expert now!

PM: *(Attempting to belittle her)* Pooh! After a week!

JUDITH: A week is enough when you're doing the job yourself. A day is enough when one is miserable and surrounded with misery as I have been for the last week. I've been so harrowed I feel I shall never be the same again. Oh, it's awful, awful! *(Bursts into tears)*

PM: *(Scornfully)* Awful? What's awful? You're getting hysterical. Don't take any notice of her Marchmount.

JUDITH: *(Taking a tear-stained face out of her handkerchief)* To see those women having all the life taken out of them – quite young girls, some of them, and so pretty, or would be if they weren't as washed out as the clothes they handle – wrung out, mangled, and sweated, at three and four shillings a week! *(Turning to* Marchmount*)* Do you know they go there at seven, and don't come out till eight or nine in the evening sometimes, and then they are so tired, they hardly have the energy to crawl home. I call it beastly. I never knew such things existed. It makes me sick to think of!

PM: *(Sneering)* I can see, they found out who you were, and laid it on to get your sympathy.

JUDITH: *(Rising and facing him in a fury)* You don't believe me? You think I'm a liar? Go and see for yourself, then, you – you – *(Chokes)* But if you *did* go, you wouldn't see anything. You're blind to everything in the world except yourself and what will serve your narrow, puny, petty, miserable, selfish, old interests!

(The PM, *with his arm raised, advances threateningly towards her.* Judith *defies him.* Featherstone *appears at the door, looking scared)*

FEATHERSTONE: *(In a terrified tone)* Miss Isabella is here, Sir. She's ill. Something has happened! I think she has fainted!

(They all rush pell-mell into the ante-room. Babel of voices, the PM's *raised above the rest)*

PM: Bring her in here, can't you? Quick! Lift her up. Here. Put her on the sofa.

(Enter Featherstone *and* Marchmount, *carrying a tall, deathly pale girl in a servant's cotton frock, cap and apron. The long white streamers of her cap drag on the floor. They lay her on the sofa and stand round.* Featherstone *fans her face with a notebook,* Judith *kneels down by her side, the* PM *rings the bell frantically)*

ISABELLA: *(Sitting up, looking dazed)* What is it? Where am I? *(Looks blankly at her father)* Do you want me, Sir?

PM: There, I told you she was all right. A lot of fuss over nothing.

JUDITH: *(With her arm round her sister)* It's all right, Belle, you're at home. There's nothing to be frightened about.

ISABELLA: *(Putting her feet to the floor)* I remember now. Am I really home again? Oh dear! I had the most awful difficulty to get back. I had no money, so I've walked the whole way from Lavender Hill!

JUDITH: Oh, Isabel! No wonder you're half dead!

ISABELLA: It's a wonder I'm here at all, with that row of policemen at the bottom of the street! They insisted I was a suffragette, and two of them twisted my arms when I ran up the steps. If George hadn't opened the door at that moment, and recognised me, they would have arrested me, I believe!

PM: *(With a groan)* Great Scott! It will be all over London in half an hour! You fool, why can't you keep quiet, instead of coming up and disgracing me? I ought never to have let you out of the house. I might have known you'd go and make a mess of it. Women can't do a thing alone. You're all fools, damned fools, every one of you!

JUDITH: You forget Mr Marchmount is here, father, with half a dozen newspapers to put everything you say into. And if we *are* fools, I'm sure it isn't our fault. I didn't know I was a fool until I went into the Snowdrop Laundry. I can thank them for teaching me that much!

MARCHMOUNT: *(His journalistic senses alert)* Perhaps Miss Foljambe could give us some of the causes that led to her taking this step?

ISABELLA: Causes! I was starved and sweated and bullied and insulted! I suppose that's cause enough?

PM: As parlourmaid in a Member of Parliament's family! A staunch Labour Member too! You expected to do the grand lady, I suppose?

ISABELLA: I never expected anything of the sort. But I thought at least Labour Members would treat their servants properly, since they're supposed to stand for the down-trodden classes and all that sort of thing! I don't believe in Labour Members any longer. They're a lot of humbugs!

PM: *(Angrily)* Take care! I will not allow those faithful, humble colleagues of mine to be insulted.

ISABELLA: Humble! They may be humble in the House of Commons, but they're not humble in their homes! You should have heard Mr Robinson shouting for his supper when he came home!

MARCHMOUNT: Ah, this sounds interesting. Tell us all about it, Miss Foljambe.

ISABELLA: To begin with, I was general servant, not parlourmaid at all. They expected me to do all the work of the house, even cleaning the boots and minding the baby! I had to get up at five, and never got to bed till twelve, and when Mr Robinson was late in the House of Commons, Mrs Robinson had to sit up for hours because he insisted on having something hot when he came home! I told her she ought to go on strike and refuse to do it any longer!

PM: I hope she had more sense than to listen to such rubbish.

ISABELLA: She *did* listen. Last night she went to bed and left him a cold supper on the table.

JUDITH: Oh, Belle, what happened?

ISABELLA: Oh, an awful scene. He woke up everyone in the house, and this morning I was sent for.

JUDITH: Weren't you terrified?

ISABELLA: I was rather. I took the kitchen shovel to defend myself with, in case anything happened!

PM: Disgraceful! To think that a daughter of mine should do such a thing!

ISABELLA: Well, Papa, Mr Robinson was so furious, I thought I'd better be on the safe side. He said I'd been making revolution in his house, and he wouldn't stand it, and he'd like me to know that woman's proper position was to serve man. That's what she was made for, and he would jolly well see that I understood it.

JUDITH: What did you say?

ISABELLA: I told him he ought to stop talking about Social Reform when he kept a slave in the house, and I said Social Reform was rotten if it didn't reform things for women before anything else! I got so fired up I never noticed he was getting purple with rage. The next thing that happened was finding myself being hurled down the front door steps. I was so frightened, I ran away up the street as fast as I could. He hasn't paid me a penny for all the work I did. I'm quite looking forward to going down to claim my wages and letting him know who I am!

MARCHMOUNT: We'll send a special reporter down with you, Miss Foljambe.

ISABELLA: Well, Papa, now you can understand why I have come home, can't you? I feel I ought to devote the rest of my life to freeing slaves; the married slaves in the home!

JUDITH: You can't do anything worth while if you haven't got a vote. The Suffragettes told us that at a meeting outside the laundry one night.

ISABELLA: Then the sooner I get one the better!

(Enter Enid Foljambe. Door opens very quietly, admitting a good-looking, fair-haired girl, dressed in an exaggeration of the latest fashion)

ALL: *(In chorus)* Enid!

ISABELLA & JUDITH: Have you left, too?

(The PM sits down heavily in his chair, with the air of a beaten man)

PM: To be at the height of my ambition, and have the cup dashed from my lips by my daughters! Oh, it's cruel, cruel! *(Buries his face in his hands)*

ENID: What *is* the matter? *(Sighs with satisfaction as she sinks into a chair)* Oh, dear, I've been on my legs for a week, and I'm tired! Thank goodness I'm at home again, and can sit down in peace!

PM: *(Turning fiercely upon Enid)* What have you returned for? Come on, give us your reasons. Your sisters haven't spared me. It's your turn now. *(Sits down with his back to her)*

ENID: *(Ignoring him)* Just fancy, every time I sat down in shop I was fined! *(Turning to her father)* I was fined so often that I thought I'd better come away before my bill got too large for you to pay. Oh, you can scarcely breathe in a shop without being fined! Really, I've had such an unpleasant time I feel I shall never get over it!

PM: You! It's I that will never get over this. You've ruined me, you three. I may as well retire from office at once. I shall resign tomorrow.

ISABELLA: Don't talk nonsense, Papa. You'll do nothing of the sort. You've got to give Votes to Women first!

PM: *(Desperately)* Never.

JUDITH: Very well, then. I shall go straight to the RHO's and put my name down for anything militant they want done. It will be rather awkward for you, won't it, to have snapshots of your daughters being arrested in all the papers! *(Turning to her sisters)* Of course, you are coming with me?

ISABELLA: It's very sad, but it seems, the only way to get anything done is to be violent; at least, if it's anything to do with *this* Government. Yes, I'll come.

EDITH: So will I. I feel so roused up at the way they've neglected shop-girls that I could blow up the House of Commons without a qualm!

(The PM *hides his face and groans)*

JUDITH: *(Bending over him and patting his shoulder)* Don't be silly, Papa. Remember you are in public, and face the situation. You shouldn't have sent us where our eyes would be opened, if you didn't want this to happen. Be thankful that we have all returned home safe and sound! Really, it's high time women who know came and stopped men making fools of themselves. Don't you think so, Mr Marchmount?

MARCHMOUNT: Well, if the rest of the women have their eyes opened as quickly as you, Miss Foljambe, there won't be much of a look-out left for us!

JUDITH: I daresay it will be all you deserve! Now, then, Papa — 'Yes' or 'No'? A Woman Suffrage Bill this session, introduced as a Government measure, and to pass through all its stages. *(Turns to* Featherstone*)* That's right, isn't it, Featherstone? *(Featherstone nods)* Or — your three daughters in Holloway Gaol? Choose!

(The PM *stands up and looks at his three daughters, who have also risen and stand close together, facing him unflinchingly. He tries to address them, but is overcome by their resolute attitude. Appeals to* Marchmount*)*

PM: What shall I do Marchmount?

MARCHMOUNT: I hardly like to say, Sir. I shall get such first-rate copy for my papers if you refuse! Of course, I might suppress it, but these things have a way of coming out, somehow. Better give in. After all, it won't make much difference, when all's said and done, this Votes for Women business, and just think, you will go down to posterity as the bravest Prime Minister that ever existed — the one who wasn't afraid of women! There's something to be said for that, too, you know!

PM: *(Seeing his foundations crumbling)* You've forced me to it. I give in; but remember, you have brought your father's grey hairs in sorrow to the grave and shamed me to the world.

ISABELLA: *(Laughing)* Nothing of the sort. Mr Marchmount won't tell, and the policemen outside had better have a bribe out of the Treasury! Let's have it drawn up formally. Write it down, Featherstone. *(Featherstone seats himself at the desk)* You and Mr Marchmount are the witnesses. Give me the Women's National

Service Bill, Father. *(PM hands it to her obediently and she tears it in several pieces and drops it in the waste-paper basket)*

JUDITH: There! No legislation without women in future! Hurrah! Votes for Women! Say it, Papa! Practise it now, in the right tone, so that it shall come easy to you in the House on Monday. Votes for Women! *(Urging him)* Go on.

PM: *(Sulkily)* Votes for Women.

JUDITH: This session.

PM: This session.

CURTAIN

MISS APPLEYARD'S AWAKENING

by Evelyn Glover

CHARACTERS:

Miss Appleyard
Mrs Crabtree (her visitor)
Morton (her parlourmaid)

DESCRIPTION OF SCENE:

Small chamber Set
Window, C. Door, U. R. E.
Writing-table and chair, C.
Table and chair, D. R.
Sofa, L: Bell in wall down L below sofa.

SCENE: A drawing-room

TIME: During an Election

(Morton *is discovered arranging blind, tidying up room, etc. Enter* Miss
Appleyard *in outdoor things*)

APPLEYARD: Oh Morton, I must have some tea now — I really can't
wait till half-past four. I don't think there's anything in the world so
tiring as canvassing! *(Sits at table, R)*

MORTON: I hope you got a proper lunch 'm?

APPLEYARD: *(Drawing off gloves)* No, it wasn't at all proper — two stale
sandwiches at Owen's — but I couldn't get home. The dinner hour
was the best time for catching some of the men. Fancy, Morton. I've
got three fresh promises for Mr Sharp!

MORTON: How splendid, 'm! Were you up by the factory?

APPLEYARD: Yes, in Dale Street and Quebec Street. I begin to think half the idiots in Mudford must have settled there judging from the intelligence of some of the voters I've been arguing with this morning!

MORTON: Won't you go and lie down a bit, 'm? You look tired out.

APPLEYARD: Oh no, I shall be all right when I've had some tea. I should have been home earlier only I simply couldn't get through the crowd in Nevil Square where one of those dreadful suffragists was speaking. I really could shake the whole lot of them!

MORTON: *(Evidently interested)* I suppose she was talking about votes for women, 'm?

APPLEYARD: Oh yes I suppose so — I didn't really listen. I heard something about some bill they wanted to get passed. The less women have to do with bills the better, to my mind — Parliamentary *and* other kinds.

MORTON: *(As if wishing to hear more)* I daresay she'd plenty to say, 'm?

APPLEYARD: *(Suppressing a yawn)* I daresay she had, Morton. I wish I'd been near enough to tell her to go back and look after her home and leave parliament to manage its own affairs! *(Pauses a moment, then speaks as if on a sudden recollection)* Oh by the way, Morton, if you and Cook would like to go to Mr Sharp's meeting at the Town Hall tonight I think the house might be shut up for a couple of hours. I can take my key in case I get back first.

MORTON: Thank you, 'm, we should very much.

APPLEYARD: Well tell Cook then. You could manage to get off by half-past seven, couldn't you, as I'm having dinner earlier? She'll have no washing up to speak of.

MORTON: Oh yes, 'm.

APPLEYARD: Don't leave it later because the place is going to be crowded. *(Looks at her hands)* I'm too dirty to eat — those factory chimneys were simply raining blacks! I'll be ready in two minutes! *(Crosses L, and exits)*

(Exit Morton and returns with tea cloth, putting it on table, R and humming March of the Women. While she is doing this a bell rings outside. She ignores it, and it rings again)

MORTON: All right — All right! Somebody else has got things to do as well as you!

(Exit to reappear almost immediately and usher in a visitor)

MORTON: *(About to leave room)* What name shall I say, please?

CRABTREE: *(Crosses to R on entrance)* Miss Appleyard wouldn't know my name. Just say that a lady from the Anti-Suffrage Society would be much obliged if she could speak to her.

MORTON: Thank you, 'm. *(Crossing to door L)*

CRABTREE: *(Sitting down R)* I won't keep her more than a moment or two. Oh – er – *(Morton stops)* I shall be asking her to allow you and your fellow-servants to sign a petition I've got with me. How many of you are there?

MORTON: *(Evidently surprised)* Two, 'm.

CRABTREE: *(Disappointedly)* Not more? Still, two names are something.

MORTON: *(Hesitatingly)* What is the petition about 'm?

CRABTREE: *(As though she thought the question unnecessary)* About? – Oh it would take rather long to explain. But *you* don't want women to sit in Parliament and leave their homes to go to rack and ruin, do you?

MORTON: Oh no, 'm.

CRABTREE: And you don't want every woman in England to have a vote so that they can swamp the men and govern the country themselves?

MORTON: That's never what the Suffragists want, is it 'm?

CRABTREE: Oh they'll all *tell* you they don't, but of course they do really. When a woman leaves her own duties to take up a man's she soon loses her sense of truth and everything else.

MORTON: Really, 'm?

CRABTREE: Why this very petition you were asking about is against a set of women who pretend that they don't think their sex ought to meddle with politics and yet they're working themselves in this Election as hard as they can!

MORTON: Oh that doesn't seem right 'm does it?

CRABTREE: Right? It's very wicked and deceitful of course, but that's just an example of the sort of thing that happens when a woman interferes with – *(She stops short as* Miss Appleyard *enters the room and looks round enquiringly)*

MORTON: A lady to see you, 'm. *(Exit)*

CRABTREE: *(Rising)* Good afternoon, Miss Appleyard. I hope I'm not disturbing you? I'm afraid you're just going out?

APPLEYARD: No, I've just come in. Please sit down.

CRABTREE: *(Seating herself again)* I won't detain you more than a few

minutes. My name is Crabtree, Mrs Crabtree. I've come as a delegate
from the Mudford ASS – I understand that you belong to it?

APPLEYARD: *(Puzzled)* The ASS? *(Sitting on sofa)*

CRABTREE: The Anti-Suffrage Society.

APPLEYARD: *(Laughing)* Oh, I beg your pardon. I didn't recognise
those rather unfortunate initials for the moment. Yes, I've been a
member for nearly a year, I think. A friend of mine gave me no peace
till I said she might send in my name.

CRABTREE: We have one or two noble proselytisers! They stop at
nothing!

APPLEYARD: Oh, I'd no real objection – I've always steadily declined
to listen to anything on the subject of Women's Suffrage.

CRABTREE: I wish there were more like you! I've really come to ask
if you would be good enough to sign a petition that some of us are
getting up?

APPLEYARD: Oh certainly. I never refuse my name to any Anti-
Suffrage Petition. I should think I've signed four this last month.

CRABTREE: *(Looking at her admiringly)* How splendid of you! And yet
Suffragists say we don't work for our cause!

APPLEYARD: Oh but Suffragists will say anything! I suppose you've
read the accounts of the disgraceful disturbances in Liverpool last
night?

CRABTREE: *(Indifferently)* No. Were there any? I can't say that I
trouble my head much about that sort of thing.

APPLEYARD: *(Astonished)* But don't you think it's abominable?

CRABTREE: There are worse things in connection with the Suffrage
movement than disturbances.

APPLEYARD: Worse?

CRABTREE: *(Impressively)* Very much worse.

APPLEYARD: But what *could* be worse?

CRABTREE: Oh my dear Miss Appleyard, if a woman's in a
policeman's arms – of course it's very deplorable but at least you
know where she *is*!

APPLEYARD: Certainly – but –

CRABTREE: *(Interrupting)* And if she's shouting in the market-place
like the female I saw addressing crowds in Nevil Square just now – at
all events she's fighting you in the open!

APPLEYARD: *(Puzzled)* Of course.

CRABTREE: Even if she's never done anything for her side but join a

Suffrage Society — well, you do know she's against you.

APPLEYARD: Certainly, but I'm afraid I don't quite see what you mean to imply.

CRABTREE: *(Drawing her chair closer to* Miss Appleyard *and lowering her voice)* What should you say to *traitors within the camp*?

APPLEYARD: *(In bewilderment)* Traitors within the camp?

CRABTREE: Traitors within the camp, Miss Appleyard. Women who join *Anti*-Suffrage Societies and under the cloak of such a membership go about propagating the very ideas they pretend to abhor!

APPLEYARD: *(Incredulously)* You can't possibly be serious!

CRABTREE: *(Triumphantly)* I thought I should startle you. My firm belief is that they're in the pay of the Suffragists.

APPLEYARD: But how perfectly disgraceful! I hadn't the slightest idea that such a thing existed! Surely it can be stopped?

CRABTREE: We hope so — we believe so. That is the object of the petition I'm asking you to sign. *(Draws paper from long envelope)* We want some pronouncement from headquarters in London that will make treachery of this kind impossible.

APPLEYARD: That's an excellent idea. I'll sign it with pleasure.

CRABTREE: Thank you very much. And I hope you'll allow your servants to do the same?

APPLEYARD: *(A little astonished)* My servants?

CRABTREE: Well it swells a list of signatures so beautifully, especially if a large staff is kept. Lady Carter's signed to the boot-boy!

APPLEYARD: I'm afraid I don't keep a boot-boy and I have only two servants. I've really never asked them their views on the Suffrage.

CRABTREE: Their views? I didn't ask my servants their views. I merely sent the petition to the kitchen for signatures. Nobody will think we're in earnest if we don't get plenty.

APPLEYARD: Well to be quite frank with you, one rather hesitates — I mean it might be a little difficult for a servant to refuse her mistress mightn't it?

CRABTREE: *Refuse? (She is apparently about to go on, then looks at* Miss Appleyard *again and checks herself)* Oh, of course I don't press the point for a moment Miss Appleyard. We shall be only too pleased if you will give us your own signature.

APPLEYARD: May I have the petition? *(Takes paper from* Mrs Crabtree *and goes to writing-table, where she sits down, picks up a pen and examines it)* I always write particularly badly when I inscribe my name on a public document. Do you want full Christian names? I'm afraid I've got four.

CRABTREE: They would look imposing.

APPLEYARD: *(Putting new nib in penholder and talking rather absently)* As you say, treachery within the camp must be put down at any cost. One can hardly believe that women would stoop to it!

CRABTREE: I'm surprised at nothing in connection with the Suffrage.

APPLEYARD: I wonder if you're right in thinking that the Suffragists are responsible?

CRABTREE: I'm convinced of it.

APPLEYARD: *(Still manipulating penholder)* Of course the quickest way to stop anything so flagrant would be to show it up in the papers. *(Draws petition towards her)* If you'll give me a few particulars I don't in the least mind writing a letter to the *Spectator*.

CRABTREE: Oh that would be splendid! There's every excuse for a woman to come out into the open in an exceptional case like this. Besides you could use a *nom de plume*.

APPLEYARD: *(Rather surprised)* I haven't the slightest objection to signing my name to any letter I write.

CRABTREE: *(Hurriedly)* Just as you like, of course. A name often does work wonders. I've got twenty-three to my petition already.

APPLEYARD: *(Smiling)* I'd better complete your second dozen before we discuss the matter further. *(Turns to petition again)* After all, though one must make a stand against it, conduct of this sort is bound to defeat its own ends. Every decent-minded woman will turn from it in disgust.

CRABTREE: *(Gloomily)* How many decent-minded women will there be left in England if this Suffrage movement goes on?

APPLEYARD: *(Laughing)* Oh come, Mrs Crabtree, we're not all going to bow the knee to Baal! I can't think that the Suffrage has made any open headway in Mudford and you must get this petition sent in time to prevent any secret proselytising.

CRABTREE: *(Sighing significantly)* Prevent? I wish we *were* in time for that!

APPLEYARD: *(Sitting back in chair)* You surely can't mean that there are any of these atrocious women among *us*?

CRABTREE: I do, Miss Appleyard. I have only too good reason to believe that we are warming a viper in our bosoms!

APPLEYARD: Tell me her name! Don't hesitate to mention a name in a case like this!

CRABTREE: I don't know it yet unfortunately. I'm waiting to discover it before I denounce her openly.

APPLEYARD: Nothing would give me greater pleasure than to help you!

CRABTREE: I wonder if you could! Do you know anything of the streets behind the factory? *(Rises, and comes to writing-table)*

APPLEYARD: What – Dale Street and Quebec Street do you mean?

CRABTREE: Yes – with the little red houses where so many of the hands live.

APPLEYARD: *(Excitedly)* You don't mean to say she's dared to go there?

(Mrs Crabtree looks round, draws a little closer, and lowers her voice)

CRABTREE: Miss Appleyard, I've just been told on excellent authority that a member of our own Anti-Suffrage Society was seen canvassing in Quebec Street and Dale Street this very morning!

(There is a moment of absolute silence. Miss Appleyard's pen falls to the ground and she gazes at Mrs Crabtree as if petrified. Mrs Crabtree picks up pen, and gives it back to Miss Appleyard. Miss Appleyard pulls herself together and ejaculates faintly)

APPLEYARD: C-canvassing?

CRABTREE: Dear Miss Appleyard, you evidently haven't grasped the brazen tactics of these women. They pretend to be Anti-Suffragists and they *canvass*!

APPLEYARD: *(Much embarrassed)* But surely I – they –

CRABTREE: *(Excitedly)* They subscribe – openly – to the tenet that woman is incapable of forming a political opinion, and they not only form one for themselves, but they go about trying to influence those of *men*!

APPLEYARD: Yes, but you surely –

CRABTREE: *(Working herself up and ignoring any interruption)* They assert – with us – that woman's place is the home and spend long hours away from their own in the arena of politics!

APPLEYARD: *But do you seriously mean that an Anti-Suff –*

CRABTREE: *(Striking the table with her hand)* They profess to leave imperial matters to men with one hand and force their way into meetings at which such matters are discussed with the other!

APPLEYARD: But is it possible that –

CRABTREE: *(Still more heatedly)* They proclaim that political activity tends to break up the harmony of the home and go straight out and address envelopes in Committee rooms by the hour! The insidiousness of it! Of course the ignorant women to whom they talk are drawn into politics in spite of themselves and the way is paved for the Suffragist who works openly! It's a far more dangerous crusade than the militant one, in my opinion, because it wears the guise of an angel of light!

APPLEYARD: *(Faintly, as Mrs Crabtree pauses for breath)* I see what you mean of course. But perhaps it hasn't occurred to them that they're doing — doing all you say!

CRABTREE: *(With a snort)* Don't tell me!

APPLEYARD: Don't you think they might never have looked at it in that light?

CRABTREE: *(A little impatiently)* Oh, my dear Miss Appleyard, one either is or isn't in favour of a thing. You can't do it in practice and denounce it in print, you know!

APPLEYARD: I — I — never thought of that. Of course it *is* inconsistent.

CRABTREE: It's worse than inconsistent, to my mind. Personally I strongly disapprove of the way in which I'm sorry to say some of even the leaders of our party try to defend the municipal vote for women. I prefer to be honest and deplore the mistake which granted it to them.

APPLEYARD: You don't think women should have the municipal vote?

CRABTREE: Of course I don't! What is it but a smaller edition of the parliamentary one? There's merely a difference of degree. The qualities that unfit a woman for one naturally unfit her for the other.

APPLEYARD: What qualities do you mean, exactly?

CRABTREE: Why, Lord Cromer has told us. Hasty generalisation — vague and undisciplined sympathies — extreme sentimentality — I can't remember all he said, but it was in the papers. He said they were characteristic of a majority of the female sex.

APPLEYARD: *(Grimly)* Oh, did he?

CRABTREE: Yes — at a meeting for men only, in Manchester.

APPLEYARD: Perhaps it's as well that women weren't admitted.

CRABTREE: Well, I believe there were a few on the platform, but I quite agree with you. I'm not at all in favour of women attending public meetings as a rule, though I *have* made an exception myself to hear Lord Cromer.

APPLEYARD: Really?

CRABTREE: He has such a marvellous grasp of this subject. There's Lord Curzon too – of course you know his fifteen reasons against Women's Suffrage?

APPLEYARD: No, I'm afraid I don't.

CRABTREE: Oh, I must send them to you! I'm always meaning to learn them by heart. I know the first – *(shuts her eyes and repeats as from a lesson book)* – 'Political activity will tend to take away woman from her proper sphere and highest duty, which is maternity.'

APPLEYARD: But we can't *all* be mothers.

CRABTREE: Oh, he recognises that! Only no doubt he considers married women particularly because, as he says in a later reason, they, if any, are best qualified to exercise the vote.

APPLEYARD: But I thought he said it would interfere with maternity?

CRABTREE: So he did.

APPLEYARD: Then how can he say that married women are best qualified to exercise it?

CRABTREE: I don't altogether follow that myself, I admit. I'm content to leave it to a superior brain to my own.

APPLEYARD: *(After a pause)* And even in the case of mothers – of course I've never been in favour of their having votes, but supposing they *had* – *would* they be constantly engaged in political activity? Fathers aren't!

CRABTREE: Men are political by nature – women are not. If women got votes they would have so much to learn that they'd never have time for anything else. *(Goes on as* Miss Appleyard *is evidently about to demur but thinks better of it)* But you must read the reasons for yourself – that is if you think it advisable to go into the subject. They set forward so plainly the awful dangers of adding a host of unbalanced judgements to a logical male electorate.

APPLEYARD: *(Dryly)* I happened to be talking to one of the logical male electorate this morning. He's my chimney-sweep. He informed me that he was going to vote for Mr Holland because his own wife is a Dutchwoman.

CRABTREE: Really? Which is Mr Holland?

APPLEYARD: *(Curiously)* Do you mean to say you didn't know that he was the Labour candidate?

CRABTREE: *(Indifferently)* Oh, I must have seen the placards and heard people talking, of course. But I naturally don't take any interest in politics. I don't consider them to be a woman's concern.

APPLEYARD: What *do* you consider to be a woman's concern?

CRABTREE: *(Impressively)* Her HOME! *(Crosses L, and sits on sofa)*

APPLEYARD: But – do excuse me – you're putting things in rather a new light to me. Don't vague sympathies and sentimentality and – what else did Lord Cromer say? – hasty generalisation? – matter in the home?

CRABTREE: *(A little taken aback)* Oh – er – well – of course, it would be better *without* them, but as Lord Cromer says, most women *are* like that. I mustn't trespass longer on your time, Miss Appleyard. If I may have your signature I won't detain you any more.

APPLEYARD: *(Taking up petition)* I haven't really looked at the text of this – I'd only surmised it from what you told me. *(Scans paper in silence, then looks up)* I see that it's a request to headquarters that some rule may be framed which shall debar any member of an Anti-Suffrage Society from canvassing.

CRABTREE: We thought it better to confine ourselves to the canvassing to start with. Later we hope to attack more of these abominable tactics. *(A bell is heard outside)*

APPLEYARD: *(Folding up paper deliberately and handing it back)* Well, Mrs Crabtree, I may as well tell you quite frankly that you won't attack them through me. *(Rises)*

CRABTREE: *(In astonishment)* Miss Appleyard – I don't understand you!

APPLEYARD: I can't sign that paper.

CRABTREE: May I ask why not? *(There is a tap at the door)*

APPLEYARD: Come in! *(Enter Morton)*

MORTON: Excuse me disturbing you a moment, please 'm.

APPLEYARD: What is it, Morton? *(To Mrs Crabtree)* Excuse me, Mrs Crabtree!

(Mrs Crabtree bows, and crosses over to R)

MORTON: *(At door – Miss Appleyard goes up to her)* Miss Allbutt's called, 'm, and she won't come in, but she says could you kindly send word if it's ten or half-past that she's to go canvassing with you tomorrow.

(There is a gasp from Mrs Crabtree who stares at Miss Appleyard in absolute horror. Miss Appleyard after a moment's pause turns to Morton)

APPLEYARD: *(Firmly)* Say ten o'clock, please.

MORTON: Yes 'm. *(Exit)*

APPLEYARD: I beg your pardon, Mrs Crabtree. You were asking –

CRABTREE: *(Very excitedly)* I am answered, Miss Appleyard – I am answered! Little did I think when I denounced the women among us who are secretly undermining our influence that they had so far worked upon your feelings as to persuade you to join them!

APPLEYARD: I really don't understand you. Nobody has worked on my feelings. I offered to help with canvassing this time as I did at the last Election. I was just going to tell you so when my maid came in.

CRABTREE: *(Agitatedly)* Then – then is it possible that *you* are the woman who was canvassing in Dale Street and Quebec Street this morning?

APPLEYARD: *(Quietly)* It's more than possible – it's a fact.

CRABTREE: This – this is beyond everything! You consider yourself capable of forming a political opinion?

APPLEYARD: Well – shall we say at least as capable as the gentleman who's going to vote for Mr Holland because his own wife's a Dutchwoman!

CRABTREE: *(Almost in a scream)* You don't think that woman's place is the home?

APPLEYARD: Place – certainly. Prison – no. You might as well say that a man's place is his office and blame him for coming home in an evening or taking an interest in his wife's duties or his children's lessons!

CRABTREE: *(Solemnly and loudly)* Man is Man and Woman is Woman!

APPLEYARD: *(With a twinkle in her eye)* Oh I'm quite prepared to concede that.

CRABTREE: And conceding it, you actually think that a woman ought to meddle with politics?

APPLEYARD: Meddle? How can any intelligent woman help taking an interest in the affairs of her country?

CRABTREE: *Her* country? It's the country of the men who fight for it!

APPLEYARD: You mean that only soldiers and sailors should be politicians?

CRABTREE: This is ridiculous! It is only too easy to see what influences have been at work!

APPLEYARD: *(Coldly)* Would you kindly explain what you mean?

CRABTREE: I mean that your line of reasoning is taken straight from the publications of the Suffrage Societies!

APPLEYARD: The publications of the Suffrage Societies? I've never seen any!

CRABTREE: I cannot, of course, dispute your word. But Suffragists think that a woman should take what they call an intelligent interest in the affairs of her country! Suffragists maintain that a woman doesn't unsex herself by political activity. Suffragists declare that the average woman is as capable of forming an opinion in these matters as hundreds of the men voters of today!

APPLEYARD: *(Defiantly)* And so do I!

CRABTREE: Then, Miss Appleyard, all I can ask is, what are you doing among *us*?

(There is a silence. Miss Appleyard, after a moment's pause, turns down L below sofa, and is evidently nonplussed. Mrs Crabtree prepares to leave and continues speaking)

CRABTREE: I am glad that you see the absurdity of your position for yourself. It would be waste of time to argue further with you today, but I shall never rest until you are back within the true fold. *(Slowly and solemnly)* I want every woman to be a perfect woman!

APPLEYARD: *(Nettled)* It seems to me that you want every woman to be a perfect fool!

CRABTREE: *(After an indignant glance)* Good afternoon, Miss Appleyard.

APPLEYARD: *(Rings bell)* Good afternoon, Mrs Crabtree!

(They bow stiffly. Exit Mrs Crabtree with head in air. Miss Appleyard stands in a listening attitude until an outer door bangs; then goes up to the door)

APPLEYARD: *(Calls)* Morton!

MORTON: I'm just bringing your tea 'm. *(Morton enters with tea things on a tray, and puts on table, R)*

APPLEYARD: *(Coming down to table, R, and sitting)* Morton, some papers came by post this morning – printed papers from a Suffrage Society. I put them in the waste-paper basket. I suppose they'll have been thrown away by now?

MORTON: No 'm, they've not. Cook and me have got them in the kitchen.

APPLEYARD: I should rather like to have a look at them.

MORTON: I'll bring them, 'm. *(Hesitating)* If you'll excuse my saying so, 'm. Cook and me think there's a deal of sound commonsense in this Suffrage business.

APPLEYARD: *(Slowly)* D'you know, Morton, I'm beginning to think it's quite possible that you may be right!

CURTAIN

NOTES

The dates and venues accompanying the titles of plays in these notes refer to the productions mentioned in the text. For publisher's names and dates of publication see bibliography.

CHAPTER I – HEDDA IS ALL OF US

1 George Rowell, *The Victorian Theatre*.
2 Henry James, *The Galaxy*, May 1877.
3 H. Bolitho, *Marie Tempest*, p. 19.
4 Eva Moore, *Exits and Entrances*, p. 4.
5 Violet Vanbrugh, *Dare to be Wise*, p. 19.
6 Interview recorded by author.
7 Interview recorded by author.
8 Margaret Webster, *The Same Only Different*, p. 120.
9 Irene Vanbrugh, *To Tell My Story*, p. 30.
10 Eva Moore, *Exits and Entrances*, p. 16–17.
11 Violet Vanbrugh, *Dare to be Wise*, p. 30.
12 Interview recorded by author.
13 Lena Ashwell, *Myself a Player*, p. 60–1.
14 Cicely Hamilton, *Life Errant*, p. 37.
15 *Ibid.*, p. 52.
16 London Museum Suffrage Collection.
17 Eva Moore, *Exits and Entrances*, p. 20–1.
18 Margaret Webster, *The Same Only Different*, p. 123.
19 Eva Moore, *Exits and Entrances*, p. 37–8.
20 H. Bolitho, *Marie Tempest*, p. 33–4.
21 Lena Ashwell, *Myself a Player*, p. 115.
22 Eva Moore, *Exits and Entrances*, p. 141.
23 *Ibid.*, p. 175.
24 E. Sprigge, *Sybil Thorndike Casson*, p. 96.
25 Lena Ashwell, *Myself a Player*, p. 133.
26 I. Duncan, *My Life*, p. 206–7.
27 Sarah Bernhardt, *Memoirs*, p. 320.
28 Violet Vanbrugh, *Dare to be Wise*, p. 157.

29 Vesta Tilley, *Recollections of Vesta Tilley*.
30 *Ibid.* p. 233–4.
31 Cicely Hamilton, *Life Errant*, p. 47.
32 H. Bolitho, *Marie Tempest*, p. 33–4.
33 Ellen Terry, *Ellen Terry Memoirs*, p. 162–3.
34 William Archer, *Fortnightly Review*, May 1889.
35 Michael Meyer, *Ibsen*, p. 547.
36 *Ibid.*, p. 631.
37 *Ibid.*
38 *Ibid.*, p. 632.
39 *The Dramatic Review*, 24 December 1892.
40 Elizabeth Robins, *Ibsen and the Actress*, p. 17.
41 G. B. Shaw, *Collected Letters 1898–1910*, to Ada Rehan, 2 August 1904.
42 George Moore, *The Hawk*, 8 July 1890.
43 Clement Scott, *The Illustrated London News*, 21 March 1891.
44 G. B. Shaw, *An Autobiography*, p. 235.
45 *Ibid.*, p. 165.
46 Elizabeth Robins, *Ibsen and the Actress*, p. 17.
47 *Ibid.*, p. 18.
48 *Ibid.*
49 G. B. Shaw, *An Autobiography*, p. 267.
50 *Ibid.*, p. 164.
51 G. B. Shaw, *Collected Letters 1898–1910*, to Ellen Terry, 1 August 1899.
52 G. B. Shaw, *Collected Letters 1898–1910*, to Lady Barrington, 8 August 1905.
53 *Ibid.*, to Mrs Patrick Campbell, 3 July 1912.
54 *Ibid.*, to Eleanor Robson, 24 December 1905.
55 Jane Marcus, 'Elizabeth Robins', dissertation, p. 54.
56 G. B. Shaw, *Collected Letters 1898–1910*, to William Archer, 24 January 1900.
57 *Ibid.*, to William Stead, July 1904.
58 *Ibid.*, to Ada Rehan, 2 August 1904.
59 *Ibid.*, to Octavia Wilberforce, 13 January 1903.
60 G. B. Shaw, *Votes for Women*, 17 June 1910.
61 *The Suffragette*, 25 October 1912.

CHAPTER 2 – DRAMATIC JOAN OF ARCS

1 G. B. Shaw, *Our Theatre in the Nineties*, Vol. II, p. 148.
2 A. Pinero, *The Second Mrs Tanqueray*, St James's Theatre, 27 May 1893.
3 Oscar Wilde, *Lady Windermere's Fan*, St James's Theatre, 22 February 1892.
4 Oscar Wilde, *A Woman of No Importance*, Theatre Royal, Haymarket, 19 April 1893.

5 Oscar Wilde, *The Importance of Being Earnest*, St James's Theatre, 14 February 1895.
6 H. Ibsen, *Little Eyolf*, Avenue Theatre, 23 November 1896.
7 A. Pinero, *The Second Mrs Tanqueray*, Act IV.
8 A. Pinero, *The Notorious Mrs Ebbsmith*, Garrick Theatre, March 1895.
9 Alan Hyman, *The Gaiety Years*, p. 81.
10 Elizabeth Robins, *Ibsen and the Actress*, p. 33.
11 Elizabeth Robins, *Theatre and Friendship*, p. 28-9.
12 Charles E. Pearce, *Madame Vestris*, p. 168.
13 *Ibid.*, p. 54.
14 *Ibid.*, p. 150.
15 *Ibid.*, p. 276.
16 Violet Vanbrugh, *Dare to be Wise*, p. 30.
17 Alfhild Agrell, *Karin*, Vaudeville Theatre, May 1892.
18 H. Ibsen, *The Master Builder*, Trafalgar Square Theatre, 20 February 1893.
19 Elizabeth Robins, *Book News Monthly*, p. 242.
20 H. Ibsen, *Rosmersholm*, Vaudeville Theatre, 23 February 1891.
21 Rex Pogson, *Miss Horniman*, p. 22.
22 E. Sprigge, *Sybil Thorndike Casson*, p. 71.
23 Stanley Houghton, *Hindle Wakes*, Aldwych Theatre, 16 June 1912.
24 Lena Ashwell, *Myself a Player*.
25 Interview recorded with author.
26 Elizabeth Robins, *Ancilla's Share*, p. 131-2.
27 Elizabeth Robins and Gertrude Bell, *Alan's Wife*, 28 April 1893.
28 William Archer, *Alan's Wife*, introduction, p. xlvii.
29 Cicely Hamilton, *Life Errant*, p. 60.
30 Cicely Hamilton, *Diana of Dobson's*, Kingsway Theatre, 12 February 1908.
31 *Ibid.*, Act II.
32 Cicely Hamilton, *Life Errant*, p. 63.
33 Elizabeth Robins, *Votes for Women!*, Court Theatre, April 1907.

PART II – THE ACTRESSES' FRANCHISE LEAGUE

1 *Votes for Women*, 13 October 1911.

CHAPTER 3 – KISSES OR VOTES

1 *Stage*, 24 December 1908.
2 *Votes for Women*, 24 December 1908.
3 Interview recorded by author, 1977.
4 *Ibid.*
5 Sylvia Pankhurst, *The Suffragette Movement*, p. 278.
6 *Ibid.*, p. 285.
7 Eva Moore, *Exits and Entrances*, p. 94.
8 Irene Vanbrugh, *To Tell My Story*, p. 83-4.

9 Eva Moore, *Exits and Entrances*, p. 96.
10 Souvenir programme, London Museum Suffrage Collection.
11 London Museum Suffrage Collection.
12 *Ibid.*
13 *Ibid.*
14 *Votes for Women*, April 1910, p. 494.
15 Eva Moore, *Exits and Entrances*, p. 90–1.
16 Interview with author, 1977.
17 Evelyn Glover, *Showin' Samyel.*
18 L. S. Phibbs, *Jim's Leg.*
19 H. M. Paull, *The Other Side.*
20 *Votes for Women*, 28 May 1909.
21 *Ibid.*, 30 April 1909.
22 Eva Moore, *Exits and Entrances*, p. 95.
23 *Votes for Women*, 28 May 1909.
24 Beatrice Harraden, *Lady Geraldine's Speech*, Prince's Skating Rink Exhibition, May 1909.
25 Inez Bensusan, *The Apple*, Southampton and Portsmouth NUWSS, 14 March 1910.
26 *Ibid.*, p. 28.
27 Cicely Hamilton, *How the Vote Was Won*, Prince's Skating Rink Exhibition, May 1909.
28 Interview with author, 1977.
29 Allan Wade, *Edy,*, ed. by E. Adlard, A Thread of Memory, p. 69.
30 *Croydon Advertiser*, 15 November 1909.
31 *Reigate and Redhill Gazette*, 3 December 1909.
32 G. B. Shaw, *Press Cuttings*, Court Theatre, 9 July 1909.
33 G. B. Shaw to Bertha Newcombe, letter dated 30 August 1909. Fawcett Collection.
34 Cicely Hamilton, *A Pageant of Great Women*, Scala Theatre, 10 November 1909.
35 *Ibid.*, p. 25.
36 *Votes for Women*, 8 October 1909.
37 Interview with author, 1977.
38 Cicely Hamilton, *Edy,* ed. by E. Adlard Triumphant Women, p. 42–3.

CHAPTER 4 – CHINA TEA-CUPS

1 Lena Ashwell, *Myself a Player*, p. 168.
2 *Ibid.*, p. 164–5.
3 Lillah McCarthy, *Myself and My Friends*, p. 148.
4 Virginia Woolf, *The Letters of Virginia Woolf Vol. II*, Chatto & Windus, London 1976, letter to Vanessa Bell, Saturday 22 April 1916, p. 91.
5 *Votes for Women*, 31 March 1911.

6 *Ibid.*, 27 January 1911.

7 Lena Ashwell, *Myself a Player*, p. 167–8.

8 *Votes for Women*, 7 April 1911.

9 Arncliffe-Sennett, *An Englishwoman's Home*, Croydon Branch of WSPU, Spring 1910.

10 *Ibid.*, p. 24–5.

11 *Ibid.*, p. 16.

12 *Votes for Women*, 7 April 1911.

13 Interview recorded by author, 1979.

14 *Votes for Women*, 28 November 1911.

15 Eva Moore, *Exits and Entrances*, p. 96–7.

16 Sylvia Pankhurst, *The Suffragette Movement*, p. 395.

17 Vera Wentworth, *Allegory*, Rehearsal Theatre, 23 April 1911.

18 *Ibid.*, p. 11.

19 *Votes for Women*, 8 December 1911.

20 Graham Moffat, *The Maid and the Magistrate*, Eustace Miles Restaurant, performance organised for the Women Sanitary Inspectors and Health Visitors Suffrage Group, 27 February 1911.

21 *Ibid.*, p. 17–18.

22 Evelyn Glover, *A Chat with Mrs Chicky*, WFL International Suffrage Fair, 13 November 1911.

23 *Ibid.*, p. 13.

24 Evelyn Glover, *Miss Appleyard's Awakening*, Rehearsal Theatre, 20 June 1911.

25 Fawcett Collection.

26 Antonia Raeburn, *Militant Suffragettes*, p. 214.

27 Cecil Armstrong, *Physical Force*, 15 December 1911.

28 *Votes for Women*, 23 May 1913.

29 Souvenir Programme, Fawcett Collection.

30 *Ibid.*

31 Bjornstjerne Bjornson, *A Gauntlet*, Coronet Theatre, December 1913.

32 *Votes for Women*, 19 December 1913.

33 Eugène Brieux, *Woman on Her Own*, Coronet Theatre, December 1913.

34 Souvenir Programme, Fawcett Collection.

35 *Votes for Women*, 12 December 1913.

36 *The Suffragette*, 12 December 1913.

37 Lena Ashwell, *Myself a Player*, p. 184.

38 Cicely Hamilton, *Life Errant*, p. 138.

39 Lena Ashwell, *Modern Troubadours*, p. 11.

40 J. M. Barrie, *The Twelve Pound Look*, Portman Rooms, December 1911.

41 Lena Ashwell, *Myself a Player*, p. 199.

42 Lena Ashwell, *Modern Troubadours*, p. 36.

43 Cicely Hamilton, *Life Errant*, p. 67.

PART III – EDY AND HER PIONEERS

1 Sybil Thorndike, *Edy*, ed. by E. Adlard, A Festival in the Barn Theatre, p. 81.
2 E. Sprigge, *Sybil Thorndike Casson*.

CHAPTER 5 – AILSA CRAIG

1 Ellen Terry and Bernard Shaw, *A Correspondence*, 10 October 1896.
2 Ellen Terry, *Ellen Terry Memoirs*, p. 89.
3 *Ibid.*, p. 80.
4 *Ibid.*
5 *Ibid.*
6 *Ibid.*, p. 82.
7 Edward Craig, *Gordon Craig*, p. 47.
8 Edward Gordon Craig, *Ellen Terry and Her Secret Self*, p. 57.
9 Ellen Terry, *Ellen Terry Memoirs*, p. 80.
10 Edward Gordon Craig, *Ellen Terry and Her Secret Self*, p. 56–7.
11 Margaret Steen, *A Pride of Terrys*, p. 186.
12 Ellen Terry, *Ellen Terry Memoirs*, p. 236.
13 Edward Gordon Craig, *Ellen Terry and Her Secret Self*, p. 71.
14 Ellen Terry, *Ellen Terry Memoirs*, notes compiled by Edith Craig and Chris St John, p. 194.
15 *Ibid.*, p. 194.
16 Chris St John, *Edy*, ed. by E. Adlard, Close Up, p. 23.
17 Ellen Terry and Bernard Shaw, *A Correspondence*.
18 Ernest Milton, *Edy*, ed. by E. Adlard, Heart and Hand, p. 88.
19 Chris St John, *Edy*, ed. by E. Adlard, Close Up, p. 19.
20 Ellen Terry and Bernard Shaw, *A Correspondence*, 4 November 1896, p. 104.
21 Ellen Terry, *Ellen Terry Memoirs*, p. 257.
22 Margaret Webster, *The Same Only Different*, p. 171.
23 Ellen Terry, *Ellen Terry Memoirs*, p. 321.
24 *Ibid.*, notes to Chapter 6.
25 Ellen Terry and Bernard Shaw, *A Correspondence*.
26 *Ibid.*, 4 September 1897, p. 229.
27 *Ibid.*, 13 April 1898.
28 Small Hythe Collection.
29 Chris St John, *Edy*, ed. by E. Adlard, Close Up, p. 20.
30 Dame May Whitty, *Edy*, ed. by E. Adlard, Edy the Magician, p. 52.
31 Chris St John, *Hungerheart*, p. 184.
32 *Ibid.*, p. 224.
33 *Ibid.*, p. 226.
34 Chris St John, *Edy*, ed. by E. Adlard, Close Up, p. 22.

35 Jeffrey Weeks, *Coming Out*, p. 95.
36 Chris St John, *Hungerheart*, p. 219.
37 *Ibid.*, p. 108.
38 Cicely Hamilton, *Edy*, ed. by E. Adlard, Triumphant Women, p. 39–40.
39 Margaret Webster, *The Same Only Different*, p. 178.
40 Isadora Duncan, *My Life*, p. 199.
41 Edward Gordon Craig, *Ellen Terry and Her Secret Self*, p. 132.
42 Ellen Terry and Bernard Shaw, *A Correspondence*, 15 May 1903.

CHAPTER 6 – 'ONE PLAY IS WORTH A HUNDRED SPEECHES'

 1 Chris St John, *Hungerheart*, p. 262.
 2 *Ibid.*, p. 269.
 3 Cicely Hamilton, *Edy*, ed. by E. Adlard, Triumphant Women, p. 40–1.
 4 *The Stage*, 8 May 1911.
 5 Irene Cooper Willis, *Edy*, ed. by E. Adlard, The Squares, p. 109.
 6 *Stageland*, May 1911.
 7 Chris St John, *The First Actress*, Kingsway Theatre, 8 May 1911.
 8 Cicely Hamilton, *Jack and Jill and a Friend*, Kingsway Theatre, 8 May 1911.
 9 *Ibid.*, p. 19.
10 *Sheffield Daily Telegraph*, 9 May 1911.
11 *Evening Standard*, 9 May 1911.
12 *The Stage*, 8 May 1911.
13 Hugh De Selincourt, *Beastie*, 15 December 1912.
14 Edith Lyttleton, *The Thumbscrew*, King's Hall, 15 December 1912.
15 Margaret Wynne Nevinson, *In the Workhouse*, Kingsway Theatre, 8 May 1911.
16 *Reference*, 14 May 1911.
17 *Daily Mail*, 9 May 1911.
18 *Reference*, 14 May 1911.
19 L. Housman, *Pains and Penalties*, Savoy Theatre, 26 November 1911.
20 *Standard*, 21 November 1911.
21 Jess Dorynne, *The Surprise of His Life*, King's Hall, 21 April 1912.
22 J. Sackville Martin, *Nellie Lambert*, King's Hall, 5 May 1912.
23 *Votes for Women*, 28 April 1912.
24 *Referee*, 28 April 1912.
25 *Yorkshire Post*, 6 May 1912.
26 H. M. Harwood, *Honour Thy Father*, King's Hall, 15 December 1912.
27 *Ibid.*, p. 42–3.
28 *Votes for Women*, 20 December 1912.
29 *Ibid.*
30 Antonia Williams, *The Street*, Little Theatre, 30 November 1913.
31 *Ibid.*, p. 128–9.

32 L. Irving, *Godefroi and Yolande*. Roswitha, *Paphnutius.*

33 R. Wright Kauffman, *The Daughters of Ishmael*, adapted by A. D'Este Scott, King's Hall, March 1914.

34 Interview recorded by author.

35 Margaret Webster, *The Same Only Different*, p. 282.

36 Cecil Fisher, *The Great Day*, Little Theatre, 18 May 1913.

37 *Ibid.*

38 Herman Heijermans, *The Good Hope*, King's Hall, 3 November 1912.

39 *Votes for Women*, 8 November 1912.

40 Githa Sowerby, *Rutherford and Son*, 29 March 1912.

41 *Ibid.*, p. 78–9.

CHAPTER 7 – BREAKING THE MOULD

1 Gwen John, *Luck of War*, Kingsway Theatre, 13 May 1917.

2 *Ibid.*, p. 24–5.

3 Yevreinov, *The Theatre of the Soul*, Little Theatre, 7 March 1915.

4 *Ibid.*, introduction.

5 *Ibid.*

6 *Ibid.*

7 *Ibid.*

8 Margaret Webster, *The Same Only Different*, p. 267.

9 Khori Torahiko, *Kanawa*, Criterion Theatre, 16 December 1917.

10 Yevreinov, *The Merry Death*, Savoy Theatre, 2 April 1916.

11 Leonid Nikolaevich Andreiev, *The Dear Departing*, 6 February 1916.

12 Paul Claudel, *The Tidings Brought to Mary*, Strand Theatre, 10 June 1917.

13 Chris St John, *Edy*, ed. by E. Adlard, Close Up, p. 32.

14 Paul Claudel, *The Hostage*, Scala Theatre, 23 March 1919.

15 Clare Atwood, *Edy*, Edy's Ways, p. 140–1.

16 Sybil Thorndike, *Edy*, ed. by E. Adlard, A Festival in the Barn Theatre, p. 78.

17 *Ibid.*, p. 79.

18 Susan Glaspell, *Trifles*, King's Hall, 9 February 1919.

19 *Ibid.*, p. 352–3.

20 *Observer*, 8 March 1925.

21 Ellen Terry, *Ellen Terry Memoirs*, notes to Chapter 3.

22 Susan Glaspell, *The Verge*, Regent Theatre, 29 March 1925.

23 Small Hythe Collection.

24 *Yorkshire Post*, 3 March 1925.

25 Susan Glaspell, *The Verge*, p. 45–6.

26 *The Lady*, 29 March 1925.

27 *Evening Standard*, 30 March 1925.

28 Small Hythe Collection.

29 Ernest Milton, *Edy*, ed. by E. Adlard, Heart and Hand, p. 85–6.

CHAPTER 8 – THE SMALL HYTHE *MÉNAGE À TROIS*

1 Vita Sackville West, *Edy*, ed. by E. Adlard, Triptych.
2 *Ibid.*, p. 129.
3 Quentin Bell, *Virginia Woolf 1912–1914*, p. 117.
4 Jeffrey Weeks, *Coming Out*, p. 106–7.
5 Chris St John, *Edy*, ed. by E. Adlard, Close Up, p. 25.
6 Harcourt Williams, *Edy*, ed. by E. Adlard, Bygones, p. 49.
7 Ellen Terry, *Ellen Terry Memoirs*, notes, p. 307.
8 Edward Craig, *Gordon Craig*, p. 327.
9 *Ibid.*, p. 327.
10 Allan Wade, *Edy*, ed. by E. Adlard, A Thread of Memory, p. 74.
11 Florence Locke, *Edy*, ed. by E. Adlard, An American Rehearses with Edy, p. 103–4.
12 Chris St John, *Edy*, ed. by E. Adlard, Close Up, p. 27.
13 Sheila Kay-Smith, *Edy*, ed. by E. Adlard, More Distant Views, p. 131.
14 *Ibid.*, p. 130.
15 Chris St John, *Edy*, ed. by E. Adlard, Close Up, p. 28.
16 Jane Marcus, *Virginia Woolf Miscellany*, Some Sources for Between the Acts, Winter 1977.
17 Virginia Woolf, letter to Vita Sackville West 15 September 1933, *The Letters of Virginia Woolf, Vol. V*.
18 Virginia Woolf, *Between the Acts*, p. 48.
19 Ernest Milton, *Edy*, Heart and Hand, p. 89.
20 Virginia Woolf, *Between the Acts*, p. 107.
21 Margaret Webster, *The Same Only Different*, p. 280.
22 Violet Pym, *Edy*, ed. by E. Adlard, A Great Treat, p. 114–15.
23 Chris St John, *Edy*, ed. by E. Adlard, Close Up., p. 32.
24 Edward Craig, *Gordon Craig*, p. 354.

SELECT BIBLIOGRAPHY

GENERAL

Adlard, Eleanor, *Edy: Recollections of Edith Craig*, Frederick Muller, London 1949.

Ashwell, Lena, *Modern Troubadours*, Gyldendal, London 1922.

Bell, Quentin, *Virginia Woolf 1912-1914*, Triad/Paladin, St Albans 1976.

Bolitho, H., *Marie Tempest*, Cobden-Sanderson, Gloucester 1936.

Craig, Edward, *Gordon Craig: The Story of His Life*, Victor Gollancz, London 1968.

Craig, Edward Gordon, *Ellen Terry and Her Secret Self*, Sampson Low, Marston & Co., London.

Dangerfield, George, *The Strange Death of Liberal England, 1910-1914*, Capricorn Books, New York 1961.

Findlater, Richard, *The Player Queens*, Weidenfeld & Nicolson, London 1976.

Gilder, Rosamund, *Enter the Actress*, Theatre Arts Books, New York 1960.

Hall, Radclyffe, *The Well of Loneliness*, Barrie & Jenkins, London 1976.

Holton, B., *British Syndicalism 1900-1914*, Pluto Press, London 1976.

Hyman, Alan, *The Gaiety Years*, Cassell, London 1975.

Hynes, Samuel, *The Edwardian Turn of Mind*, Oxford University Press, London 1968.

Kauffman, R. Wright, *The Daughters of Ishmael*, Stephen Swift & Co., London 1911.

Liddington, J. and Norris, J., *One Hand Tied Behind Us*, Virago, London 1978.

Meyer, Michael, *Ibsen*, Penguin, Harmondsworth 1974.

Nicoll, Allardyce, *English Drama 1900-1930*, Cambridge University Press, Cambridge 1973.

Pankhurst, Sylvia, *The Suffragette Movement*, Longman, London 1931; reprint Virago, London 1977.

Pearce, Charles, *Madame Vestris and Her Times*, Stanley Paul & Co., London.

Pearsall, Ronald, *The Worm in the Bud*, Weidenfeld & Nicolson, London 1969.

Pogson, Rex, *Miss Horniman and the Gaiety Theatre*, Barrie & Rockliff, London 1952.

Raeburn, Antonia, *Militant Suffragettes*, Michael Joseph, London 1973.

Robins, Elizabeth, *Ancilla's Share: An Indictment of Sex Antagonism*, Hutchinson, London 1924.

Robins, Elizabeth, *Ibsen and the Actress*, Hogarth Essays, Second Series, No. XV, London 1932.

Robins, Elizabeth, *Theatre and Friendship*, Jonathan Cape, Life and Letters Series, London 1932.

Rowell, George, *The Victorian Theatre*, Oxford 1956.

Rowell, George, *Victorian Dramatic Criticism*, Methuen, London 1971.

Shaw, George Bernard, *Our Theatre in the Nineties*, 3 vols, Constable, London 1932.

Shaw, George Bernard, Collected Letters, 1898-1910, ed. Dan H. Laurence, Dodd, Mead, New York 1965, 1972.

Sprigge, E., *Sybil Thorndike Casson*, Victor Gollancz, London 1971.

Steen, Margaret, *A Pride of Terrys*, Longmans, London 1962.

Stokes, John, *Resistible Theatre*, Paul Elek Books, London 1972.

Strachey, Ray, *The Cause*, G. Bell & Son, London 1928, reprint Virago, London 1978.

Terry, Ellen and Shaw, Bernard, *A Correspondence*, Constable, London 1931.

Webster, Margaret, *The Same Only Different*, Victor Gollancz, London 1969.

Weeks, Jeffrey, *Coming Out*, Quartet Books, London 1977.

Woolf, Virginia, *Between the Acts*, Penguin, Harmondsworth 1976.

Woolf, Virginia, *The Letters of Virginia Woolf*, Vol. II *The Question of Things Happening*; Vol. V *The Sickle Side of the Moon*, Hogarth Press, London 1976 and 1979.

AUTOBIOGRAPHIES

Ashwell, Lena, *Myself a Player*, Michael Joseph, London 1936.

Bernhardt, Sarah, *Memoirs*, William Heinemann, London 1907.

Duncan, Isadora, *My Life*, Victor Gollancz, London 1928.

Hamilton, Cicely, *Life Errant*, J. M. Dent & Son, London 1935.

McCarthy, Lillah, *Myself and My Friends*, Thornton Butterworth, London 1933.

Moore, Eva, *Exits and Entrances*, Chapman & Hall, London 1923.

Pankhurst, Emmeline, *My Own Story*, reprinted Virago, London 1979.

St John, Chris, *Hungerheart, The Story of a Soul*, Methuen, London 1915.

Shaw, George Bernard, *An Autobiography*, ed. Weintraub, S., Reinhardt, London 1970.

Terry, Ellen, *Ellen Terry Memoirs*, Victor Gollancz, London 1933.

Tilley, Vesta, *Recollections of Vesta Tilley*, London 1934.

Vanbrugh, Irene, *To Tell My Story*, Hutchinson, London 1948.

Vanbrugh, Violet, *Dare to be Wise*, Hodder & Stoughton, London 1925.

PLAYS

Arncliffe-Sennett, H., *An Englishwoman's Home*, Actresses' Franchise League. London 1911.

Andreiev, Leonid Nikolaevich, *The Dear Departing*, Hendersons, London 1916.

Barrie, J. M., 'The Twelve Pound Look' in *Half-Hours*, Hodder & Stoughton, London 1914.

Bensusan, Inez, *The Apple*, Actresses' Franchise League, London 1911.

Bjornson, Bjornstjerne, 'A Gauntlet' in *Three Comedies*, J. M. Dent, London 1912.

Brieux, Eugène, *Woman on Her Own*, Herbert Jenkins, London 1916.

Claudel, Paul, *The Hostage*, Oxford University Press, London 1971.

Claudel, Paul, *The Tidings Brought to Mary*, trans. Louise Morgan Sill, Chatto & Windus, London 1916.

Glaspell, Susan, *Trifles*, French's Acting Editions, London 1932; reprint in *Women in Drama*, Mentor, New York 1975.

Glaspell, Susan, *The Verge*, Small, Mayward, Boston 1922.

Glover, Evelyn, *A Chat with Mrs Chicky*, Actresses' Franchise League, London 1913.

Glover, Evelyn, *Miss Appleyard's Awakening*, Actresses' Franchise League, London 1913.

Glover, Evelyn, *Showin' Samyel*, Suffrage Recitation, 1914.

Hamilton, Cicely, *Diana of Dobson's*, French's Acting Edition, London 1925.

Hamilton, Cicely, *How the Vote was Won*, Suffrage Press, London 1910.

Hamilton, Cicely, *Jack and Jill and a Friend*, Lacy's Acting Edition of Plays No. 160, London 1911.

Hamilton, Cicely, *A Pageant of Great Women*, The Suffrage Shop, London 1910.

Harraden, Beatrice, 'Lady Geraldine's Speech', *Votes for Women*, 2 April 1909.

Harwood, H. M. with F. Tennyson Jesse, *Honour Thy Father*, *Three One Act Plays*, Ernest Benn, London 1926.

Houghton, Stanley, 'Hindle Wakes' in *Late Victorian Plays 1909-14*, ed. George Rowell, Oxford Paperbacks, London 1972.

Housman, Laurence, *Pains and Penalties*, Sidgwick & Jackson, London 1911.

Irving, Laurence, *Godefroi and Yolande*, J. Lane, London and New York 1898.

John, Gwen, *Luck of War*, Repertory Plays, London and Glasgow 1922.

Khori, Torahiko, *Kanawa*, Repertory Plays, London 1910.

Moffat, Graham, *The Maid and the Magistrate*, Actresses' Franchise League, London 1913.

Nevinson, Margaret Wynne, *In the Workhouse*, International Suffrage Shop, London 1911.

Paull, H. M., *The Other Side*, Actresses' Franchise League, London 1913.

Pinero, Arthur, *The Second Mrs Tanqueray*, *Late Victorian Plays, 1890–1914*, ed. George Rowell, Oxford Paperbacks, London 1972.

Robins, Elizabeth, and Bell, Gertrude, *Alan's Wife*, Henry & Co., 1893.

Robins, Elizabeth, *Votes for Women!*, Mills and Boon, London 1909.

Roswitha, *Paphnutius*, *Plays of Roswitha*, trans. Chris St John, Medieval Library, London 1923.

Shaw, Bernard, 'Press Cuttings' in *Collected Plays & Prefaces Vol. III*, The Bodley Head, London 1971.

Sowerby, Githa, *Rutherford and Son*, Sidgwick& Jackson, London 1912.

Wentworth, Vera, *Allegory*, Actresses' Franchise League, London 1913.

Williams, Antonia, *The Street*, *Three New Plays*, T. Werner Laurie, London 1908.

Yevreinov, Nikolai Nikolaevich, *The Theatre of the Soul*, trans. Marie Potapenko and Chris St John, Hendersons, London 1915.

Yevreinov, Nikolai Nikolaevich, 'A Merry Death' in *Five Russian Plays*, Kegan Paul & Co., London 1916.

UNPUBLISHED WORK

Bensusan, Inez, collection of AFL playscripts, Manders & Mitchinson Theatre Collection.

Marcus, Jane, 'Elizabeth Robins', dissertation for North Western University, Evanston, Illinois, June 1973.

INDEX